Consumer Data Research

Consumer Data Research

Paul Longley, James Cheshire
and Alex Singleton

UCLPRESS

Acknowledgements

The editors are grateful to the Economic and Social Research Council for funding and supporting the work of the Consumer Data Research Centre (CDRC), an ESRC Data Investment, grant ES/L011840/1 and all the research featured in this book.

Sarah Sheppard (CDRC Project Manager) has been particularly instrumental in the success of CDRC and, by extension, this book. Her efforts to coordinate researchers as well as maintain close working relationships with data providers are greatly appreciated! Thanks also to Patrick Morrissey (Unlimited) for his excellent work designing and typesetting the book.

The authors and the CDRC would also like to thank our Data Partners for making the data available for the research featured and for their continued support.

Consumer Data Research Centre

An ESRC Data Investment

Contents

Consumer Data Research – An Overview

Paul Longley, James Cheshire and Alex Singleton

It has become a cliché to observe that new sources of Big Data are becoming available in ever greater variety, in unprecedented volumes and with ever more frequent temporal updating (velocity). This book is about 'consumer data' that arise out of every-day transactions for goods and services, carried out between individuals and organisations. Such data account for an increasing real share of all of the characteristics and activities of active citizens today, and offer the prospect of better understanding the nature and functioning of society.

Consumer data are not created for the edification of researchers and analysts. Instead, they are a by-product of the myriad consumer transactions that created them. This has important implications for the data's content and coverage when they are reused for research purposes. First, the traces of (some kinds of) transactions or those people conducting them may be more evident or detailed than others, and this outcome is usually well beyond the control of the analyst. Second, different individuals have different wants, needs and spending power, and so some individuals in the population at large will be represented more prominently than others – and at the other extreme, those that consume nothing from a particular retailer / service provider will not be represented at all. A related point is that few consumer organisations have a monopoly of their markets, and many focus upon particular market niches. Taken together, this means that there is bias in the content and coverage of consumer data sources, and that the source and operation of bias cannot be ascertained without reference to external sources. In many ways these issues are akin to those that characterise volunteered or crowd sourced data – in that individuals need to feel motivated in order to contribute data, and the distinctive characteristics of those that feel motivated may affect the content and coverage of the resulting dataset (Haklay, 2010).

This situation contrasts sharply with the design of conventional social surveys, where the principles of scientific sampling are used to ensure complete coverage of the relevant population of interest at the design stage. Nevertheless the quality of social surveys is diminished where acceptable response rates are not achieved, or there is bias in the relevant characteristics of those that respond to the surveys and those that do not. In this context, it is important to recognise that recent years have seen cumulative declines in response rates throughout the developed world (e.g. Sax et al 2003) and that in important respects social surveys are no longer a panacea for social science research. More generally, there is also no guarantee that we will be able to rely on the long-term availability of those traditional sources of data such as a Census of the Population, as within many countries these expensive and time-consuming surveys have come under increasing threat in line with fiscal constraint (Singleton et al, 2017).

Many of the chapters in this book arise out of shared challenges that are faced by academics and the organisations that, to differing degrees, create consumer data. There are, of course, differences too: the timescales that characterise academic research offer horizon scanning that business organisations are less likely to have resource to facilitate; usually focused upon more operational matters, such as optimising the next set of sales figures. There may be tensions too, in that consumer data providers may safeguard their competitive position, while contributing to research that ultimately increases the competitiveness of their industrial sector as a whole. There are also differences of emphasis in method, technique and application that have evolved in different ways between the academic and business sectors. But it is also possible that there is shared interest in better understanding the form and functioning of social systems.

The research reported in this book has developed using the Consumer Data Research Centre's (CDRC) 'ladder of engagement', whereby initial collaborations with consumer organisations are focused upon specific small MSc projects. A number of these have developed into co-sponsored PhD projects, or shared projects staffed by CDRC Data Scientists. Some data providers then progress to providing data for wider use by the academic community, under agreed terms set out in data licensing agreements. Finally, it is also possible to engage data providers in the co-production of data with the CDRC itself. Good examples are provided by our engagement with players in the domestic energy provision and retail sector who have participated in the Master's Research Dissertation Programme before going on to co-sponsor PhD research. This latter development in turn led to providing CDRC with a nationwide dataset; which is available to access by other researchers through the CDRC service. The collaboration with the Local Data Company (LDC) reported in this book represents the highest rung of this 'ladder of engagement' and follows successful collaboration on MSc and PhD projects as well as the co-production of nationwide data with CDRC for further research and development.

Many consumer-facing organisations are highly sensitised to the risks of disclosure, although these risks are absolutely minimal where data are anonymized prior to transfer, and appropriate resources to access them are put in place. To this end, CDRC uses a number of secure data facilities (one of which is accredited by the London Metropolitan Police), and CDRC researchers are familiar with using novel data access technologies such as secure links to sensitive data-sets held by different organisations.

The approaches to consumer data research that are reported in this book come at an interesting time in the evolution of data landscapes in advanced economies. There is emerging consensus that data are the world's most valuable resource (The Economist, 2017). To the behemoths of the Internet age – Alphabet, Amazon, Apple, Facebook, Microsoft – data are a strategic resource, largely to be acquired and siloed within corporate organisations. From the broader public good perspective, data provide infrastructure for individual and societal decision-making. For example, there is abundant evidence that Open Data platforms and open Application Programming Interfaces (APIs) lead to wide economic and social benefits, with the data feeds from Transport for London (TfL) providing one of the most well-known exemplars. Such initiatives can lead to the creation and successive updating of new data infrastructures, although in many cases this process is impeded by difficulties in apportioning the cost of infrastructure creation and maintenance. Whilst there has been significant progress, the freer movement of data within and between jurisdictions and industrial sectors still presents daunting challenges for government, not least because there exists no open market for many sources and forms of data.

Without a strong precedent, the work of CDRC relies heavily upon the attitudes to data licencing of a wide range of industrial partners with their own policies and procedures (over 20 data licensing agreements have been signed to date). These partners provide their data for the public good and pursue research questions that contribute to a more competitive economy and fairer society. Some of these shared objectives were integral to the 2017 Digital Economies Act, which includes provisions to require business to assist in the compilation of national statistics. The spirit of the approach underpinning the chapters of this book is to go beyond narrow official requirements and engage in truly collaborative inter-sector research of common concern. It is our hope that these arrangements might flourish further in the future, for example through the

'passporting' of data originally acquired for government statistical purposes to researchers. Such arrangements would also have favourable implications for the preservation and curation of many sources of consumer data under the provisions for research exemptions of the General Data Protection Regulation (GDPR).

This vision begs a number of important strategic questions concerning the form and detail of the emerging data landscape:

1) Are Big Data to be thought of as a rival or non-rival resource? The siloed approach of large corporations suggests that data are a valuable commodity and strategic resource, the potency of which is diluted if data are shared with competitor 'rivals'. Seen from this perspective, they are not to be traded or otherwise shared. Yet data sharing has been shown to leverage wide benefits, particularly if data platforms can be made open to the widest constituency of users.

2) Does GDPR present a threat to the creation and maintenance of datasets for research purposes, or an opportunity for researchers to create, maintain and preserve data-rich representations of social systems?

3) How can the Big Data 'exhaust' of consumer transactions and interactions be reused in representations of social systems that are genuinely inclusive? How can scientific methods be repurposed to analyse data that are created and possibly assembled without any scientific research design?

4) How can public trust and understanding of science be developed and maintained in support of research that realises more of the potential of consumer data?

CDRC's mission includes the creation and maintenance of new measures of the ways in which 'smart' urban systems function, for example with respect to pedestrian flows, household activity patterns and residential and social mobility. Any representation of a 'smart' system is necessarily incomplete, and it is important for analysts and public alike to understand the nature and extent of this incompleteness. Furthermore, improved scientific understanding of the public is inextricably linked to improved public understanding of science, since only this is likely to bring informed consent for acquisition of the best data and the best research practices to take place.

There are rapid developments and changes in the digital data economy, ranging from renewed open data initiatives to the creation of new data silos within industry. Given its increasing real share of all data collected and its salience to understanding individual activities, attitudes and preferences, it seems clear that consumer data have an important role to play in developing tomorrow's data infrastructures. The contributions to this book illustrate many of the ways in which academic engagement with customer-facing organisations can release consumer data that will help us to better understand what is going on in contemporary society. Yet effective representation of consumer behaviour will not be achieved unless the sources and operation of bias in consumer datasets can be successfully accommodated. This argues for a research agenda that seeks to triangulate rich, salient and timely consumer data with more conventional census, administrative data and social survey sources.

Further Reading

Haklay, M. (2010). How good is volunteered geographical information? A comparative study of OpenStreetMap and Ordnance Survey datasets. *Environment and Planning B: Planning and Design,* 37(4), 682-703.

Sax, L. J., Gilmartin, S. K. and Bryant, A. N. (2003). Assessing response rates and nonresponse bias in Web and paper surveys. *Research in Higher Education,* 44, 409-32.

Singleton, A. D., Spielman, S. and Folch, D. (2017). *Urban Analytics.* London: Sage.

The Economist (2017). 'The world's most valuable resource is no longer oil, but data'. May 6. https://www.economist.com/news/leaders/21721656-data-economy-demands-new-approach-antitrust-rules-worlds-most-valuable-resource

PART ONE

PROVENANCE AND CONSUMER DATA INFRASTRUCTURE

Consumer Registers as Spatial Data Infrastructure and their Use in Migration and Residential Mobility Research

Guy Lansley and Wen Li

1.1
Introduction

This chapter outlines efforts to devise modelled estimates of population change at a small-area level using annual registers that blend consumer and voter registration data. Names and addresses of individuals are routinely collected by governments and commercial organisations. However, there have been few attempts by academics to pool the data in order to track population changes despite the registers representing the majority of the adult population. Therefore, the possibility of linking databases for chronological pairs of years could provide a unique insight into population dynamics on an annual basis. Aligned with consumer data analytics, this information could reveal important statistics about the United Kingdom's changing social structure and how it varies geographically – with far more frequent refresh than available from comprehensive government sources such as the Census of Population. Comprehensive models of

migration at a household level would give us the opportunity to develop an understanding of social mobility and asset accumulation through linkage to other geographic datasets.

In this chapter, we present work on the 2013 and 2014 Consumer Registers produced by CACI Ltd (London, UK). The registers comprise the public version of the Electoral Register (sometimes termed the 'edited register') and are supplemented by a range of unattributed consumer data sources. Together, these population databases provide near complete coverage of the adult population at the individual level and are consolidated on an annual basis. However, the data only contain information on adult individuals' names and postal addresses and lack any demographic variables. In addition, due to the nature of their data collection and amalgamation, the consumer data are of unknown provenance. We have therefore developed novel data-linkage techniques in order to assess the completeness of the population recorded prior to modelling apparent trends from these pooled data.

Set in the context of harnessing information on population dynamics from data linkage between two registers, this study has three broad aims. First, to devise an appropriate technique to match addresses. Second, to estimate household dynamics by linking names at matched addresses. And finally, to estimate migration by modelling the movements of those that have left and joined addresses – specifically between 2013 and 2014. We will explore the feasibility of this model as a means of representing migration and social mobility.

1.2
The data source

The consumer registers potentially provide an invaluable source of population data as they comprise the vast majority of the adult population at an individual level. The data are routinely collected throughout the year, although collection methods vary between the registers' different data sources. The latest public Electoral Register enumerates about 50% of the population, it is usually updated in bulk in the autumn (with a deadline for inclusion being 15th October) and then released a few months later. However, following the introduction of Individual Electoral Registration in 2014, the proportion of those who decided to opt out of the edited versions of the Electoral Registers has increased (Electoral Commission, 2016). Therefore, the consumer sources are becoming more important underpinning components of the consumer registers.

In this study we have acquired registers for 2013 and 2014. In total, the 2013 register has 54,380,747 records, whilst the 2014 register represents 55,397,463 individuals. There are slightly over 27 million unique addresses in both datasets.

1.3
Consumer representation

Issues of representation are paramount to all consumer datasets (Kitchin, 2014). Therefore, we have been considerate of possible data biases, and how they may vary geographically. The Electoral Register has historically been considered a representative source of data on the voting population. Many social researchers have used the registers to create effective sample frames for surveys (Hoinville and Jowell, 1978). However, there are three main issues with accessing the data for social research today. Firstly, not all adults living in the UK are eligible to vote and are therefore excluded from the registers. Secondly, not all eligible adults are on the register due to political disengagement or changes of address that are untimely from the perspective of voter registration. Finally, not all adults agree to have their names and addresses shared on the public versions of the Electoral Registers. Consequently, the public versions do not fully enumerate the adult population. In this case, only about 50% of the adult population could be recorded by the edited version of the Electoral Register in 2013 and there has been considerable variation around this mean figure in recent years. The opt-out rates for the edited register have also steadily increased since its introduction in November 2001. Data made available from the UK Office for National Statistics (ONS) revealed that the opt-out rate in 2014 ranged between 19% and 88% between local authorities. However, the accuracy of the records is unknown. For example, it is estimated that 91% of entrees were accurate at the time of release of the 2015 register (Electoral Commission, 2016).

Previous research by the Electoral Commission found that Electoral Registers have an inherent demographic bias. As few as 67% of adults aged 20 to 24 were included in the data (Electoral Commission, 2016). There was also an under-representation of adults of black and minority ethnic backgrounds and foreign individuals who were eligible to vote due to their country of citizenship (i.e. Irish and Commonwealth citizens). In addition, only 57% of respondents in privately rented properties were found to be in the Electoral Register. This suggests that it is the geographical mobile population that are typically under-enumerated or inaccurately recorded. It is highly likely that the remaining data sources in the Consumer Registers will also under-enumerate those who recently changed address as there are little incentives to immediately update your details for many services following a change of address. It is also possible that different sources of consumer data may have particular demographic and socio-economic biases.

Previous research has focused upon issues of under-representation when discussing the provenance of big datasets. The Consumer Registers appear to over-represent the size of the adult population. We have compared the number of records to the estimated population of persons aged 17 and above from the ONS mid-year population estimates. For example, the 2013 and 2014 Consumer Registers each contain over three million more individuals than the ONS population estimates for the same year. This could be due to a number of reasons such as the duplication of those who live at multiple addresses, failure to delete old records and issues of cross contamination when data are pooled (Bollier, 2010). There are also likely to be some individuals below the age of 17 in the consumer data who cannot be distinguished due to the unavailability of demographic variables. We should also consider that population estimates do not represent the actual population counts.

We have attempted to identify if there are geographic patterns of overrepresentation. Firstly, we have considered local authority (or district) level variations at the national level through comparisons to the 2011 Census population (adults aged 17 and

above) (Figure 1.1). It can be observed that two main areas of under-representation are London and Northern Ireland. Whilst under-enumeration in London can possibly be accounted for by the higher proportion of (non-voter) migrants and individuals in rental properties, the low counts in Northern Ireland are probably due to different administrative procedures of their Electoral Office or a low presence of participating retailers. Indeed the pattern across the UK is rather serendipitous; whilst the most over-represented districts are generally less densely populated, this is not always the case. As the electoral roll is administered by local authorities, it is possible their varying practices have contributed to these differences. In addition, some of the consumer data may come from companies which have regional customer biases. We have also considered the spatial distribution of representation at the intra-urban scale. We have taken the City of Bristol as an example due to its pronounced socio-spatial inequalities and observed the rate at the census output area (OA) level. Census OAs had an average population of just over 300 in 2011. Indeed, Figure 1.1 also highlights that most under-representation occurs in the centre of the city. This part of the city has the greatest proportion of young adults, ethnic minorities and those in privately rented accommodation. All three of these characteristics were found to be associated with under-enumeration in the Electoral Register (Electoral Commission, 2016). Generally, it is neighbourhoods with the greatest rate of homeownership which have the highest counts in the consumer registers.

1.4
Address matching

The addresses recorded in the registers are formatted into six text columns representing distinctive lines of their postal addresses, such as house numbers or names, streets, cities, etc. In addition, there is also a postcode column. However, unfortunately,

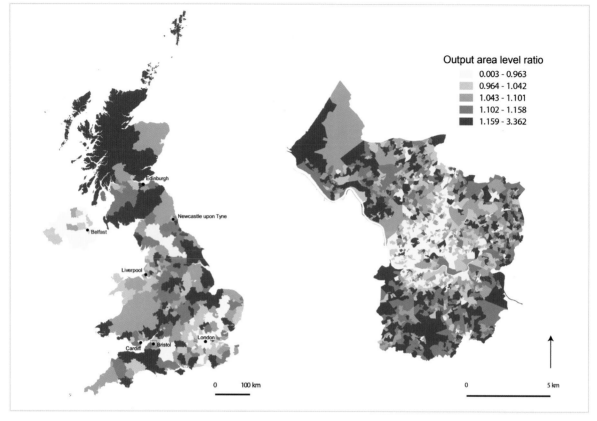

the addresses are not consistently structured. For example, the first line of an address may represent a flat number for some addresses, whilst it could represent the street name and house number for others. In addition, the number of lines in each address varies; many records do not include the county or region name. Although the data provider did include a unique reference number for each address, there were inconsistencies between its recording in 2013 and 2014.

Our aim was to create a methodology to match as many addresses as possible, regardless of how they are formatted. Due to inconsistencies within the database, we could not match all dwellings via a simple string match. To improve the quality of joining via textual addresses, we devised a method for matching addresses based on similarity of text strings. The method combines three similarity functions

derived from the intuition based on UK addresses. The first one is based on the numbers used in the addresses including property numbers and flat numbers. Examples are '14', '14a'. The second is based on the word difference between two addresses which measures how close the word sets respectively are used in the two addresses. This will cover the cases where addresses do not contain a house number. The function also takes into account the common words in addresses (such as road, street) by weighting the difference between words inverse proportionally to their frequency in the data, as well as their abbreviations. The third function is a variant of Levenshtein Distance (a.k.a. Edit Distance) which measures the difference in terms of characters. The adaption incorporates a weighting scheme to emphasise the difference at the beginning of the textual addresses. To match addresses from a set of

Figure 1.1
The ratio of the number of recorded persons in the 2013 Consumer Register by the population of persons aged 17 and above from the 2011 Census at the district level for the UK (left) and output area level for Bristol (right).

candidates, we combined the scores from the three similarity functions by weighted sums. The parameters were tuned by inspecting the matching pairs with large dissimilarity with respect to each similarity function.

Using our methodology, between 2013 and 2014 we were able to match 26,757,456 addresses, 98.9% of records in 2013.

We also acquired the addresses of all dwellings that were sold in 2013 and 2014 from the Land Registry. This data would be useful to determine where changes in residence were very likely to have occurred. In total, the databases contained 683,842 sold homes in 2013 and 794,929 in 2014. Through our methodology, 100% of these addresses could be matched to addresses from the Consumer Registers.

1.5
Identifying household change

With a valid means of linking addresses, it was possible to detect household level changes between years by matching the residents. We considered both the total number of residents in each year, and also changes in household composition. This was possible by matching residents' full names between different years in order to detect reoccurring residents. For example, if in one year 'John Smith' and 'Sally Smith' resided at a dwelling, and the following year 'John Smith' and 'David Jones' lived there, our model would assume one adult has remained, one adult left the property and one adult joined or came of age. We also created a key to represent the small number of individuals who may share their full name with another resident in their household. As this accounted for roughly 100,000 individuals in each dataset, we have presumed that many of these are not duplications and could be senior/junior name variants.

However, this method would fail to account for individuals whose names may have been recorded differently in different registers. Many individuals may have changed their names. There are roughly 120,000 marriages a year in England and Wales and many married women will take their husbands' surnames. We therefore applied heuristics to detect name changes due to marriage. Titles were not found to be useful discriminators of gender, many records were missing titles and there were also occurrences of gender neutral titles such as 'Dr'. Therefore, we used a lookup table of genders by forenames to estimate gender where the titles 'Mr', 'Mrs', 'Miss' or 'Ms' were not present. The database was built from birth certificate and consumer data files and represented over 17 million individuals (as described in Lansley and Longley, 2016). With the ability to differentiate between genders, our next task was to identify occurrences of where a female's forename matched between both datasets within a household but her surname did not. We then checked to see if a male was also present in the same household in both years. If the female's surname in the second year was identical to that of the male's, then we assume her surname changed following marriage. Between 2013 and 2014, 100,439 individuals were identified as having names that changed due to marriage. This figure is plausible given that many wives may not change their names after marriage and a proportion may not have lived with their husband in the preceding year.

Although punctuation was removed from the name matching process, we also created a flag to identify those with double-barrelled names. It was observed that some adults may have double-barrelled surnames in one register and just one of their singular surnames in the other. Aside from marriages, the main cause of this could be inconsistencies in name entry procedures between data suppliers. In addition to the identified marriages, we found that over 11,743 individuals had double-barrelled surnames that were inconsistently recorded. Finally, we also

Household type	Number of households
Stable household	19,940,359
Complete change	3,153,518
Growth	1,614,979
Shrinkage	1,218,182
Unstable household [1]	830,418
Present in 2013 only	289,808
Present in 2014 only	512,244

Table 1.1
Changing household characteristics, 2013–14.

considered surnames that were misspelled using a similar approach. This time we identified occurrences of identical forenames and surnames which were different by up to just three characters. In addition to those identified as recently married, or with inconsistently formatted names, 73,532 persons were identified as having differently spelt surnames. In total, 185,714 persons were matched despite being recorded with different surnames; these were subsequently reassigned as stable residents.

Although the registers contain personal information, our analysis was automated and the outputs have been aggregated to avoid issues of privacy. Throughout the chapter we have used some names as fictitious examples to demonstrate key concepts.

Following name cleaning, our household matching model identified that the vast majority of households remained stable, by which we mean their composition of recorded residents were identical in both registers. The frequency of different types of household change between 2013 and 2014 are outlined in Table 1.1.

We would expect there to be a geography to the rate of churn identified by linking the 2013 and 2014 databases. Taking Bristol as an example, the proportion of households with at least one continuing resident (by which we mean a name appearing at an address in both 2013 and 2014) have been mapped (Figure 1.2). It can be observed that the central parts of the city have the lowest

proportion of addresses which represent the same households in both years, identifying that more population churn occurs in cosmopolitan areas.

It is very difficult to determine who may have joined a household due to a change of address or due to coming of age. One possibility is to filter adults who join households where at least one other household member shares their surname as a large proportion of these are likely to be the offspring of other household members. Indeed, just over 2 million people met this criterion between 2013 and 2014. However, this number is very high considering the population of 18 year olds in this period was just over 770,000 according to the mid-year population estimates from the ONS. Therefore, many of these may be young adults returning to their parents' homes due to rising rent costs or elderly family members moving in. Indeed, between 2008 and 2015 the number of young adults who resided with their parents rose drastically to 3.3 million (ONS, 2015). Through linkage to our forenames database, it was possible to obtain inferences about age structures. Names have been found to be associated with age groups due to changes in baby name popularity over time, and changing rates of migration (Lansley and Longley, 2016). The forenames database provides models for the typical age structures for over 10,000 given names and was built from birth certificate records and consumer data sources (Lansley and Longley, 2016). It was observed that the median estimated age of those who have joined the family household

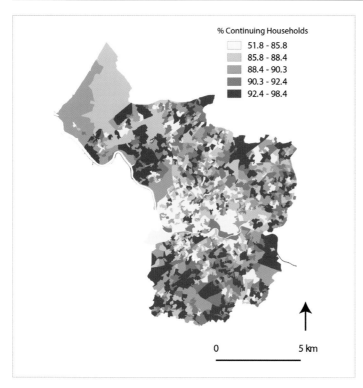

% Continuing Households
- 51.8 - 85.8
- 85.8 - 88.4
- 88.4 - 90.3
- 90.3 - 92.4
- 92.4 - 98.4

0   5 km

Figure 1.2
The proportion of addresses with at least one continuing resident in Bristol by output area.

is substantially younger than the average for the rest of the data.

1.6
Estimating migration

Having established a means of data linkage in order to detect population changes at a household level, our next objective was to model a substantive proportion of residential mobility which occurred between 2013 and 2014.

As the data lack any associated attributes, modelling migration had to be computed from novel data linkage techniques based on given and family names. Our heuristics are relatively straightforward. If we subset the data to create a database of adults who were present at a given address in the initial time period and were not rerecorded there in the subsequent time period – we could term these individuals as 'leavers'. Then a second subset of 'joiners' who were recorded at a dwelling during the subsequent time period but not the earlier.

It is highly probable that many of the leavers have also been recorded as joiners at their new address. However, it is difficult to confidently match them. Our first approach is to consider only adults with one occurrence of their full name in each subset of movers. If a name is recorded only once in the leavers subset and only once in the movers subset, it is highly probable that they represent the same individual who has changed address between 2013 and 2014. It is, therefore, possible to record their origin and destination. To increase the number of adults who we are able to match we will also consider residential mobility at the household level. By grouping all of the movers from the same household into a single household name composition key, it is possible we may be able to link household units that moved together. In many cases, we could also identify individuals with more common names using this approach. For example, potentially thousands of John Smiths could have moved house between our sample years. However, if one John Smith was originally a resident at an address with an individual with a less common name, there is a stronger likelihood that they are the only household unit which contains those individual names together. Of course, this model can only identify the moves of household units if members move together and are, therefore, recorded identically at their new address in 2014.

Therefore, to predict migration we utilised two models. The first model attempts to identify singular joins between household units from households that left an address in 2013 and are present in households in 2014. A second model then found additional movers by focusing only on adults with unique full names, as not all moved household units will remain intact following a move (i.e. household deformation or due to delays in recording specific members). Although the models may neglect individuals with more common names, their results could be informative of broader migration trends. For instance, it will be possible to generate statistics on moves, such as distance and deprivation. This insight can then be used to allocate the non-unique name holders into the most likely origin-destination pairings.

1.6.1
Unique names

As our models are largely based on the linkage of unique occurrences of names between our movers databases, it is important to understand the connotations this may have when attempting to represent the wider population. Most full names are relatively uncommon. For example, in the 2013 register, 18.3% of the population have unique full names and 50% of adults share their names with less than 16 other individuals. Figure 1.3 displays the cumulative frequency for full names in 2013. However, in addition to considering unique names alone, by pooling all of the names within households that change address, our models will also consider many individuals with more common names. For example, while there are over 11,000 David Smiths and 6,000 Margaret Smiths (the most common male and female names respectively) in the 2013 register, there are less than 140 households comprising of these two names together, despite it being the third most common household name composition.

Figure 1.3 also labels the nine most popular names in the 2013 data, all of which are white British male names. We have considered that a large proportion of adults with unique names may have international heritage. Therefore, to explore the relationship between ethnic heritage and name popularity we ran all of the names from the 2013 register through a names classifying tool called Onomap (www.onomap.org). The tool assigns each name (considering both forenames and surnames) to their most likely cultural, ethnic and linguistic group and was produced from clustering an extensive database of forename-surname

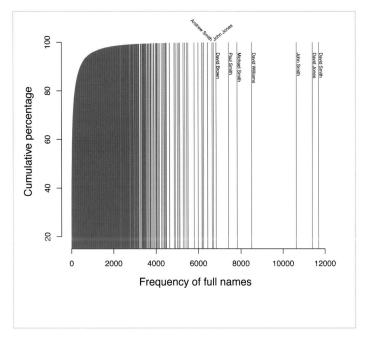

pairs (Mateos et al, 2007). The proportion of name-inferred ethnic groups for the 2013 Consumer Register and a subset of those with unique names only is shown in Table 1.2. The percentage of British ethnic groups as recorded in the 2011 Census have also been included for comparison.

Although reliant on names as proxies of cultural heritage, the analysis suggested that the Consumer Register slightly over-represents the White British population. This assumption is reasonable given that the Electoral Register is known to under-enumerate ethnic minorities. Although the precise sources of the consumer data are not known, ethnic minorities are also known to be under-represented in large customer loyalty databases. As anticipated the under-representation of the White British population is considerable amongst adults with unique names. For example, names identified as 'other white' background were over 3.5 times as prominent in the unique names subset relative to the original data. This reflects the range and diversity of European names. We, therefore, need to consider that although we have devised a

Figure 1.3
A cumulative percentage of the frequency of full names in 2013.

2001 Census Ethnic Group	Consumer Register	Unique names only	2011 (Excl. NI)
A) WHITE – BRITISH	84.36%	60.56%	81.47%
B) WHITE – IRISH	3.79%	4.55%	0.95%
C) WHITE – ANY OTHER WHITE BACKGROUND	3.77%	13.30%	4.32%
H) ASIAN OR ASIAN BRITISH – INDIAN	2.02%	4.48%	2.36%
J) ASIAN OR ASIAN BRITISH – PAKISTANI	1.78%	3.18%	1.91%
K) ASIAN OR ASIAN BRITISH – BANGLADESHI	0.40%	0.70%	0.73%
L) ASIAN OR ASIAN BRITISH – ANY OTHER ASIAN BACKGROUND	0.17%	0.74%	1.40%
M) BLACK OR BLACK BRITISH – CARIBBEAN	0.04%	0.14%	0.98%
N) BLACK OR BLACK BRITISH – AFRICAN	0.79%	2.67%	1.66%
R) OTHER ETHNIC GROUPS – CHINESE	0.43%	0.86%	0.70%
S) OTHER ETHNIC GROUPS – ANY OTHER ETHNIC GROUP	1.67%	4.68%	0.55%
Y) UNCLASSIFIED	0.78%	4.14%	NA

Table 1.2
The proportions of ethnic groups for the 2013 Consumer Register, a subset of adults with unique names only, and the UK 2011 Census.

novel way of estimating internal migration, a greater proportion of the modelled flows may be representative of those with international heritage.

1.6.2
Representing migration

In total, our model estimated the origin and destination of 762,359 individuals. In addition to these, our model also identified a further 100,000 cases where adults moved within the same postcode. We have considered that these movers may have remained in the addresses that could have been recorded differently in both registers. Therefore these individuals are not included in the subsequent results.

By joining the postcodes to the ONS Postcode Directory, it was possible to observe spatial trends in modelled migration. Most moves tended to occur over relatively short distances which corresponds with known migration traits within the UK (Stillwell and Thomas, 2016). Our median distance was just 19.7 miles as the crow flies, whilst the mean was 66.1 (Figure 1.4). The Royal Mail identified that the average distance of movers which could be identified by their redirection service is just 25.83 miles (Royal Mail, 2017). However this service is likely to be biased towards home owners.

We have presented the key spatial trends as a flow map below, which displays the interactions between local authorities in Great Britain (Figure 1.5). In order to only convey the key trends in the data and avoid issues of disclosure, only flows of at least 40 persons are shown. In addition, we have also included moves within each district. These are displayed as proportional symbols in the centre of each authority.

Most moves between 2013–14 occurred within the same local authority district. It is also observable from Figure 1.5 that a large proportion of flows are between neighbouring local authorities. It is also interesting to predict migration between regions, and observe how it may vary from officially recorded statistics from the 2011 Census. Although recorded differently and

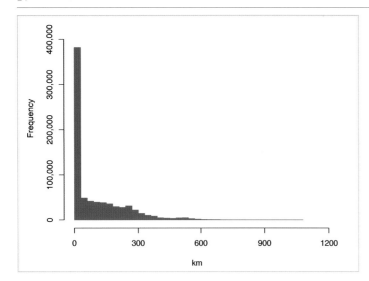

Figure 1.4
A histogram of the distance
moved by adults in the
Consumer Registers.

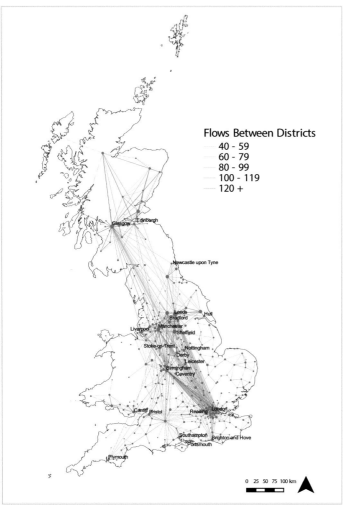

Figure 1.5
Flows of home movers
between local authorities.

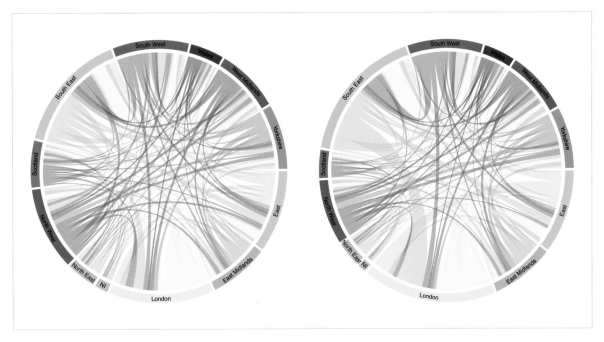

Figure 1.6
Chord diagrams representing the proportion of moves between regions as identified from the Consumer Registers (left) and the 2011 Census (right).

absent of any children, the trends identified by the Consumer Registers were similar to the official statistics from 2011. Flows between regions as recorded from the Consumer Registers and the 2011 Census are displayed in Figure 1.6.

The migration model also presents an opportunity to gain an understanding of segregation, social mobility and asset accumulation through geographic data linkage. There is an assumption that geographic mobility and social mobility are extrinsically linked as people generally move to improve their life chances (Savage, 1998). Focusing on the English Index of Multiple Deprivation (IMD), it is possible to observe the social trajectory of internal migrants by considering the deprivation ranks of their origin and destination Lower Super Output Areas (LSOAs). To demonstrate the key trends in our data, we have aggregated all of the English LSOAs into IMD quintiles and observed the flows of migrants between them (Figure 1.7).

For each quintile, the most popular out-flow feeds back into the same group. The next largest flows are those into the

adjacent quintiles which suggests that there is still only limited social mobility in England. There are only a minority of migrants that move between places of drastically different levels of deprivation. Interestingly, there was only a slight majority of upwardly mobile flows over downwardly mobile flows. Whilst this could highlight that migration is no longer more abundant amongst socially mobile adults, it is probably also due to adults moving between living with parents, rental accommodation and eventually home ownership. House prices have made many of the least deprived neighbourhoods unaffordable for first-time buyers (Dorling, 2015). In addition, there are also occurrences of elderly relatives moving in with family or to assisted accommodation. Indeed, these results can also be explained by the fact that most moves occur over relatively short distances and deprivation is positively spatially autocorrelated. Figure 1.7 also identifies addresses that were sold in 2013 or 2014. It is also noteworthy that a greater proportion of moves where a house was purchased occurred for movers moving to and from the least deprived parts of the country.

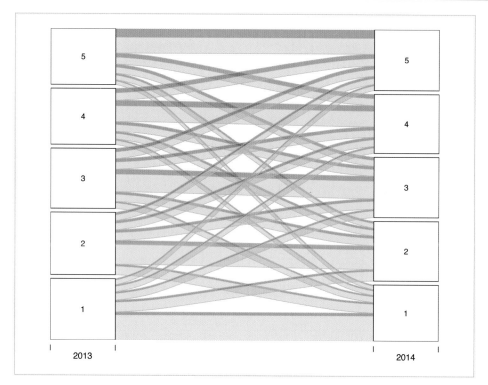

Figure 1.7
An alluvial plot of migration between different quintiles of the 2015 English Index of Multiple Deprivation, where the lowest quintiles are most deprived. Moves to addresses that were sold in 2013 have been coloured green.

1.7
Conclusion

Our analysis has presented a novel means of estimating migration from population registers for two given years. Given that similar datasets are built each year, such models could fill the data void on internal migration which occur between census years. Although the model presented in this chapter identified a larger sample of movers than any other available dataset on internal migration, excluding the decennial Census, there are a couple of means which could be employed to increase the number of moves that could be identified from the registers. The social and geographic trends from the modelled data could be used to allocate the duplicated records that could not be definitively matched before. Indeed, we have found that distance is an obvious influencer, although geodemographic characteristics are also worth considering. However, this approach is based entirely on assumptions built from a particular sample of movers. A second feasible approach is

through matching registers which are recorded more than one year apart. Research from the Electoral Commission identified that there is a data lag in the electoral register which occurs when individuals change address (Electoral Commission, 2016). Only a minority of individuals are correctly updated within a year of a change of address. It is conceivable that a similar lag may be inherent in the consumer data files too, although it is not possible to determine the rate due to the anonymity of the sources.

This research has demonstrated that it is viable to model household dynamics and migration from population registers through novel data linkage techniques. Although collected for administrative purposes, the coverage of the data presents us with a unique opportunity to harness detailed information on the population at a small-area level. Through a household matching algorithm, it was possible to create indicators of churn which corresponded with results from the

2011 Census. It was also possible to determine internal migration flows for hundreds of thousands of individuals. Whilst the Consumer Registers are the most comprehensive data on the population at an individual level, there were still undoubtable issues of representation, and these vary at regional and intra-urban scales. Therefore future work should attempt to understand the provenance of the data in order to scale back the data and fill in data gaps.

Further Reading

Bollier, D. (2010). The promise and peril of big data (p. 1). Washington, DC: Aspen Institute, Communications and Society Program.

Dorling, D., (2015). Policy, politics, health and housing in the UK. *Policy & Politics*, 43(2), 163-180.

Electoral Commission (2016). *The December 2015 electoral registers in Great Britain: Accuracy and completeness of the registers in Great Britain and the transition to Individual Electoral Registration.* The Electoral Commission Report, July 2016.

Hoinville, G. and Jowell, R. (1978). *Survey Research Practice.* London: Heinemann Educational Books.

Kitchin, R. (2014). *The data revolution: Big data, open data, data infrastructures and their consequences.* London: Sage.

Lansley, G. and Longley, P. (2016). Deriving age and gender from forenames for consumer analytics. *Journal of Retailing and Consumer Services*, 30, 271-278.

Mateos, P., Webber, R. and Longley, P. (2007). The cultural, ethnic and linguistic classification of populations and neighbourhoods using personal names. CASA Working Paper 116, Centre for Advanced Spatial Analysis, University College London.

ONS (2015). Families and households: 2015. Office for National Statistics, Statistical bulletin.

Royal Mail (2017). UK's first home move map reveals nation's habits. Online: http://www.royalmailgroup.com/uk%E2%80%99s-first-home-move-map-reveals-nation%E2%80%99s-habits

Savage, M. (1988). The missing link? The relationship between spatial mobility and social mobility. *British Journal of Sociology*, 39(4), 554-577.

Stillwell, J. and Thomas, M. (2016). How far do internal migrants really move? Demonstrating a new method for the estimation of intra-zonal distance. *Regional Studies, Regional Science*, 3(1), 28-47.

Acknowledgements

We are grateful to CACI for providing the Consumer Register data under a special research licence to enable us to carry out this research.

Note

1. Unstable households refer to addresses that have remained the same household size, but some of the residents have changed.

2

The Provenance of Customer Loyalty Card Data

Alyson Lloyd, James Cheshire and Martin Squires

2.1
Introduction

Loyalty card schemes have become extremely popular for both retailers and consumers. They create a system of marketing incentives that encourage customer loyalty by offering rewards for repeat shopping behaviour. These schemes, facilitated by technological innovation, have placed retailers at the forefront of the 'Big Data' revolution since they now retain and interpret an immense body of data about their customers and their consumption patterns. These data underpin a burgeoning consumer insight industry, but have been subject to relatively little appraisal from the academic community. This oversight is, in part, a symptom of disaggregate loyalty card data being hard to access outside commercial settings. Thanks to the efforts of the Consumer Data Research Centre (CDRC) this hurdle is slowly being overcome, offering the potential to tackle societal and geographical questions

in an entirely new way. However, as is prominent in 'Big Data' research, many uncertainties arise when they are utilised in contexts beyond those for which they were originally created.

There has been a wealth of academic research on loyalty card schemes, which has primarily focused on the concept of loyalty and whether or not schemes are effective in increasing shopping behaviours. However, sparse evidence is available regarding the applications of loyalty card data outside of commercial contexts. The emergence of large, spatially and temporally referenced data, such as is produced by loyalty cards, has caused a considerable paradigm shift from quantitative geographic research to data-driven geography. This has fundamentally challenged withstanding research practices through its blending of abductive, inductive and deductive approaches. For example, data-driven methods advocate descriptive insights of voluminous populations, rather than theory driven research supported by sampled observations of individuals. Such data allow for the creation of theories from observed behavioural patterns rather than self-reported responses, such as are a feature of traditional methods (i.e. surveys). They allow us to infer spatiotemporal dynamics directly, on a multitude of scales, and are collected on an ongoing basis, meaning that both mundane and unplanned events can be captured. This has allowed researchers to now analyse the world through large-scale digital systems.

This chapter provides an overview of the provenance of loyalty card data and the utility of these data in population research. Examples are presented from a loyalty card dataset obtained from a major high street retailer (HSR) in the UK, made available through the CDRC. These data represent approximately 18 million UK customers and 500 million transactions collected between 2012 and 2014, from an expansive national network of stores, providing a powerful tool for exploring the dynamics of loyalty card data.

2.2
Data provenance

Loyalty card data have attracted substantial interest from retailers, marketing agencies and the wider research community for two fundamental reasons. Firstly, the proliferation of loyalty card schemes amongst major retailers since the 1990s has provided a means of gathering data pertaining to a large proportion of the consumer population. For example, it is estimated that approximately three-quarters (76%) of consumers carry between one and five cards with them at all times (YouGov, 2013) and collectively, almost 46.5 million people, or 92% of the adult population, are currently registered with at least one loyalty card programme (Loyalive, 2015). Secondly, these schemes provide rich data about consumers. Data collected typically comprise of customer metadata such as age, gender and address, in addition to transactional data describing store visiting and product buying characteristics, spending patterns and timestamps of when interactions occur. From a retailer's perspective, these data are principally collected and analysed for Customer Relationship Marketing (CRM) purposes, allowing a greater understanding of individual customers. For example, variations in loyalty behaviour are typically quantified using segmentation; the notion that a market can be divided up into several behavioural, demographic and/or psychological groups, over a variety of behavioural indicators such as transaction frequency, average intervals, duration of activity and basket size. Facilitated by customer postcodes, these segments are then enriched through linkage to (geo)demographic classifications. These classifications provide a useful context about social structures and common characteristics between people and places, which have been widely applied by businesses to infer lifestyles, social attitudes and identify the best locations from which to serve and retain their customers (Longley, 2017). Postcodes are also typically utilised for marketing strategies such as mail-based rewards or location-based targeting, yet also for spatial applications such as location planning and catchment area mapping.

From an academic perspective, this relatively new form of data has attracted considerable interest due to its potential to inform a broad spectrum of social, economic, political and environmental patterns and processes, and represents a huge opportunity for endeavours in human geography. The provision of customer postcodes and store locations provide a valuable geographic reference that can be regarded as the key to utilising these data for a broad range of spatial applications, and the data are high in temporal granularity, providing detailed timestamps of consumption patterns. Equipped with these data there is the potential to build a finer-grained − in both spatial and temporal terms − depiction of societal phenomenon than previous work with more 'traditional' datasets such as national censuses. These depictions would have widespread applications in a broad range of public service decision-making processes from transport planning to health.

It is therefore paradoxical that despite the growing abundance of these data, their use by academic researchers has been limited. This, perhaps understandably, is partly due to the data's origins in privately owned businesses and their secure storage requirements since they provide information about consumer transactions, residential locations, movements and interactions. This raises substantial ethical and legal considerations in regards to disclosure control, anonymisation and privacy. Safeguards are therefore required, especially where geographic information technologies facilitate the linkage of these data to the likes of administrative or alternative spatial data sources. Combined, these aspects have generated substantial barriers to advancing understanding of their fitness for purpose outside of commercial contexts. Yet, access to these data via the CDRC has provided a means of beginning to overcome such obstacles, allowing exploration of their dynamics and the challenges encountered when attempting to apply these data in research. For example, these data are adequate from a retailer's perspective, as variables are created and data interpreted with the primary focus of understanding and maximising the buying behaviours of their customer base. Conversely, academic endeavours strive to obtain rigorous representative data for their population of interest and therefore tend to prefer official statistics collated by government. It would be impractical to assume that these kinds of consumer data will meet the 'gold standards' of national statistical datasets in terms of both their quality and representativeness; therefore, understanding their applications for research purposes requires preliminary considerations such as the completeness, accuracy, bias and validity/plausibility of

the data. As we demonstrate below, access to the CDRC HSR loyalty data has facilitated a better understanding of the nature of these data in their raw form. These insights are foundational to a pragmatic approach to utilising these data in wider research and facilitate an appraisal of the potential for such research to offer substantive insights into social and geographical phenomena.

2.3
Loyalty cards as social and spatial data

Loyalty cards typically produce very rich temporal data on consumption patterns. Whilst these behaviours may arguably provide a very useful context of socio-demographic characteristics, loyalty data comprise little explicit socio-demographic information. However, customer postcodes provide a valuable means of linkage to conventional statistical geographic units and data associated with them such as existing national statistics. This provides a number of advantages. For example, it allows measures of neighbourhood type, population characteristics or cultural background to be appended to individual customer records, which permits interpretation of how consumer behaviours may vary with population characteristics. This also allows for the identification of potential biases in the data. Conversely, these data offer a variety of attractions for our current understanding of geodemographic phenomena. Geodemographic classifications are widely used in business and public service organisations, yet are typically derived from surveys such as national Censuses, which may have limited sample sizes that can be affected by non-response rates, a coarse spatial scale and low temporal granularity (collected on a decennial basis). In addition, whilst traditional classifications provide valuable local indicators, and there have been contributions towards daytime indicators with the production of small area workplace statistics, human identity

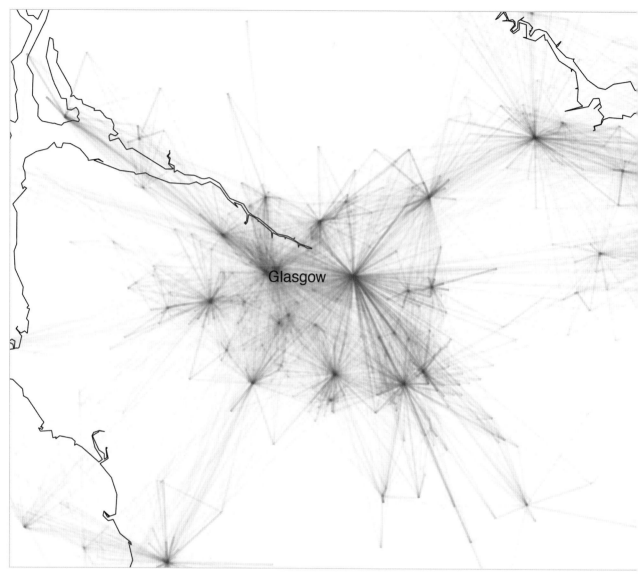

Glasgow

encapsulates more than the duality of work and residence (Longley, 2017). It is therefore increasingly important to incorporate more appropriate representations of individual trajectories with finer temporal granularities, such as those that represent the dynamics of day-to-day activities. The emergence of novel forms of Big Data such as from loyalty cards offer the potential to facilitate a more sophisticated view of this phenomenon, providing voluminous consumer data that are not compromised by uneven response rates, can be updated on a regular basis and permit consistent comparison between different behavioural datasets on a relatively granular scale (over 1.4 million postcode units across the UK). Such information may provide an enriched description of what makes people, or groups of people, distinctive. However, utilising these data in this context also gives rise to a number of shortcomings, such as the well-established issue of ecological fallacy when aggregating data to a small-area level (i.e. confounding the characteristics of areas with particular

Figure 2.1
Customer residence to store flows – Central Lowlands, Scotland.

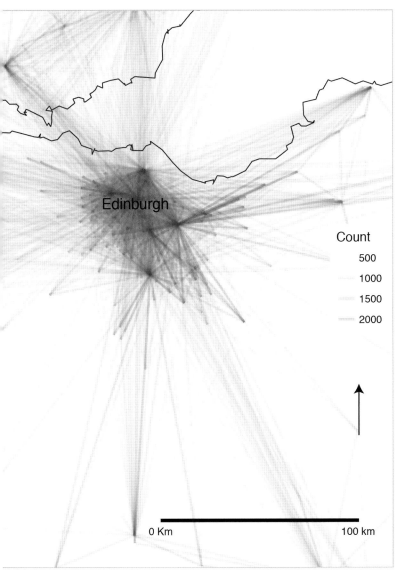

Count

500
1000
1500
2000

Edinburgh

0 Km   100 km

therefore are able to capture both short-term changes in buying behaviours and long-term trends of changing consumer attitudes and lifestyles. An example comes from Tesco's Clubcard, where analysis of their loyalty data resulted in the linkage of customers buying nappies for the first time also correlating with an increase in buying beer. Further investigation revealed that this could be attributed to the behaviours of new fathers, who showed an increase in drinking in the home rather than socialising. These kinds of analysis will likely increase our understanding of the linkage between consumption patterns and geodemographics, providing insights for both contemporary classifications and retailers alike.

An additional dimension of loyalty card data is that they not only provide insights into what consumers buy, but also the network of stores that they use to service their needs. Spatial patterns can be observed in this instance by utilising customer postcodes and store location information. For example, Figure 2.1 shows HSR journeys made from places of residence to store locations across part of the Central Lowlands of Scotland. Darker lines indicate more popular trips, which can be generated by convenience of access, or the range of activities that different destinations offer.

Detailed analyses of individual-level daily activity patterns in loyalty card data have the potential to be useful in a number of contexts. Research regarding human activity spaces (i.e. the choice of routes through time and space that individuals take in order to meet their daily obligations) have important applications not only for understanding travel and commuting behaviour, but also under-researched areas such as trip chaining. Very little research has been able to utilise large, temporally granular and longitudinal data for research in such domains. For example, there is a need for greater insight into how consumers incorporate store visits

individuals who live within them). In addition, linkage of these data is wholly dependent on the assumption that addresses provided by loyalty cards are accurate, which may not always be the case (i.e. see Section 2.4).

Nevertheless, a prominent advantage of loyalty card data is that they allow us to analyse trends at both individual and aggregate levels. In addition, the transactional data offer high temporal granularity over long time periods,

Census Data

Loyalty Card Data

Figure 2.2
Daytime flows card vs. census.

into their daily travel obligations, of which the majority of research to date has only been able to utilise self-reported travel diaries of relatively small sample sizes. In addition, the vast majority of research into trip chaining has focused on home to work based trips only, despite work-related travel not representing all activities that are undertaken (i.e. leisure and tourism; Primerano et al., 2008). Loyalty consumption patterns could provide insight into how activities change over time, or how interactions with increasingly popular online alternatives (such as click and collect or home delivery) may affect subsequent behaviours. The data produced by loyalty cards allows us to investigate a broad number of variables relating to mobility, such as distances travelled, size of store networks and the characteristics of locations that individuals visit over time. These insights have important implications for planning decisions and policies in urban environments and also issues relating to high street retail e-resilience.

By incorporating the temporal element of these movements, we can further utilise these data to understand more complex socio-spatial characteristics. This evolving research may enable us to summarise daily activity patterns in both time and space. Figure 2.2 shows an example of patronage flows from customer residences using lunchtime, weekday transactions of HSR customers, compared to self-reported origin to workplace destination flows from the 2011 Census.

Such comparisons suggest that loyalty card data may be able to provide us with the means to understand daytime activities within the general population, help us to better understand aspects such as the connectedness of various locations over different temporal periods (i.e. daily, weekly, seasonal) and – ultimately – aid the construction of geo-temporal profiles. These temporally integrated analyses postulate that people are influenced not only by where they live, but also by places they visit, when they visit them and who they interact with. It is our expectation that loyalty card data, both alone and in combination with other datasets, will advance our knowledge of the functional relationships between places given the volume of interactions between different social, economic and demographic groups that they are able to capture.

Figure 2.3
Summary diagram of
issues affecting data.

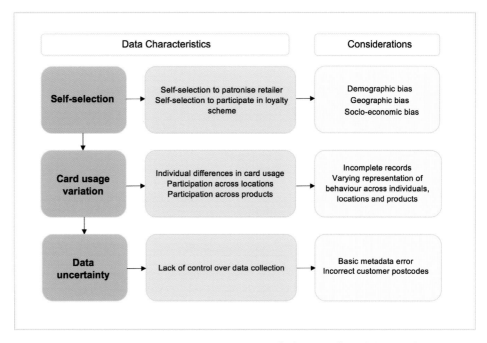

Figure 2.3
Summary diagram of
issues affecting data.

2.4
Data quality and uncertainty

The creation of data in a purely commercial setting leads to a complete absence of researcher control in the data collection process. This raises substantial methodological questions when applying commercial data in research; it is therefore necessary to determine data quality, uncertainty and fitness for purpose in order to extract and interpret meaningful insights. For example, initial assessments in this context require identification of potential bias in the sample (i.e. ascertaining both demographic and geographic coverage of customers), determining the quantity, consistency and completeness of data pertaining to individual customers, and also the plausibility of observed trends. The evaluation of these dynamics in loyalty card data is made possible through exploratory analyses of the CDRC's HSR data, and the proceeding section aims to highlight a number of pragmatic measures that should be considered when implementing loyalty card data in research practice. These can be understood in terms of a number of major themes that influence both the loyalty population sample and data quality (see Figure 2.3).

In loyalty card data, issues of representation and bias are inherent due to the effects of self-selection since only those choosing to participate in a loyalty scheme will be represented. Traditional sampling techniques uphold that every member of a population has a known probability of being selected as part of the sample, and if it is to be valid, we must ensure that the sample is independent and random. However, loyalty card samples are neither designed nor collected and it is therefore improbable to assume that such a dataset will warrant a random sample of the general population. Retailers attract and target certain demographic groups, therefore over-representing those who fall within the scope of the particular markets or activities that are being tracked. In addition to these initial self-selection biases, there is ambiguity as to whether information gathered about the retailer's loyalty population can be applied to all purchases taking place at a given outlet, or if behaviours can only be attributed to the loyalty card holding segment of customers.

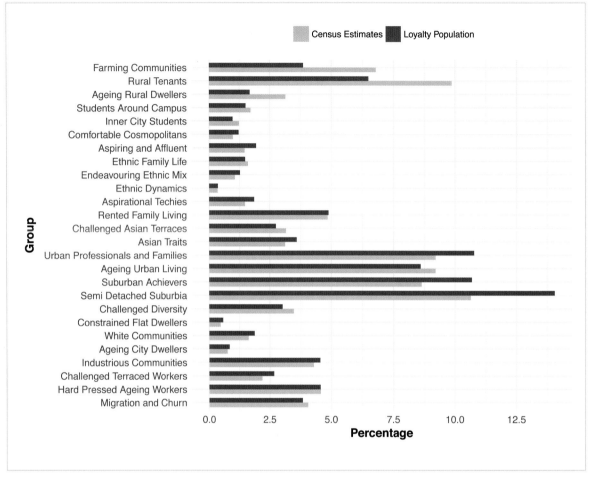

For example, the loyalty customer base may be subject to an underlying self-selection process such as customers who are more money conscious or receptive to special offers being more likely to participate, whereas those with privacy concerns likely being deterred. Variations in behaviour as a result of individual/psychological dispositions to participate can be investigated to some extent by comparing loyalty card and non-card transactional data. However, making direct comparisons can be problematic due to non-card data also comprising instances where a cardholder did not use their card with a transaction. Yet, using a data-driven approach, demographic biases can be investigated by drawing comparisons with existing national population statistics,

for example, by analysing distributions of age and gender characteristics present in the data. In addition, we can attempt to quantify dynamics by drawing comparisons between existing geodemographic classifications. Figure 2.4 demonstrates an example of the volumes of HSR customers across Output Area Classification (OAC) groups in comparison to Census estimates. These classifications categorise the general UK population based on socio-economic characteristics obtained from the 2011 Census.

It is clear that certain groups are disproportionately represented by these data in terms of both their characteristics and geographic locations, with more affluent groups likely being over-represented (particularly ageing suburban

Figure 2.4
Proportions of customers by OAC for loyalty customers vs. census – group level.

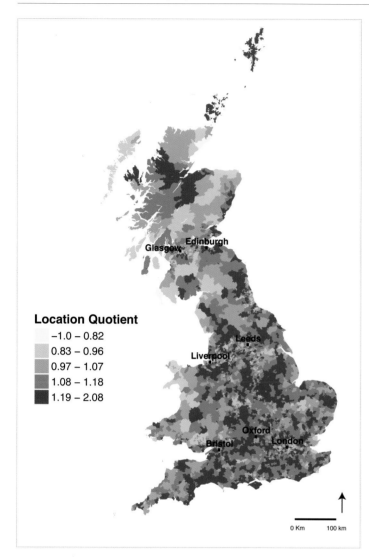

Location Quotient
- −1.0 – 0.82
- 0.83 – 0.96
- 0.97 – 1.07
- 1.08 – 1.18
- 1.19 – 2.08

Figure 2.5
LQ of cardholders per MSOA.

volumes as estimated by the 2011 Census. Customers may also be more likely to participate in loyalty schemes if they live in close proximity to a store; therefore, the distribution of customers may also be dependent on the retailer's store locations relative to their consumer base.

Further considerations of bias and uncertainty arise from individual differences in card usage, which can result in a disproportionate representation of customers across the database. Firstly, data may not include all of the purchases made by card-holding accounts, due to not having the card or feeling that it is not worth using for small purchases (Wright and Sparks, 1999). In addition, many seldom or never utilise the cards after signing up (Cortiñas, Elorz, and Múgica, 2008) and it is improbable to assume that consumers will patronise only one chain, meaning there is a limited completeness in utilising the records of a single loyalty card. Therefore, it is important to consider one retailer's loyalty data will represent a variable fraction of an individual's full spending habits. Due to the lack of available data outside of commercial settings, very little research has been able to quantify the effects of card usage on data quality. However, within the HSR database, approximately a third of customers (33%) transacted less than 10 times over a two-year period, and approximately 23.4% of all customers were responsible for 60% of all transactions. Overall, only 9% were active on a weekly basis, yet selecting customers that exhibit monthly activity patterns over a two-year period represents approximately 7 million, or 38%, of HSR customers. Therefore, in relation to the total sample size, these data still represent a significantly large and rich source of data in comparison to traditional studies of population activity over longitudinal periods.

Variations in card usage are also evident across different retail locations. For example, significantly lower levels of participation are observed in more transient locations, such as 'convenience'

cohorts and young professionals), and deprived neighbourhoods/less affluent segments of the general population under-represented. Importantly for applications in human geography, this may bias the resulting spatial distribution of customers who are signed up to the scheme, with volumes of customers across areas reflecting underlying socio-economic characteristics rather than a representation of the general population. Figure 2.5 demonstrates an example of the distribution of cardholders across Middle Layer Super Output Area's (MSOA) in Great Britain, taking into account underlying population stores (i.e. smaller stores located in urban areas). Conversely, higher levels of participation are observed in destination locations, such as city centre flagship stores. This is likely due to the importance of larger basket sizes in these store types, which produce higher loyalty participation (i.e. due to the perceived benefits of more expensive purchases). A product type bias is also evident, with cards more likely to be used with higher value items. The implications of these trends are that, firstly, the distribution of behavioural data will be influenced by the characteristics of a store location, and secondly, if analysing individual product buying behaviours, it is important to consider that the purchasing of certain products may be over- or under-represented based on the propensity to use a card for that particular item. These aspects have important implications for the mobility and product-buying analyses outlined in Section 2.3, as the completeness of individual trajectories may be influenced by these differing motivations to participate. Despite this (due to the enormous volume of overall data) there are still a vast amount of data produced by loyalty cards available across all store locations and product types.

Finally, due to the lack of data collection control, there may be elements of uncertainty regarding the completeness, accuracy and validity of these data. Assessment of data completeness and accuracy may be particularly important in the case of loyalty card metadata, as this information is entirely dependent on accurate human input at the time of enrolment. Simple exploratory analyses can be applied to identify basic errors in these data, such as invalid postcodes or illogical age ranges. However, a more complex issue is that the accuracy of customer postcodes is also dependent on the motivation of a customer to update this information in the event of a location change. For example, we have demonstrated that through the linkage of locational and behavioural attributes, we are able to identify those in the loyalty

card population (approximately 3.5%) with stated addresses that may no longer be their usual place of residence. Although this is reassuring since it indicates that the vast majority of loyalty data likely contain valid spatial references, it does also suggest errors assumed not to be present in official statistics. This has important implications if using the postcode information as a key spatial reference to infer social and spatial processes, and efforts should be made to identify potentially spurious patterns before utilising the data. However, we also highlight how these errors are not random and can be disproportionately ascribed to certain segments of the loyalty population - primarily students and other groups who are likely to have particularly transient residential locations. Therefore, we can make attempts to identify customers who are most at risk of exhibiting these data errors.

2.5
Conclusion

Loyalty card data offer an untapped opportunity for researchers to analyse societal and geographical questions in an entirely new way. They represent large numbers of people and allow analyses at a variety of spatio-temporal scales. However, there are a number of preliminary considerations and pragmatic steps required to ensure these data are fit for purpose in a research context. For example, loyalty cards represent large but selective samples, are inherent with socio-economic and spatial biases and present elements of data uncertainty. It would be impractical to assume that these kinds of consumer data will meet the standards of national statistical datasets, yet it is suggested here that pragmatic actions can be taken to ensure the quality of these data are both understood and considered. As such, the preliminary focus when applying these data should be suitably based on the initial assessment and quantification of inherent data quality issues, such as those outlined in Section 2.4. Careful consideration of these characteristics may facilitate extraction of insights that were not previously possible nor practically obtainable using traditional methodologies. These cautions mirror those adopted in traditional methods of data handling in regards to data quality and sampling bias; however, due to the nature of Big Data collection, efficient methods of revealing these inherent data issues require exploration.

An important future direction is therefore to continue to develop new methods of handling and analysing these data. Traditional statistical methods have been focused on data-scarce science, where aims are to identify significant relationships from small, controlled sample sizes with known relationships. Developments in Big Data research may involve applying data-driven approaches to quantify uncertainty within the data, continual critique and truth propagation and using contemporary social and geographical theory to support the reliable use of these new kinds of data sources. Beyond this, future prospects are concerned with gaining a robust understanding of the applications of these data to advancing our knowledge of population dynamics in respect to consumption behaviour, daytime activities, mobility patterns, spatio-temporal dynamics and the relationship of these patterns in regards to consumer attitudes and lifestyles. Moving towards constructing spatio-temporal classifications using these kinds of data may advance our knowledge of relationships between places in terms of the volumes of interactions generated by different social, economic and demographic groups over different temporal periods. It is further possible, through the availability of common spatial keys such as postcodes, to draw comparisons between classifications derived from alternative spatially referenced datasets. This offers the potential to, firstly, bridge gaps between issues of representation that are inherent in these data, but also to create an enriched view of social and spatial processes based on a broader range of information. We may expect to see correspondence between the clusters derived from loyalty cards and the categories of traditional classifications for example, which will ultimately provide an enhanced description of what makes certain groups of people distinctive.

The development of these applications will be made possible through the continuing data collaborations facilitated by the CDRC, which provides a means of utilising data of a personal nature, whilst adhering to important disclosure controls. It is critically important that analyses of this nature endeavour to achieve outputs that are both informative and safe, especially where data linkage is concerned. Nevertheless, the prospects of loyalty card data as a social and spatial data source present promising applications for the use of large consumer datasets in social science research.

Further Reading

Cortiñas, M., Elorz, M. and Múgica, J. M. (2008). The use of loyalty-cards databases: Differences in regular price and discount sensitivity in the brand choice decision between card and non-card holders. *Journal of Retailing and Consumer Services*, 15(1), 52-62.

Longley, P. A. (2017). Geodemographic profiling, In *The International Encyclopedia of Geography*. Wiley and the American Association of Geographers (AAG).

Loyalive (2015). Loyalive – an introduction. URL no longer available.

Primerano, F., Taylor, M. A., Pitaksringkarn, L. and Tisato, P. (2008). Defining and understanding trip chaining behaviour. *Transportation*, 35(1), 55-72.

Wright, C. and Sparks, L. (1999). Loyalty saturation in retailing: Exploring the end of retail loyalty cards? *International Journal of Retail & Distribution Management*, 27(10), 429-440.

YouGov (2013). British shoppers in love with loyalty cards. Online: yougov.co.uk/news/2013/11/07/british-shoppers-love-loyalty-cards/

Acknowledgements

The authors thank 'High Street Retailer' for providing transaction data to enable us to carry out this research. The first author's PhD research is sponsored by the Economic and Social Research Council through the UCL Doctoral Training Centre.

3

Retail Areas and their Catchments

Michalis Pavlis and Alex Singleton

3.1
Introduction

Shopping destinations often exist at the core of urban areas, having evolved naturally as centres for trade and exchange, but within the contemporary urban landscape they can also emerge as purpose-created retail opportunities including: regional shopping centres, retail parks, strip malls or focused shopping destinations such as designer outlets. Regardless, retail centres are complex economic systems that constantly evolve, with changing composition and spatial extent that expands or contracts over time due to changes related to their attraction, market potential and competition. By identifying shopping destinations and delineating their spatial extent it is possible to gain a better understanding of the relationship between retail space use and changes in consumer behaviour. Furthermore, such retail area boundaries can be used to implement retail analytics tasks related to store location and

demand estimation and to produce systematic metrics of retail centre morphology and performance (Thurstain-Goodwin and Unwin, 2000).

In the case of England and Wales, a national set of town centre boundaries were made available from the Department of Communities and Local Government (DCLG) in 2004, which were created using kernel density estimation from socio-economic variables including building density, diversity of building use, and tourist attraction. However, these boundaries are outdated (as they were produced in 2004) and more expansive (e.g. by including office space) than those that are specifically related mainly to retail. Apart from the DCLG town centre boundaries, in the UK, each local authority is required by law to produce a retail centre health check that typically requires the delineation of their retail area boundaries. Even though such reports produced by the local authorities are rich in information, they are typically only available in PDF format, which hampers their use for research purposes.

Given these circumstances the objective of this work was to move away from a general definition of town centre location as a centre for employment, to a more functional measure of space delineated for retail and services. This was accomplished by developing a national-scale dataset of retail agglomerations within the context of retail setting and policies in Great Britain (GB), using a dataset of approximately 530,000 retail unit locations that were provided to the Consumer Data Research Centre (CDRC) by the Local Data Company (LDC). The following methodology was used:

1) The performance of five potentially useful clustering methods were tested for the purpose of identifying agglomerations of retail units. The criteria that were used to select the candidate clustering methods included: their capability of identifying spatial clusters of arbitrary size and shape, the easiness of tuning the parameter values, and also their computational complexity.

2) Eight representative areas across GB were selected to test the performance of the clustering methods relative to those retail area boundaries produced by the respective local authorities.

3) Subsequently, the selected clustering method was further refined through calibrating the tuning parameters using existing retail area boundaries, but also by relying on the formal definitions of retail areas in GB to determine some of the parameter values. For example, by definition the smallest retail area in GB should consist of at least 10 retail units, which we used as a parameter of the clustering analysis (Wrigley and Lambiri, 2015).

4) Finally, the obtained clustering solution was validated against an independent dataset of 359 retail area boundaries that were produced by the

company Geolytix for the year 2013 and were available as open data.

3.2
Where are the retailers located?

A national occupancy dataset of 529,062 retail locations across GB was provided by the LDC through the CDRC and was collected via a large pool of local surveying teams during 2015. The data contain detailed information about the current occupier and location of retail unit and service premises. While a full postcode was available for all surveyed premises (enabling geocoding proximal to ~13 properties), more precise latitude and longitude coordinates were available for 437,260 units (about 82%), which were retained for further analysis, thus providing accuracy at building level. Other collected information for each location included the fascia (a surrogate for occupier) and the type of retail or service business (i.e. leisure, comparison, service and convenience) including vacant outlets. For retail units located in shopping centres, retail and leisure parks the respective name of the shopping centre or retail park was also provided.

Conceptually, utilising vacant units in the identification of local retail agglomerations may be problematic given that these voids may often occur as a result of failure of a particular retail setting, and as such, an indication of potential change in extent morphology. For this reason, all vacant units were removed from the dataset. Additional processing also removed units that were classified as auto services that are not typically considered part of retail agglomerations. Furthermore, miscellaneous (not related to retail or unclassified units) were also excluded. The final cleaning operation identified and removed duplicate locations (i.e. points with identical coordinates or within very close proximity), which can unduly influence clustering results as well as the identification of outliers. These duplicate locations were typically the result of the two-dimensional representation of retail units within multi-storey buildings. Thus, the removal of duplicates (any points within a 2 metre radius from another point) was carried out.

3.3
Estimating retail centre location and extent: methods and calibration

Cluster analysis is a collection of unsupervised learning methods that address the issue of grouping a set of objects based on similarity. Many commonly used clustering algorithms make group allocations with the objective of increasing similarity within a cluster and increasing dissimilarity between clusters. Other commonly used clustering techniques such as density-based algorithms seek dense regions separated by low density regions, while model-based methods assume that the data come from a mixture of probability distributions, each of which represents a different cluster. Cluster analysis is a multivariate technique (multiple attributes of the phenomenon under investigation can be used), but in this study it is strictly spatial, utilising only the locations of the retail units. This is an appropriate approach for the identification of retail agglomerations where the extent of the clusters are determined by spatial discontinuity in unit distribution (Dearden and Wilson, 2011).

To estimate the definition of retail centres, the following clustering methods were evaluated: DBSCAN (Ester et al, 1996), Quality Threshold (Scharl and Leisch, 2006), Kernel Density Estimation (Azzalini and Torelli, 2007), Random Walk (Csardi and Nepusz, 2006) and K-means (Lloyd 1982). As will be described, all of the clustering methods evaluated require the calibration of tuning parameters that we selected to optimise using the S_Dbw internal evaluation indicator (Halkidi and Vazirgiannis, 2002). As such, the process of calibrating each clustering method was

carried out prior to implementation in the evaluation by identifying suitable starting values (for those tuning parameters that a single value could not be determined), then producing a number of different models within a range of values and finally selecting the optimal model based on the S_Dbw index.

DBSCAN is probably the most prevalent density-based clustering method, and it requires the specification of two tuning parameters: the radius and the minimum number of nearest neighbours from a focal point. It can identify clusters of arbitrary size and shape, it is computationally efficient and is robust to the presence of outliers. However, the biggest drawback of DBSCAN is its limited sensitivity for datasets with varying point densities.

K-means is the most frequently used clustering method and requires the specification of a single parameter which is the number of clusters in the dataset. It has the disadvantage of producing clusters of convex hull shape but it has low computational complexity; however, given its popularity, it was used as a benchmark against the other clustering methods.

The quality threshold method requires specification of two parameters: the maximum diameter of the clusters and the minimum number of neighbours within a cluster. The method has the advantage that its parameters are relevant in the context of identifying retail agglomerations and it is also robust in the presence of outliers. However, given that it is stochastic, it suffers from long running times.

The non-parametric Kernel Density Estimation (KDE) method combines KDE with graph structures and algorithms. It requires the specification of a single tuning parameter, and given that it is non-parametric, it is insensitive to the data distribution. However, similar to the quality threshold method, it is stochastic and suffers from long running times.

The random walk is a graph-based clustering method that requires the specification of a single parameter which is the maximum number of steps required by the algorithm to find the optimal solution. The method relies on the assumption that random short walks tend to stay within the same densely connected area. It can identify clusters of arbitrary size and shape, it is relatively fast but it is difficult to identify the optimal number of steps required by the algorithm.

Obviously, there are a plethora of other methods that have been shown to be useful for clustering spatial data; however, an important factor for inclusion in the evaluation was that the methods were accompanied by useful documentation that facilitated their implementation. It was also important that the methods were under active development or well established as well as being available within most programming languages.

3.4
Centre definition and evaluation

The candidate methods were evaluated over eight case study areas that are representative in terms of GB retail location density and size. These included: Abertillery and Cardiff in Wales, Bristol, Clapham Junction, Winchester and Wolverhampton in England, Glasgow and Inverurie in Scotland (Figure 3.1).

Although there is a larger pool of other representative areas, within these specific locations additional supplementary data were also available for cross validation and included two sources. Firstly, local authorities within GB are required to perform a town centre 'health check' (NPPF, 2012), which typically requires them to delineate boundaries for retail centres. The reports are publicly available in PDF format and, given the small number of (qualitative) comparisons that can be made against these sources without extensive re-digitising, the reports were used to

Figure 3.1
The locations of the eight case study sites in Great Britain.

Case study area	Retail centre type	Preferred method
Abertillery, Wales	Small town centre	KDE, Random Walk
Bristol, England	Large urban area	DBSCAN
Cardiff, Wales	City centre	DBSCAN
Clapham Junction, England	Large high street	DBSCAN
Glasgow, Scotland	Large city centre	DBSCAN
Inverurie, Scotland	Small high street	DBSCAN
Winchester, England	Historic town centre	DBSCAN
Wolverhampton, England	Regional town centre	DBSCAN, Random Walk

Table 3.1
Results from the qualitative comparison of the clustering methods in eight locations across Great Britain.

assist with input parameter specification and testing during the calibration process described in the previous section. Secondly, boundaries for the 339 largest 'retail places' in GB were acquired from Geolytix, and although they represent only a subset of total retail boundaries, they nevertheless provide an additional and relatively large sample of independently created retail area extents suitable for comparison.

Table 3.1 presents the overall evaluation results from the qualitative comparison for all of the eight study areas. In most cases, the DBSCAN method provided results that were more consistent with those formal definitions created from the respective local authorities. Importantly, DBSCAN was the most efficient method in terms of computing resources, which is particularly significant for a national extent study. In addition, it was easier to identify starting values for the parameters of the method,

while one of the strongest advantages of DBSCAN was the identification of outliers.

It is clear from the results that DBSCAN performed well for the case study selection; however, this method is known to underperform in areas where the density is not uniform (Everitt et al, 2011). Such an issue also becomes apparent when looking at the range of the optimal epsilon values that were used for the selected areas (Table 3.2). If a single global epsilon value had been used for all case studies, it would have resulted in suboptimal local results. As such, we developed a refinement to the method which involves splitting of the national-scale data into more homogeneous areas for separate treatment; with the challenge being that unlike the case study evaluations, this required automation given that coverage was for the national extent.

Table 3.2
Optimal epsilon values used by DBSCAN in the selected study areas.

Study Area	DBSCAN epsilon (metres)
Abertillery	84
Bristol	119
Cardiff	120
Clapham Junction	70
Glasgow	70
Inverurie	120
Winchester	80
Wolverhampton	91

3.5
Development and application of a modified DBSCAN method

Addressing the issue of heterogeneous density, a modified approach to DBSCAN was developed by introducing three important concepts:

1) The use of k-nearest neighbours to represent the point data as a sparse graph, which allows the partition of the data into areas of more homogeneous point density.
2) The use of a maximum distance to constrain the points that can be member of a cluster. The maximum distance within a retail context represents the distance that a location can still be considered well connected to a shopping area by foot. The rationale behind this decision is that distance is an important parameter of retail agglomerations, and that it enhances the sensitivity of the method to gaps and discontinuities.
3) The third concept that we introduced was the iterative application of DBSCAN, to select one cluster per iteration based on the condition that the cluster's density is representative of the global point density.

More specifically, in the first step of the proposed methodology, a sparse graph representation of the spatial dataset is created based on a k-nearest neighbour matrix and the maximum distance constraint. The vertices of the graph are the locations that have at least one neighbour within the specified maximum distance. Next, a Depth First Search algorithm is implemented to decompose the sparse graph to create more homogeneous (in terms of point density and distance between the retail units) subgraphs, under the condition that each subgraph has at least 10 vertices, which is the minimum number of retail units required for an area to be classified as a local centre (Wrigley and Lambiri, 2015),

and that each location has at least one neighbour within the maximum distance. The vertices that are not part of any subgraph are removed as outliers. The maximum distance value in this study represents the maximum distance that a location can still be considered well connected to a shopping area on foot. Different distance values have been suggested as indicators of walking distance, ranging between 300 to 500 metres (NPPF, 2012). Based upon the definition of edge of centre for retail purposes in the UK (DCLG, 2009), the maximum distance value was set equal to 300 metres. Three k values were tested to split the study area into subgraphs, and included 4, 10 and 15. As it would be expected, the lower the k value the greater the number and the more homogeneous the density of the subgraphs that were produced. On the other hand, using lower k values (between 4 and 10) can result in splitting areas with low point density (mostly chained clusters, i.e. high streets) into different subgraphs. For this reason the k value was set equal to 15.

Given that the spatial extent of each subgraph depends on the connectivity and number of points within an area, each subgraph can represent a town centre, a city centre or even a metropolitan region. DBSCAN, however, assumes that the epsilon value is a representative indicator of the local density. To fulfil that assumption, in the third step of the methodology, DBSCAN is first applied (within each subgraph) in an exploratory approach to identify and select the cluster that has density (as estimated by the local epsilon, i.e. the 95th percentile of the 4-nearest neighbours' distances) closer to the overall density.

Following the selection of a single cluster, all the neighbouring clusters (i.e. the clusters that share a common edge in the graph) with similar density are selected along with those neighbouring points that were identified by the exploratory DBSCAN

Figure 3.2
The point data are represented as a sparse graph using a distance-constrained k-NN sparse matrix. DBSCAN is first applied in an exploratory approach. The neighbouring clusters (that share a common edge) with similar point density are selected forming a new study area of homogeneous point density, where DBSCAN is iteratively applied until no cluster can be formed.

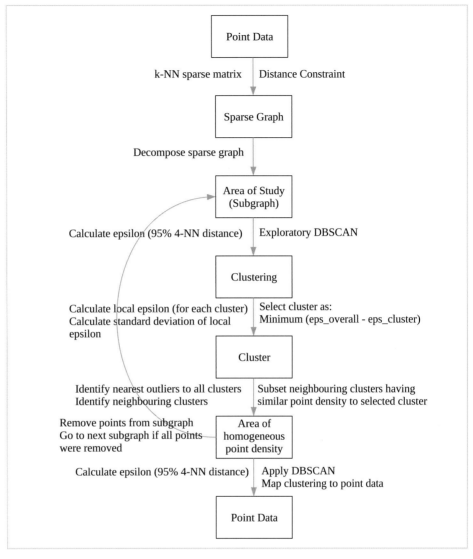

as outliers. Following this, a new study area of homogeneous point density is created from the selected points and DBSCAN is applied again to identify the clusters. The selected clusters are then removed from the graph representation of the point data, and the process of using an exploratory DBSCAN model to identify a cluster and select those neighbouring clusters with similar point density is iteratively carried out until no cluster can be formed. This process is summarized in Figure 3.2. It should be noted that one of the advantages of the methodology is that

it is no longer required to optimise the clustering solution using the S_Dbw index, which results in a faster algorithm.

To evaluate the point density similarity among clusters, the standard deviation of point density in a subgraph was used. More specifically, those neighbouring clusters with point density within 1 standard deviation from the point density of the initially selected cluster were also selected, with the assumption being that they define an area of homogeneous point density. To test the sensitivity

Models	Number of Clusters	Distribution of epsilon values (metres)						
Standard Deviation Threshold	Count	Minimum	25%	50%	Mean	75%	Maximum
0.6	2,928	80	80	80	100.3	113.0	170.0
0.8	2,922	80	80	80	100.3	113.0	170.0
1.0	2,920	80	80	80	100.3	113.0	170.0
1.2	2,923	80	80	80	100.1	113.0	170.0
1.4	2,921	80	80	80	100.1	113.0	170.0

of the method to the standard deviation threshold, five different values were considered, 0.6, 0.8, 1.0, 1.2 and 1.4. As can be seen in Table 3.3, the clustering solutions are practically identical when looking at the number of clusters produced and the distribution of the local epsilon value.

For the parameter values required by DBSCAN, as detailed earlier, the value of the minimum points parameter was set equal to 10 and the epsilon value was calculated as the 95th percentile of the 4-nearest neighbour distance. However, the epsilon value was only allowed to vary within the range between maximum 170 metres, which was found to be useful to exclude outliers from being identified as members of clusters, and a lower bound of 80 metres which was used to avoid identifying certain large shopping malls as clusters. This necessity is a consequence of the hierarchical nature of retail centres within GB given that the objective of the analysis was to create clusters that were inclusive of the different functional retail forms. Following the application of DBSCAN to each subgraph and the extraction of 2,920 clusters, the final retail agglomerations were compiled and each retail location was assigned an identifying number denoting cluster membership. The results derived from this new method were compared to data supplied by Geolytix, which represent the only freely available and independently created national sample of contemporary retail centre extents. They provide frequent updates of a dataset of retail places across the UK, part of which (339 places) were licensed as open data in 2012. The Geolytix boundaries are produced using multiple variables (including the locations of retail units) with information that was collected at least three years prior to the data that were used in our analysis. Additional causes of difference between the two datasets might also include the different objectives and notion of what constitutes a retail centre (Geolytix did not use a threshold of minimum 10 retail units), and only the boundary polygons from the clustered locations of the retail units were available. Given that the creation of similar polygon boundaries for our output may have resulted in an additional source of error, it was decided to compare the Geolytix boundaries against the retail unit locations and associated clusters. The comparison was based on two metrics, the 'n-ary' relation between the two datasets, and the proportion of points within the Geolytix polygons. The n-ary relation returns a score where the higher the number of clusters that had a one-to-one relation with the clusters identified by Geolytix the better the relationship.

Data pre-processing removed the major out-of-town retail parks from the Geolytix dataset, which was followed by a spatial

Table 3.3
Summary values of five clustering models with different standard deviation thresholds.

Figure 3.3
The retail unit locations that are members of the cluster of the city of Glasgow (blue circles), overlaid on the Geolytix retail centre boundaries.

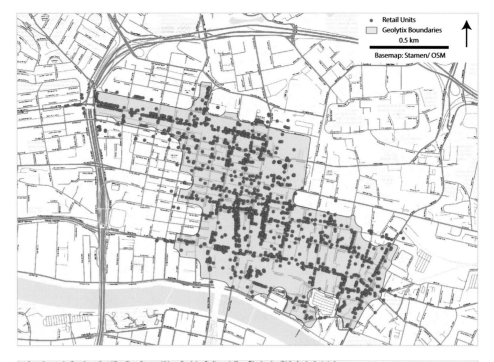

Figure 3.4
The retail unit locations that are members of the cluster of the city of Bristol (blue circles), overlaid on the Geolytix retail centre boundaries (only the area around the Broadmead shopping district was available as open data).

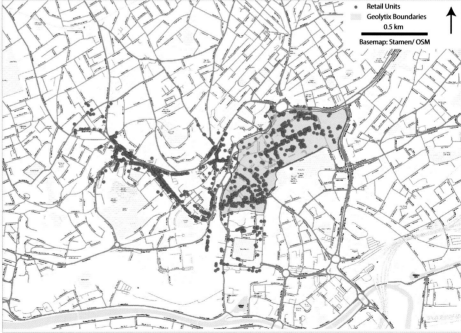

join of the Geolytix dataset with the clustered retailer locations. There were 294 spatial intersections between the two datasets, out of which 244 were one-to-one. Summary values of the spatial distribution of the clustered locations within the Geolytix boundaries are shown in Table 3.4. On average (based on the median value) almost 90% of the clustered points were within the Geolytix boundaries. Glasgow (Figure 3.3) serves as an example where the two datasets mostly overlap, but also shows that the spatial extent of the clusters produced in this analysis were on average larger, which to some extent is related to Geolytix post-processing of boundaries to be constrained by the road network. An example where the two datasets have significant differences is Bristol (Figure 3.4).

Looking at Bristol, it can be seen that Geolytix split the city centre into smaller clusters, of which only Broadmead was available as open data. However, the clustering solution for Bristol that was produced in this analysis was very similar to the one produced by the Bristol local authority and, thus, arguably more appropriate based on this local knowledge. Despite these mismatches that to some extent are related to different objectives and notions of what constitutes a retail centre, it could be argued that the two clustering solutions largely overlap in the areas that were available by the open source Geolytix retail places, which provides evidence for the validity of the retail clusters that were produced in this work vis-à-vis competing methods.

3.6
Conclusion

The objective of this analysis was to develop a clustering method that would facilitate the identification of retail agglomerations across a national extent and that could be updated over time. For this purpose, five of the most frequently used clustering methods were compared within eight representative locations across Great Britain. The DBSCAN method was selected on the basis that it provided the most accurate representation of those retail areas relative to formal definitions; it was faster to produce a clustering solution and easier to calibrate optimised input parameter values.

However, to address a well-known issue that DBSCAN does not cope well in areas of varying densities, the DBSCAN method was adapted so that it could be iteratively applied within smaller, more homogeneous sites that were created using a k-NN sparse graph representation of the retail locations. Each selected retail cluster was created by the DBSCAN algorithm with an epsilon value that was representative of the local point density. The clusters produced were comparable to those retail areas designated by the local authorities for the sample areas of study, and in some cases, were more accurate when compared to the traditional DBSCAN method. In addition, the identified clusters were in most areas similar in terms of spatial extent to those produced by Geolytix using alternative data and methodology. It should be noted that even though the suggested method is

Table 3.4
Summary values describing the spatial distribution of the clustered locations within the Geolytix boundaries.

Minimum	1st Quartile	Median	Mean	3rd Quartile	Maximum
0.68	63.97	89.81	73.99	95.99	100.00

more demanding in terms of computer resources compared to the traditional DBSCAN, it scales better as it could be applied in parallel for each subgraph.

Furthermore, the output of this analysis provides a better spatial coverage and option for automated update in comparison to the existing DCLG town centre boundaries. Given that the DCLG boundaries were widely used by academics, local authorities and private organisations across the country it can be anticipated that these results will prove to be valuable for research and analysis.

With the developed methodology being open source, it will also be straightforward to update the retail boundaries on a regular basis, and potentially apply the suggested method within a context of historic data. Finally, given the variety in point density, size and shape of the retail clusters in the dataset it would be reasonable to assume that the methodology could be applicable with different datasets and for different international locations.

Further Reading

Azzalini, A. and Torelli, N. (2007). Clustering via nonparametric density estimation. *Statistics and Computing*, 17, 71-80.

Csardi, G., Nepusz, T. (2006) The igraph software package for complex network research, InterJournal, Complex Systems 1695. Online: http://igraph.org

DCLG (2009). Practice guidance on need, impact and the sequential approach. Online: www.gov.uk/government/uploads/system/uploads/attachment_data/file/7781/towncentresguide.pdf

Dearden, J. and Wilson, A. (2011). A framework for exploring urban retail discontinuities. *Geographical Analysis*, 43(2), 172-187.

Ester, M., Kriegel, H. P., Sander, J. and Xiaowei, X. (1996). A density-based algorithm for discovering clusters in large spatial databases with noise. Online: www.aaai.org/Papers/KDD/1996/KDD96-037.pdf

Everitt, B. S., Landau, S., Leese, M., and Stahl, D. (2011). *Cluster Analysis.* 5th ed. Chichester, Wiley.

Halkidi, M. and Vazirgiannis, M. (2002). Clustering validity assessment using multi-representatives. Online: lpis.csd.auth.gr/setn02/poster_papers/237.pdf

Lloyd, S. P. (1982). Least squares quantization in PCM. *IEEE Transactions on Information Theory,* 28, 128-137.

National Planning Policy Framework (NPPF) (2012). Online: http://planningguidance.communities.gov.uk/blog/policy/achieving-sustainable-development/annex-2-glossary/

Scharl, T. and Leisch, F. (2006). The stochastic QT-clust algorithm: Evaluation of stability and variance on time-course microarray data. Online: http://www.ci.tuwien.ac.at/papers/Scharl+Leisch-2006.pdf

Thurstain-Goodwin, M. and Unwin, D. (2000). Defining and delineating the central areas of towns for statistical monitoring using continuous surface representations. *Trans. GIS* 4(4), 305-317.

Wrigley, N. and Lambiri, D. (2015). British high streets: From crisis to recovery? A comprehensive review of the evidence. Online: http://thegreatbritishhighstreet.co.uk/pdf/GBHS-British-High-Streets-Crisis-to-Recovery.pdf

Acknowledgements

The authors would like to thank Local Data Company Ltd for providing retail unit data for this research.

4

Given and Family Names as Global Spatial Data Infrastructure

Oliver O'Brien and Paul Longley

4.1
Introduction

This chapter outlines an ongoing Consumer Data Research Centre (CDRC) project that has produced a large (c. two billion record) global database of people's names, together with the approximate locations of their bearers. Although in part a 'hobby' project, the work is being reconfigured into demographic profiles of people over a full range of scales. We discuss the value and provenance of different data sources, data extraction techniques and the tools used to assemble a truly global database. We also present illustrative results from the resulting dataset, at the global scale as well as for selected countries. Case studies are used to examine some individual countries, where simple analysis of publically available data samples can reveal internal migration patterns and sub-national variations in the popularity of both given and family names.

In important respects a name is at the same time the purest and most widely used form of personal data. It is a characteristic of a person that is typically assigned at birth and often not changed or adulterated during the bearer's lifespan except for reasons of marriage. Names data are shared between individuals for many reasons core to social organisation, and sharing often follows established social patterns. Names are ubiquitous across cultures and throughout the world – nearly everyone has a name and it is rarely if ever assigned at random. A person's full (given/fore- plus family/sur-) name may thus provide a direct indicator of its bearer's gender, ethnicity and religion. Changing fashions in given naming practices often render given names a reliable indicator of age.

Additionally, most names have geographic origins, some of which may be very specific and localised. The naming practices of most societies provide for inheritance of family names, and thus comparison of present residence with historic name origins makes it possible to trace the probable migration histories of many individuals and their blood lines. It is even possible to establish links between long settled populations and their genetic make-up (www.peopleofthebritishisles.org). The accuracy with which this may be done does of course depend upon the event histories of the individuals whose names are inherited through the generations, and historically these have been overwhelmingly male – yet local marriage practices throughout history do in practice retain this signal through the generations.

Finally, the fact of geographic concentrations of clusters of surnames means that names may be associated indirectly with the economic fortunes of the areas in which their bearers live. Inheritance, along with the intergenerational inheritances of human and social capital, may also mean that a name provides clues to economic and social standing. This tendency may be reinforced if there are social dimensions to given naming practices within broader cultural, ethnic and linguistic groups.

Linking given names and family names together, and clustering, produces groups of names typically sharing demographic traits. Studying such groups, with appropriate control data, allows the geographer to assign profiles which then can be used with similar names to infer similar demographic characteristics.

The clustering process is dependent on having a large and geographically representative pool of given/family name pairs. This chapter describes an ongoing CDRC project that is gathering many name pairs, across the world, for such clustering purposes, as well as for a similar probabilistic classification process based on the fact that many names have strong country (and indeed intra-country) geographic profiles that are retained to this day, even in an era of greater increasing global mobility.

4.2
The Worldnames 2 project

The Worldnames 2 project is an outcome of a series of research grants and private initiatives stretching back to 2003 (see www.onomap.org), and attempts to collect and assemble as many name pairs as possible until global coverage is achieved. The names of resident individuals are associated with the country (and often region or locality) in which they reside. The results can be mapped in order to portray the geographic distribution of names at a range of scales, and can be analysed in order to link names and groups of names to places. It follows on from the Worldnames 1 project, which presents a website showing name distributions in around 25 mainly western countries, by expanding to cover almost every country of the world. A secondary aim is to allow public dissemination of the enlarged dataset via a more modern website than the existing Worldnames 1 platform (which is around 10 years old). The data are mainly collected from freely available governmental, administrative and other public datasets from the countries concerned – although some of the data have been obtained under licence with attendant restrictions upon reuse. The project is in an ongoing phase and this chapter describes the work to date, as well as outlining some early results and presenting a number of country-specific case studies.

4.3
Objectives, execution principles and simplifications

The general objective of the ongoing project is to obtain as many name pairs as possible, on a country-by-country basis that can be deemed to represent the established population of the country. In some senses the objective is to create a demographic framework for the world, in terms of the personal attributes that can be inferred from naming conventions at national, regional and local levels. We are in the process of creating a website that will enable users to examine these traits of any name that is part of our dataset. Users will also be able to interrogate the data in order to identify the most prevalent surname by country lists or intra-country distributions of popular single-country-origin names.

As such, the project is clearly a Big Data project that is vulnerable to the vagaries of Big Data sources that are discussed at various points in this volume. Some of the data sources are acquired under licence, with restrictions upon how they may be redistributed, particularly those that formed part of the original Worldnames 1 project. The countries that have formed the focus of our renewed attention on the project are openly available on the web, without needing a login or subscription to access, and from the original source, rather than from other consolidator sites with related foci of interest. We also exclude datasets whose custodians did not, in our opinion, intend the data to be made available for wide public use, albeit in aggregate form. These judgments are inevitably subjective and our intention is to avoid any legal infringements arising from reuse of data for new purposes. In particular, we have avoided using data published by third parties without the consent of the original owner to this end. From this standpoint, newspaper republishing of time-restricted electoral lists would be considered to be valid but database dumps, obtained as a result of a breach of security or insider leaks, would not be used. This distinction is not always clear cut, and require decisions to be made on a case-by-case basis – for example, data obtained from the WikiLeaks service and similar investigative journalism projects, or those where the original source and authority to publish is unclear. To simplify processing a vast array of diverse datasets, a number of simplifications are applied. The western-style naming convention of a given (assigned) first name followed by a (typically hereditary) family name is assumed, with other name structures (e.g. Spanish double surnames) simplified.

The 'Western Latin' alphabet is used, with accents and capitalisations removed and the only non-alphabetic characters allowed are apostrophes and dashes – these being combined anyway with pure-alphabetic variants. This is necessary to accommodate the inconsistent ways which names are stored on the official records are typically used in the project. For example, MacDonald can appear, in different datasets across different countries, as Mac Donald, MACDONALD, Mac.Donald and Mac-Donald. Other non-alphabetic characters, such as spaces and underscores, are replaced or removed as judged appropriate.

It is acknowledged that, with a project of this scale, using hundreds of diverse datasets, such simplifications will potentially obscure helpful demographic information; this is minimized where practical. We have retained the names in the original forms captured, however, in order to allow the incorporation of other accents in future spin out projects from the research.

4.4
Data acquisition and processing methodology

4.4.1
Search-based initial discovery

To ensure a reasonable level of quality and a high geographical and demographic representation for each country are maintained, we carry out the data collection manually, rather than creating a 'bot' or 'spider' to crawl the web automatically. This also presents opportunities to discover additional unindexed datasets with intelligent URL modification by the investigator.

This means that, for each of the ~200 countries of the world, a different collection process is employed, built up by starting from a set of common principles detailed below, but then refined as name data are discovered from the current active country.

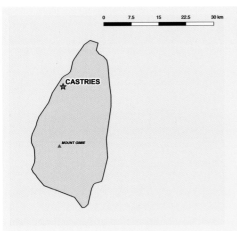

Figure 4.1
Map of St Lucia. St Lucia
is approximately 40km
in length (north to south)
and 20km in width (east
to west).

Case Study 1: Saint Lucia

Saint Lucia is an island nation in the Caribbean with a population of approximately 186,000 people (Figure 4.1). Our names data come from the polling lists published by the Saint Lucia Electoral Department at www.electoral.gov.lc/polling-list. Saint Lucia's top-level administrative areas are known as quarters, the constituencies are based on these quarters but with a number split or merged, to make 17 in total. These are then each further split into between 3 and 9 polling divisions, or precincts. The electoral data for each of the 84 precincts are listed on the website as paged tables, with a POST query needed to access each page.

The data listed on the tables include the given name, family name, street name, constituency, unique registration number, precinct and gender.

A python script was used to send POST queries and download the HTML tables, and extract the data from them using regex into a CSV file. The data are believed to be relatively up-to-date, as the most recent election was in 2016. 162,025 records were extracted in this way, at first glance matching well with official summary information for the 2016 election suggesting that there were 161,883 registered voters. However, a large number of duplicated records were found – where the same record would appear on multiple pages in a table for a single precinct. On de-duplicating, 129,685 records remained, representing around 70% of the 2016 UN estimate of 186,383 people. The reasons for this large discrepancy are not clear, but, if the official figures are at fault, it would go some way to explaining the apparently low turnout of 57% and that the numbers of reported registered voters have increased at a much larger rate than the population in general, since 2000.

70% of the 2016 estimate is a plausible percentage, as electoral lists are not population lists – they typically exclude young people and foreign residents. Voters for a general election in Saint Lucia must be at least 18 years of age and either a Saint Lucian or a Commonwealth citizen who has resided in Saint Lucia for at least seven years.

Because of the readily available geospatial boundary data for Saint Lucia's quarters, and the relatively small population of the nation as a whole, it was decided to sub-divide the population by a single level – quarters, but merged where the constituencies go across quarters, for the Worldnames 2 project – rather than further

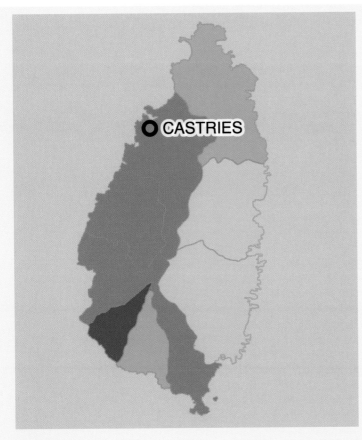

Figure 4.2
Distribution of Charlemagne surname in St Lucia, with darker shading indicating higher proportions of the population bearing this surname.

dividing into constituencies, quarters or precincts, the former of which are not sufficiently different from the merged quarters and the latter of which have some very small populations. The constituencies and precincts also do not have readily available boundaries available.

This results in nine geographical areas, with the electoral population varying from 4,962 to 45,980.

The data were considered to be relatively 'clean', because of the direct extraction from HTML tables, rather than a structure-recreation approach that is often needed when extracting from PDFs.

As is characteristic for many Caribbean countries, Western given names have come into usage as family names. In Saint Lucia's case, the most common given family names show this trait: Joseph (4.6% – the most popular), Charles (2.1%), James, Alexander and Henry. There are 10,074 distinct family names. 7,119 of these are most common in Saint Lucia, compared to other countries for which there is currently data in the Worldnames 2 database. Hippolyte and Mathurin are two popular family names in Saint Lucia that are relatively unusual elsewhere.

Looking at the names data split by the merged quarters, a number of popular family names have strong variations through the nation. For example, Charlemagne is more popular on the western side of the island than the eastern side (Figure 4.2). The 100 people with this family name on the polling list for Choiseul quarter represent a frequency of 1.7%, while the 11 in Dennery quarter equate to frequency of just 0.12%. However, as these are small numbers in total, this may just be a statistical coincidence.

A small amount of logic, however, can be shared across countries. A number of countries in West Africa, for example, use the same off-the-shelf portal software for their government or public service websites, and so file locations discovered during the search for data for one country, can then be reapplied to additional countries using the same software.

The initial stage is to perform a simple search, typically using Google Search, for 'obvious' open-access lists of the greater part of a country's population. These may take the form of public versions of electoral rolls or civil registry lists. These may be posted both on a country's official portal, but also occasionally republished by citizens on private websites, for example the Chilean electoral roll can be freely obtained on disk and implicitly republished privately, but is not itself published online by the electoral authorities.

If a comprehensive list is not obtained, then it is necessary to search using distinctive surnames and then full names for any given country. It is necessary to 'seed' the search with certain key names which are popular in the country in question, but ideally not in neighbouring countries or other jurisdictions. To do this, reliable pan-national websites containing lists of famous people from a country, for example from Wikipedia, were used, as well as government and pan-national database-driven websites of elected government ministers or national election candidates – one type of data that are nearly universally published and that a number of separate projects, such as IFES Election Guide and International IDEA, are aiming to catalogue and maintain. The latter project also contains some information about the availability of online electoral rolls for each country and its approach to open data, including direct links to them where available.

As a rule of thumb in our research we deemed that at least three distinctive 'seed' surnames were required for any country. Google Search queries were then carried out using these surnames in conjunction with various combinations of numerical, country filter, data format and/ or list keywords. Top-level country filters on Google Search were used, along with gov.xx and edu.xx second level domain filters (xx here the country's top level domain). These filters restricted results to being from subdomains of the domains specified and, due to the nature of Google Search's indexing, this more specific search often revealed additional results of interest. Format keywords can narrow large numbers of results returned to ones likely in the form of a downloadable, processable, list, for example 'pdf', 'xls' or 'xlsx'. The CSV format is probably the simplest and easiest list format to parse but is little used by non-technology focused websites. A small number of useful sources were found in the more modern JSON file format. Adding sequential numbers, e.g. 1345 1346 1347 1348 can both reveal list-focused results, and ones with a likely population of (in this case) well over a thousand names. Finally, the inclusion of other key words in the search for distinctive document classes can also be useful – as with 'cedula' (national identification document) for Spanish-speaking countries. Other more generic words were also useful in our searches, e.g. 'first name', 'given name', 'forename', 'last name', 'family name', 'surname', 'ID number', or 'candidate'. Translating these into different languages (typically using Google Translate) was also useful.

Somewhat counter intuitively, increasing the numbers of names in a query led to more search results being returned. This is another example, as mentioned above, of the heuristics applied in Google Search and other search engines, and the ways in which key words for websites are stored in the internal indices of the search engines.

Where surnames alone did not reveal useful datasets, use of distinctive individual full names was useful, since this focused searches on websites with a record for that person amongst a larger list of bearers of less distinctive or unusual names, or with a search function or directory index (as discussed below) that revealed additional data files. As a general point, we avoided searches using famous names since these directed focus away from general population names.

It was often the case that, once identified, a relevant dataset offered coverage of only a (regional or sectoral) part of the population. In such instances the issue of coverage was addressed by amending the relevant part of the URL until full population coverage had been achieved – for example after using every government regional identifier within a given country. In some circumstances this was achieved by identifying the parent directory of a relevant dataset. We became used to anticipating abbreviations and invoking other trial and error procedures in this process.

The Internet Archive was also useful for retrieving files that no longer existed at their original locations but which were still revealed through stale indices in search engines and related weblinks. Additionally, websites occasionally change their domain names but fail to provide forwarding links from the old domain. Sometimes, missing files referred to from a Google search or external web links can be retrieved simply by modifying the domain name to the new one.

As well as Google, specialized search engines, such as Docs Engine, are useful. In particular, we found Docs Engine good at revealing lists of PDFs, Microsoft Excel (XLS) and Microsoft Word files which are not readily found with Google Search – particularly when searching for a single non-celebrity full name.

Where the information was available as numerous web pages rather than

as documents, simple Python scripting was used to automate retrieval of large numbers of webpages, supplying appropriate GET/POST parameters on a consistent, sequential or known list basis, and simple processing and name extraction of the resulting HTML files retrieved. Where webpages listed a large number of documents, a bulk downloader browser extension 'uSelect iDownload' was used.

4.4.2
Targets

A minimum target number of names to be harvested was calculated for each country. In important respects, Web-based research often remains unreconciled with respect to established scientific apparatus of sampling and inference, in that:

1) Sample frames (in our case normally resident populations) are at best imperfectly defined. For example, not every country in the world has reliable and accurate procedures for measuring and monitoring population size.

2) There are multiple definitions of the eligible populations of any country. In our research, there is inherent ambiguity in the definition of 'eligible', and in practice falls back upon identifying the full names of as many of the 'ordinarily resident' population as possible. The conception and measurement of 'ordinarily resident' nevertheless varies between jurisdictions. For example, the UK uses different definitions of 'ordinarily resident' (for access to health services and formerly for tax purposes), 'indefinite leave to remain' and 'right of abode'.

3) Closest approximations to 'ordinarily resident' populations may systematically exclude some groups that have distinctive naming practices, for example lists of eligible voters will exclude many recent migrants and others that have not yet attained citizenship, voting age or other requirements for voting. In some

Figure 4.3
Map of Somalia.

Case Study 2: Somalia

There are no openly accessible names lists for Somalia (Figure 4.3) that provide widespread coverage of the country – not surprising in a country without an effective government controlling much of its territory. An additional problem, from the perspective of the Worldnames 2 project, is that documents are generally published in Somali, the native language, although this uses the Latin alphabet and so is relatively easily translated.

The best data source that was available was a number of PDF downloads from the Ministry of Education for the Federal Government of Somalia, at moesomalia. net/english/ (although the website has been updated since the data was extracted and so it is no longer available for direct download). The data files are lists of students that have received the national secondary school leaving certificate. The data include the full name of each pupil (with given and family names not split out), the mother's name, year of birth, roll number and certificate number (neither

unique to the country), academic year, score and issue date. Somalian names do not tend to follow the Western structure where family names are passed down each generation; instead the family name of a child is typically the given name of the father.

This is likely to be a highly selective sample, for example, completing secondary school may not be possible in large parts of the country due to safety concerns, there may be a tradition of only boys or only girls attending school in some areas, and so on.

The data sources, combined, contain 7,834 name pairs, representing just 0.07% of the population based on the 2015 UN estimate of around 11 million. Combined with the likely demographic biases discussed above, this means that the Somalia dataset will likely give a poor profile of given name and family name distributions in the country, and as such is included simply because of the desire to have as many countries as possible represented in the database – poor data being better than no data at all.

The data was extracted by using Tabula to detect the table structure and data fields in the PDFs and output as a CSV. The data was then combined in Excel, with the column ordering lined up. The first word and last word of the name were interpreted to be the given name and family name respectively, a necessary simplification to homogenise name structures globally for the project. No sub-national information (e.g. school name) was available to allow a first-level administrative geography to be developed; in any case the sample size is too small to allow for meaningful geographical division.

'C/' is a popular prefix for Somali names. It is short for Cabdi, and is regarded as a prefix rather than a true first name, so was not used as a first name.

Mohamed was found to be the most common last name (i.e. family name for the purposes of the project), with 8.5% of names, followed by Ali (6.5%) and Ahmed (5.4%), with 901 distinct names out of the 7,834 in total. Mohamed was also the most common given name (8.4%) followed by Ahmed (4.3%) and Abdirahman (4.2%). The tradition of the father's given name becoming the family name of the child means that it would be expected that the top lists for family and given names would be similar.

Alternative spellings of Mohamed are also popular, with Mohmed, Mohamud, Maxamed, Mohamoud, Mohmud, Mohmoud, Mahad and Maxamuud all appearing in the top 60 most popular family names. Maxamed is the direct Somali spelling of Mohamed.

Mohamed Mohamed is the most popular name pair in the list, with 101 occurrences within the list of 7,834. There were 5,375 distinct name pairs.

countries, notably in the Middle East, migrant populations may be large relative to those that are longer settled and that may consider themselves the true 'ordinarily resident' population.

4) The non-availability of population registers of any kind will often necessitate the use of available substitute sources, for example particular age cohorts or occupational groups. In each case, we tried to use sources that were unlikely to introduce bias into the sample number and frequency of names harvested.

5) The sample size required depends upon the heterogeneity of the phenomenon (in our case, given and family names) that is being recorded. Populations with heterogeneous characteristics require larger samples, and the diversity of forenames relative to surnames may itself vary within a country. Diversity of forenames may also vary between age cohorts within a country in line with other secular trends. The sample fraction required between countries will thus vary, subject also to a minimum sample size.

6) For all of these reasons, our source data are unlikely to represent a purely random sample of the ordinarily resident population. In the absence of any reliable population sources, it is not possible to reweight names by probability of selection when synthesising the complete population.

7) The jurisdictional partitioning of some of the world is in flux, and for this reason it may be necessary to use data that do not pertain to current geographic boundaries.

In practice our data harvesting criteria were to identify:
- 10% of 2016 World Bank population estimates for small countries/areas (less than 10,000 population)
- 1,000 people, for medium countries/areas (10,000–1 million)
- 0.1%, for large countries/areas (1 million+)

The targets are based on the most recent available estimated population of the country or sub-country administrative area. This is generally sourced through simple web searches for the current population. The accuracy of the resulting data is not critical, as the target thresholds are themselves very approximate. The data generally come from the Indicators section of the World Bank's Data platform. Our experience suggested that smaller countries are generally more open about publishing lists of people's names – possibly because they are inherently more open, but also possibly because their governments have not created elaborate data infrastructures. However, such smaller populations, even when considered in aggregate, are less useful for this project, as clustering and demographic prediction is only effective for high data volumes. Smaller datasets are also more prone to individual errors/omissions biasing the final result, so it is more important to have a greater proportion of the population covered. For this reason, the higher thresholds targets were necessary for such smaller countries. Conversely, for very large countries, even a relatively small sample will likely be representative for the country, at least for more common names.

A time/effort limitation guideline was also adopted, over and above the number target outlined above, to protect against unnecessary effort and diminishing returns. Many countries have vast numbers of datasets including people's names, of vastly varying quality and quantity. By contrast, other countries appear to have virtually no useable datasets on the web that contain useful ranges of first names and last names. In both cases, to provide an appropriate balance between effort and reward, a maximum of one person-day was employed to discover the datasets.

4.4.3
Data sources

At the time of writing this chapter, (September 2017) around 450 distinct sources have been used across approximately 170 countries. A single source has been used for most countries but this has not always been possible, for example Pakistan's very large population and lack of a comprehensive single source openly available on the web necessitated use of 24 sources in order to achieve the 0.1% threshold, both across the country as a whole and at Level 1 (Province) and Level 2 (Division) scales.

Where multiple sources were used, care was taken to try and avoid counting the same person twice, by looking for significant overlaps of names across sources. Where individual sources represent a very small proportion of the population, duplication concerns were, however, often disregarded, as they were expected to have only a minimal effect on the quality of the overall information about name distribution in the country.

As mentioned above, data sources generally need to be openly available on the web, or purchased for this project or its predecessor. We have generally only rarely used names derived from social media directories (by other projects) and have strictly avoided using data from commercial but otherwise similar pan-national projects such as Forebears (forebears.co.uk), Ancestry (www.ancestry.com) or Linked-In (www.linkedin.com).

Frequently used sources include:
- Electoral rolls (also known as voter lists or voter registers)
- Landline telephone directories (white pages)
- Government fund qualification records (e.g. rural hardship)
- School/national examination results/ candidates
- University matriculation/graduation/

admission lists
- Professional practice licences (doctors, lawyers, engineers)
- Candidates for elections (local/ parliamentary)
- Official statistics from national statistics agencies (e.g. Census summaries)
- Government transparency employee and contractor pay lists
- Business owners (e.g. local service providers, tax registers)
- National service callup lists (jury service, military)

Less frequently used, but still useful sources, particularly for countries with a limited web presence or a culture of significantly restricting personal data publication:
- Government lottery/scheme winners (e.g. university laptops)
- Government honours lists/award winners
- Local government employee directories
- Public meeting minutes
- Private club member lists

Other less frequently used datasets, which potentially can come from super-national data sources:
- Player league tables (e.g. chess rankings)
- Match lineup lists of international footballers and other athletes
- Social network names (used by and supplied by other projects)
- Academic paper data releases and books
- Private insurance subscribers

The project does not republish full individual records (i.e. no disclosure of both the first name and last name of a single record) but anticipates that the publication of 'most popular full name' by region will be appropriate and possible. It will not publish personally identifying information (PII), at any level, by aggregating appropriately to ensure that the statistics published are not about a single person.

Sensitive personal information (SPI) datasets – for example medical records, or full CVs – are not collected. During the data collection process, such information, surprisingly, is encountered on the open web from time to time, but is discarded.

4.4.4
Data processing and georeferencing

For each country, files were processed once sufficient names had been retrieved, and then entered into a number of database tables – individual name pairs, aggregated tables by area for given names and family names separately, and general statistical tables.

The Tabula (tabula.technology) open source software was used to efficiently extract tables and lists of names from PDFs. Microsoft Excel, TextWrangler and a standardised set of SQL queries were also heavily used for names lists, particularly to extract the given and family name components from full names, strip initials, convert accents to an unaccented approximation, standardise apostrophes, remove/convert spaces, remove certain prefixes and suffixes (e.g. Most, Dr) and normalise the way the additional demographic information was specified across multiple datasets. For example, certain data sources omitted leading zeros for national IDs while others maintained them.

More sophisticated data cleaning was occasionally required. For example, a number of data sources were mis-encoded, or double encoded in error, requiring careful manual decoding. Transliteration websites were used, mainly for Cyrillic-alphabet to Latin-alphabet conversion, which is relatively straightforward.

Geodata for Worldnames 2, for displaying name results in an online map on the project's website and helping understand geographic patterns of names, was mainly sourced from the GADM (www.gadm.org)

Case Study 3: Nepal

The Nepal data were built up from Police Clearance Report (PCR) Certificate Lists which are criminal record check application results, published in English by the Nepal Police as a PDF every few days. A complete list of nearly 1000 of these documents, published in the last three years, can be found at cid.nepalpolice.gov.np/index.php/pcr-certificate-list

By downloading the PDFs, converting them to CSVs using Tabula and combining them, 517,946 records can be retrieved, representing approximately 1.6% of the country's current population. Full names are listed, with a double space sometimes, but not always, separating the given name from the family name. Middle names are often present, but were disregarded, with the first word and last word forming the given and family name respectively, for Worldnames. The gender is also listed, along with a non-unique sequential list sequence number, passport number, district and a unique sequential dispatch number. The passport number is useful to de-duplicate the list (as someone may have applied more than once), while the district name can be used to build up the geography of the person's location.

Nepal (Figure 4.4) recently introduced a top-level administrative structure of seven provinces. However, geospatial data are more readily available for the previous 14 zones, which are split into 75 districts, and it is these latter two administrative areas that are adopted by Worldnames 2, particularly as the district is listed in the source data. One zone (with a single district) has only 1,132 names; however the rest of the zones are well populated in the dataset. Around 80% of the districts also have a population of at least 1,000 in the data, thus generally satisfying the target minimums discussed earlier in this chapter.

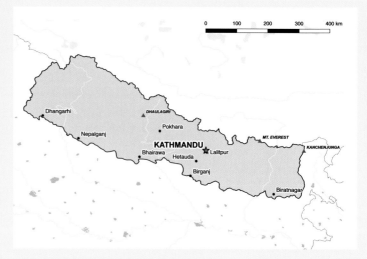

Nepal's most common family names are Tamang (4%), Gurung (3.6%) and Shrestha (1.7%), with 11,662 distinct family names in the data, while the most common given names are Ram (2.6%), Krishna (1.2%) and Santosh (0.93%), there being 37,141 unique given names detected. Ram Yadav was the most common name pair, with 1,193 occurrences, and there were 219,161 distinct name pairs.

Looking at the sub-country level, in both Manang and Mustang districts, 61% of family names were Gurung, while 23% of the population in Siraha had the given name of Yadav. Analysis at the district level confirmed that this Indian-origin name is much more common along the southern border of Nepal (Figure 4.5).

Tamang, the most common family name, is much more common in the eastern part of the country and is almost absent further west (Figure 4.6).

Figure 4.4
Map of Nepal. Nepal is approximately 800km long (east-west) and 200km wide.

Opposite top:
Figure 4.5
Distribution of Yadav family name in Nepal, with darker shading indicating higher proportions of the population bearing this surname.

Opposite bottom:
Figure 4.6
Distribution of Tamang family name in Nepal, with darker shading indicating higher proportions of the population bearing this surname.

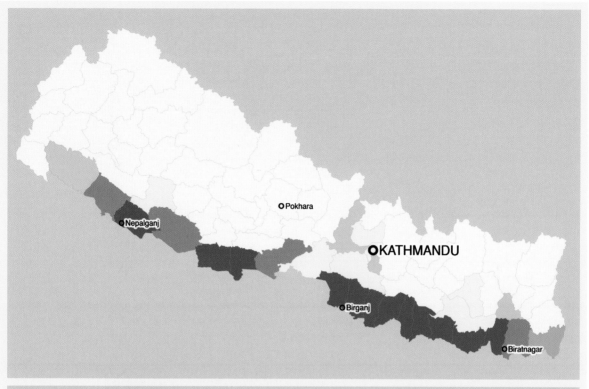

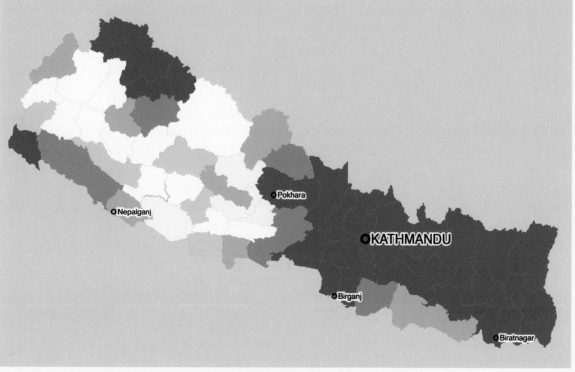

project. Some more recent (or legacy, where the names data were for jurisdictions that have recently changed) administrative boundaries were obtained from other projects – Natural Earth Data (www.naturalearthdata.com), OpenStreetMap data (osm.org) from Geofabrik Downloads (download.geofabrik.de) and the now discontinued MapZen Borders service (mapzen.com/data/borders), and various country-specific projects, often available through the GitHub (github.com) repositories. QGIS (www.qgis.org) was used to process and organise the metadata associated with the geodata.

This included the creation and population of a globally consistent ID for all countries and the first and second level subdivisions, where available and used for certain countries. While other projects maintain such a list (e.g. HASC codes and ISO 3166-2 codes), our own system was used for maximum flexibility, particularly as occasionally customized topologies and aggregations had to be employed, depending on the name data available. The system is based on the ISO 3166-1 country codes, an administrative level number and a padded integer code for the unit. Occasionally, the country's official codes were adopted for the latter part, where these were integer based.

For the world map of countries, a GeoJSON-format dataset from Natural Earth Data was used. Where countries had sub-country name data, the MapShaper website service was used to simplify the topology of the geodata, and one TopoJSON-format data file for up to two levels of sub-country area borders was created using it. TopoJSON (github.com/topojson/topojson) is a modern, flexible and highly compact file format.

4.5
Conclusion

The project thus far has collected individual data on approximately 1.7 billion individuals, plus a number of surname-only statistical breakdowns representing another 1.5 billion people (the majority of the names in this latter category being from China). Around 175 countries are represented, with an eventual aim to also include data for the remaining approximately 30 countries, albeit likely very simple statistical summaries of the most popular names.

As stated in the introduction, this project is quite different to other CDRC initiatives, both in its longevity (the first funding for this work was received in 2003), the persistently high levels of public interest that it has generated – recording nearly a million visits a year to Worldnames 1 for several years following its launch (worldnames.publicprofiler.org/webstats/index.html) and articles in large-circulation media such as the *Guardian* and *Daily Mail* newspapers, and the way that it has been conducted in spare time between funding streams. It is nonetheless important as the only CDRC project that purports to provide something approaching a global spatial data infrastructure, albeit founded on diverse, piecemeal and fragmented data sources.

This is, without doubt, a Big Data project – albeit one in which the search for and processing of appropriate data sources has been very labour intensive. We believe that this has implications for the wider practice – namely that Big Data have to be broadly understood before they are 'ingested', and that significant flaws in the content and coverage of data cannot be accommodated in subsequent analysis through blind application of sophisticated techniques. Spatial data are special by their very nature and geographic skills are foremost of those required to understand the possible sources and operation of bias in datasets such as Worldnames 2.

The greatest impact of the research to date has been upon the legions of amateur genealogists who are interested in understanding the geographies of their origins across the widest possible range of spatial scales. But, as set out in our introduction, the work is of wider importance precisely because a name is a statement of a number of facets to our individual identities – ranging from cultural, ethnic and linguistic group, to age and probable social standing in the world. In our future research we hope to address the ways in which names provide indicators of the movement of populations through the generations – both by the contagious diffusion of a surname from its known point of geographic origin (nearly a thousand years in the case of Anglo Saxon surnames, but less than a century for much of Turkey, for example) and by hierarchical diffusion cascading through the increasingly interconnected system of world cities. From these standpoints, georeferenced names provide valuable indicators of the legacies of successive waves of global migration through to measures of the social progression of migrants relative to their source and host communities.

Further Reading

Brunet, G. and Bideau, A. (2000). Surnames. *The History of the Family*, 5(2), 153-160.

Cheshire, J. A., Longley, P. A. and Mateos, P. (2010) Regionalisation and clustering of large spatially-referenced population datasets: The Case of Surnames. *GIScience conference 2010.*

Longley, P. A., Cheshire, J. A. and Mateos, P. (2011). Creating a regional geography of Britain through the spatial analysis of surnames. *Geoforum*, 42(4), 506–516.

Mateos, P., Webber, R. and Longley, P. (2007). The cultural, ethnic and linguistic classification of populations and neighbourhoods using personal names. *CASA Working Papers Series* 116 Centre for Advanced Spatial Analysis, University College London.

Munzert, S., Rubba C., Meißner, P. and Nyhuis, D. (2014). Mapping the geographic distribution of names. In *Automated Data Collection with R.* Chapter 15, 380–395. John Wiley & Sons, Ltd.

Acknowledgements

The authors would like to thank Dr Muhammad Adnan for his work on the original Worldnames, which formed the basis of much of the research and development of this project.

PART TWO

DYNAMICS AND CONSUMER DATA INFRASTRUCTURES

5

Ethnicity and Residential Segregation

Tian Lan, Jens Kandt and Paul Longley

5.1
Introduction

The preceding chapters have demonstrated the value of consumer data as an informative component of a spatial data infrastructure. This chapter focuses on applications using UK adults' names and addresses at individual level, which are commonly collected Big Data items in consumer registers. Names are potentially informative markers because their social properties permit inference of socio-demographic attributes such as age, sex, ethnicity, language and religion. Furthermore, many consumer databases can be turned into longitudinal data resources offering great potential to study the dynamics of individuals, households and place with novel insights into ethnic segregation, social and spatial mobility and local demographic change. In this chapter, we examine trends in ethnic diversity and residential segregation in contemporary Britain by using consumer data to underpin ethnicity classifications.

First, we elaborate on the value of consumer data viewed against prevailing approaches in measuring segregation. We will then explain the data and methods employed in order to explore highly detailed dynamics of ethnic geographies as well as the workflow of linking consumer data to other data sources. Subsequently, we present overall profiles of ethnic diversity and explore the changing ethnic compositions of contemporary Great Britain, including England, Wales and Scotland. As Britain becomes increasingly diverse, so the degree of residential segregation as measured by ethnicity becomes central to wider concerns about socio-spatial inequalities and the geography of economic and social opportunity. We conclude the chapter with findings and reflections on using consumer data in the study of ethnic diversity and segregation alongside their limitations.

5.2
Consumer data and ethnic geographies

Ethnicity is a taxonomy categorising people to social groups based on common ancestral, language, religion or cultural characteristics, which is not only an inherently complicated concept closely related to an individual's identity but also an important demographic and socioeconomic indicator. It constantly draws public, political and academic attentions and is currently strongly identified again as a paramount factor in social integration in the UK (Casey, 2016). In recent years, Britain has experienced increasing ethnic diversity, which has stimulated a wide public and policy debate as to whether Britain may be 'sleepwalking' into a more segregated society (Finney and Simpson, 2009). Revolving around this debate, ethnicity and residential segregation in the British context has been intensively examined in the literature. Simpson (2007) has suggested that there had been an increase in residential mixing because of growing minority populations and their more even spread across localities. Peach (2009) has also challenged the assertions that ethnic segregation in Britain was increasing and argued that Britain still does not have American-style ghettos like that of Chicago. Pointing out that increasing diversity had become an important feature of contemporary population change, Catney (2015) mapped the evolving geographies of ethnic diversity over two decades to update the knowledge of how diversity had grown. Most of these studies rely on national Census of Population data from the Office for National Statistics (ONS), which provides small area aggregated population counts for ethnic groups within pre-defined spatial units. For example, the Census Output Areas (OAs) are the lowest level of geography in the hierarchy of census boundaries and it is convenient to further aggregate OAs to higher level of geographies.

Although completion of the Census is a legal requirement, and the small area OA geography is convenient for many purposes, census data nevertheless present drawbacks for segregation research. First of all, there exist consistency issues with ethnicity classification across censuses. Questions and categorisation about ethnicity has been changed among the 1991, 2001 and 2011 Censuses (Table 5.1). For example, the White group in the 1991 Census is further divided into sub-groups as White British, White Irish, and any other White background in the 2001 Census. Mixed ethnic groups are added in the 2001 and 2011 Censuses. Categorisations like Gypsy/Irish Traveller and Arab are introduced in the 2011 Census. In the census context, it is often categorised into ethnic categories, among which some are not ethnic groups in a strict sense, such as 'White British' or 'Black British'. By asking to choose one categorisation to best describe the respondents' ethnic group, answers inevitably rely on subjective judgement. Numerous longitudinal studies (Simpson, Jivraj and Warren, 2016) have indicated that some individuals would change the perception of their own ethnicity among censuses. For the purpose of this chapter, we use the most common categories of the latest Census, merging the rare mixed ethnicities into Mixed (see Table 5.1).

Geographic boundaries such as OAs for collecting, analysing and reporting the population counts are not consistent throughout censuses, although there is generally a strong correspondence between the 2001 and 2011 data. According to the lookup file[1] between 2001 and 2011 OAs in England and Wales, there are 4,354 (2.4%) OAs among a total of 175,434 OAs that have been either split or merged to formulate 2011 OAs. In addition, the household census form for England and Wales is different from other parts of the UK. All these issues lead to comparability problems, and precautions need to be taken before comparing ethnic groups across censuses.

1991 Census ethnic groups	2001 Census ethnic groups	2011 Census ethnic groups	Merged census ethnic groups for this study
White	White British	White English/Welsh/Scottish/Northern Irish/British	White British
	White Irish	White Irish	White Irish
	Other White	White Gypsy/Irish Traveller	Other White
		Other White	
Indian	Indian	Indian	Indian
Pakistani	Pakistani	Pakistani	Pakistani
Bangladeshi	Bangladeshi	Bangladeshi	Bangladeshi
Chinese	Chinese	Chinese	Chinese
Black African	Black African	Black African	Black African
Black Caribbean	Black Caribbean	Black Caribbean	Black Caribbean
Any Other	Any Other	Any Other	Any Other
		Arab	Arab
	Other Mixed	Other Mixed	
Other Black	Mixed White-Caribbean	Mixed White-Caribbean	Mixed
	Mixed White-African	Mixed White-African	
	Other Black	Other Black	
Other Asian	Mixed White-Asian	Mixed White-Asian	
	Other Asian	Other Asian	Other Asian

Table 5.1
Comparison of ethnic groups across censuses and merged census ethnic groups for this study. Note: This table is modified from the table in Catney (2015).

Moreover, UK Censuses are usually updated only every ten years, which undermines the merits of census data when finer-grained temporal resolution is needed to capture population change in intermediate years. For example, a Polish immigration wave after Poland's accession to the European Union in 2004 can only be observed as accumulated results using 2011 data[2] on ethnicity. This issue is further compounded by the omnipresent Modifiable Areal Unit Problem (Openshaw, 1984), which is unlikely to be wholly negated by census zone design considerations.

In the remainder of this chapter we seek to demonstrate that the linkage of consumer registers and use of names-based ethnicity classifications offers promising ways to begin to address the shortcomings of census data. First, ethnicity is assessed at the individual level in a less subjective way with a consistent method applied over selected inter-Censual years. Second, ethnicity data can be generated almost continuously because consumer data are generated in real time and are consolidated at least once a year. Thus, population dynamics can be measured at a much higher temporal resolution. Third, since consumer data can be geocoded at address level, it enables the examination of ethnic geographies across the fullest range of scales. Taken together, used in association with conventional census data, consumer data can be used to identify highly granular geo-temporal patterns of segregation in contemporary Britain.

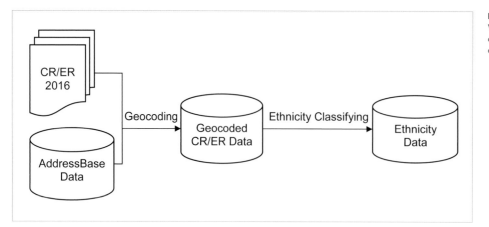

Figure 5.1
Workflow of formulating
address-level ethnicity
data from consumer data.

5.3
Deriving ethnic geographies at address level

The Consumer Data Research Centre (CDRC) currently stores consumer data for the whole UK. Consumer data are compiled from multiple data sources (see Lansley and Li, Chapter 1 in this volume), which include the full public versions of the annual Electoral Register (ER) for the earlier holdings (1998–2002) and compendium of both the redacted public ER and consumer dynamics files obtained from a range of sources for the later years (2003, 2007, 2013–2016). In what follows we describe each annual update as a 'Consumer Register' for Great Britain. In these Registers, consumer residential locations are identified only by postal addresses that are captured and retained in a non-standard form, making it necessary to link the data to a common geo-referencing framework such as Ordnance Survey AddressBase[3] or the Postcode Address File (PAF). The workflow of formulating ethnicity data from these composite registers is shown in Figure 5.1. This data processing procedure mainly consists of two steps: geocoding and ethnicity classification.

5.3.1
Geocoding

Since consumer data only contain non-geocoded postal addresses for each customer record, geographic locations need to be assigned. There are two basic input datasets for geocoding: consumer data and Ordnance Survey (Great Britain) AddressBase Premium data. The AddressBase data provide address point coordinates in both British National Grid and ETRS89 coordinate reference systems for postal addresses from the Royal Mail Postal Address File (PAF). In this study every postal address is geocoded using coordinate pairs in the British National Grid reference system. A text matching algorithm is used to match customers' addresses with postal addresses from AddressBase for data pertaining to every annual update of the Consumer Registers. The output from this step is geocoded CR/ER data with geographic coordinates.

5.3.2
Ethnicity classification

A standalone application Onomap (Mateos, Longley and Sullivan, 2011; www.onomap. org/) is used to assign every customer record into ethnic groups, based on their forenames and surnames. Onomap was developed as a series of lookup tables to predict ethnicity using fore and surnames with indicative cultural, ethnic and linguistic origins. A matching algorithm is used to classify names based on these tables. The resulting output file contains name pairs and their corresponding Onomap Group. To make the result more comparable, the Onomap ethnic

Figure 5.2
White and non-White
proportion change
over time.

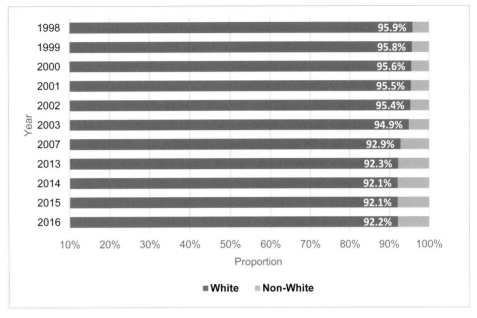

Figure 5.2
White and non-White
proportion change
over time.

classification is condensed into the merged 2011 Census ethnic groups (Table 5.1) for this study. A new version of Onomap, the Ethnicity Estimator, is currently under development and its main new feature will be its calibration with micro data on self-assigned ethnicity from the 2011 UK Census.

5.4
Ethnic diversity in contemporary Britain

We begin by exploring the ethnic composition change over time as derived from the address-level ethnicity data. The White ethnic group, including White British, White Irish, and Other White, constitutes the majority of Britain's population: White British alone accounted for 85% of the population of Britain in the 2016 consumer data. By contrast, other ethnic groups such as Pakistani, Indian, Bangladeshi and Chinese together comprised less than ten per cent (Figure 5.2). The proportion of the White majority group decreased year on year from 95.9% in 1998 to 92.2% in 2016 according to the consumer data, although the absolute size of the White population increased over this period.

The White and non-White bipartition in Figure 5.2 can be further divided into finer ethnic categorisations to gain a more in-depth picture of the ethnicity composition in Britain. Since the White British group is so predominant that it could easily overshadow patterns of other minority ethnic groups, the White British group is excluded from the selected groups of the 2011 Census ethnic classification in Figure 5.3. Three years are chosen from the timeframe: 2001, 2007 and 2016. Year 2001 is the only available directly comparable reference point to any Census year, although further acquisitions are in prospect.

As suggested by Figure 5.3, Indian is the largest group among ethnicities, with around 2.1% of the population in 2016. Pakistani is the second largest non-White community in Britain with 1.9% in 2016. Except for the Black African and Bangladeshi, an increase in the proportion across the three years can be seen for most ethnic groups. There has been a noticeable boost for the Other White group with an increase of around 1.1% in 2007 and 2% in 2016 compared with base year 2001. It is in accordance with the 2011 Census analysis on ethnicity of the non-UK born

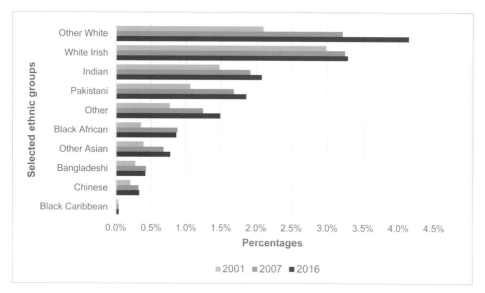

Figure 5.3
Ethnic composition
change of Britain in 2001,
2007 and 2016 (White
British excluded).

population, which claimed that 71% of the residents who identified themselves as Other White arrived in the UK between 2001 and 2011. It is suggested that the drastic increase for the Other White group is mostly due to the 2004 accession of several Eastern European countries into the European Union.

Some facts can be summarised from the ethnicity profiles above. Over the years, the relative share of the White majority population has decreased, although it has increased in absolute size. The White British group remains the largest ethnic category in Britain followed by the Other White group. Most of the minority ethnic groups are experiencing increase in their proportion of the population. Therefore, it can be concluded that Britain has become more and more ethnically diverse over time. It is also evident in Figure 5.3 that all of the ethnic minorities are growing in proportion over the three years, except for the Bangladeshi and Black African groups.

The year 2001 is the only point in time that is shared by both the Census and one of the consumer registers currently held by CDRC. Since the eligible age for electoral rolls registering was 16 in Britain in 2001, the adult (aged 17+) counts are extracted

and combined from the 2001 Census for England/Wales and Scotland for comparison purpose. Population counts of ethnic groups from consumer data are compared against adult counts of ethnic groups provided by the 2001 Census (Table 5.2). The comparison shows that consumer data only account for 87% of the 2001 Census total population and all of the individual ethnic groups are under-represented to a greater or lesser degree. Particularly, 88% of the White British group against the 2001 Census is relatively well represented in the consumer data, while only 40% of the Chinese group is represented. The representative rates for the Indian and Pakistani groups are 72% and 86% respectively.

The Black Caribbean and Other Mixed groups are severely under-represented and the Arab group is not applicable in 2001 Census ethnic categorisation. With the elimination of the above three ethnic groups, the ratios of adult counts for individual ethnic group in consumer data to counts in 2001 Census data are visualised in Figure 5.4. The red dashed line indicates 1:1 representation. The White Irish group is extremely over-represented, which suggests that a considerable amount of people who are classified as White Irish

Merged Census Groups for the study	Adult (16+) counts in 2001 Consumer Data	Adult (16+) counts in 2001 Census Data	Ratios of counts (Consumer data to Census Data)
Other Asian	151,594	189,036	0.802
Bangladeshi	106,480	174,257	0.611
Chinese	78,532	198,145	0.396
Indian	580,620	811,044	0.716
Pakistani	418,401	486,061	0.861
Black African	137,123	338,827	0.405
Black Caribbean	11,703	450,498	0.026
Other Mixed	291	337,547	0.001
Other	300,890	245,330	1.226
Arabic	4	NULL	NULL
Other White	829,458	1,226,886	0.676
White British	35,754,961	40,534,837	0.882
White Irish	1,178,502	650,658	1.811
Total	39,548,559	45,643,126	0.866

Table 5.2
Comparison between adult counts in 2001 consumer data and 2001 Census data.

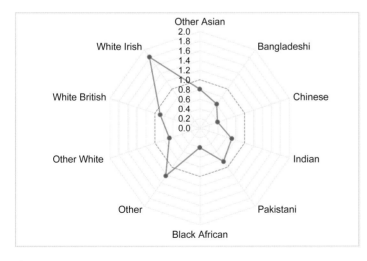

Figure 5.4
Ratios of adult counts for individual ethnic group in consumer data to counts in Census data. (The red dashed line indicates 1:1 ratio).

based on surname and forename by Onomap identify themselves as other ethnicities, most likely as White British. The varied representative rates might relate to the eligibility and willingness of different ethnic groups to register to vote in various elections. Although these ethnic groups are more or less under-represented, consumer data still remain a powerful resource to capture more details about the changes in Britain's ethnic composition.

To examine geographic patterns of consumer data's representativeness, ratios of adult counts in 2001 consumer data to 2001 Census data for the White British group are mapped across the Local Authority Districts (LADs) in Britain (Figure 5.5). The White British group are generally well represented for the whole of Britain, except for some districts in yellow colour such as South Cambridgeshire and Glasgow City, which have representativeness lower than 50%. Better or even over-representation (greater than 90%) of the White British group can be spotted in some urban areas, for instance London Boroughs, Birmingham and Manchester. Brent and Newham highlighted in dark blue in the inset map have the highest representative rate of the White British group among other LADs in Great Britain.

5.5
Residential segregation in contemporary Britain

Trends in ethnic diversity alone cannot inform the distributions of ethnic groups within Britain. A geographical perspective on ethnicity can provide information on the important research and policy issue of residential segregation. Ethnic residential segregation can be an elusive concept (Peach, 2009) without unified definition and measurement. There are various indices examining different dimensions (Massey and Denton, 1988) of residential segregation. For example, the Index of Dissimilarity and the Information Theory index for the Evenness dimension; the Exposure/Isolation index for the Exposure dimension. A single index of residential segregation could even result in different values at different spatial scales. In this study, the Index of Dissimilarity is employed to measure the evenness of ethnic residential patterns across the OAs.

A few concerns need to be addressed in advance. To demonstrate the feasibility of using consumer data on residential segregation studies, we choose the simplest and best interpretable, aspatial Index of Dissimilarity. Since the index is widely accepted in the previous studies as well as governmental reports, this choice facilitates comparisons with related studies in the British context. For the same purpose of comparability, we aggregated population counts by ethnic group to the 2011 OAs. There are 227,759 OAs in Great Britain in 2011. In addition, traditionally ethnic diversity is largely an urban phenomenon and studies of ethnic segregation focus on metropolitan areas. Nonetheless, dispersal

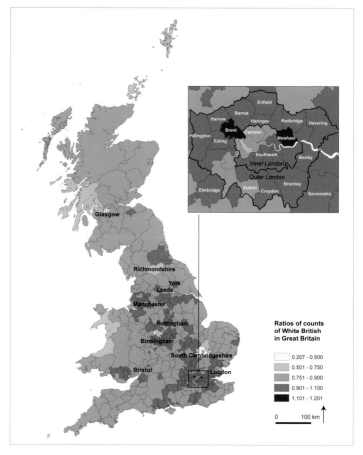

of ethnic minorities and immigrants into suburban and rural localities has been observed in the UK's changing geographies of ethnic diversity in recent decades (Catney, 2015). Therefore, this study includes both urban and rural OAs when examining the overall trends of ethnic segregation in Britain.

The national residential segregation of individual ethnic groups is measured using pairwise Index of Dissimilarity denoted as D in Equation (5.1), which captures the absolute difference between the spread of a specified group and the spread of the rest of the population across spatial units nationally. Here w_i denotes the number of residents of the ethnic group under examination in the ith OA, and denotes the number of the total population of the ethnic group under examination in Britain.

Figure 5.5
Ratios (2001 Consumer data to 2001 Census data) of counts of the White British group across the LADs in Britain.

Correspondingly, b_i is the number of the rest of residents other than the examined group in the ith OA, and B is the total number of the rest of the population in Britain. The absolute difference between the percentages is summed up over OAs and then halved to make the index value fall between 0 and 1. Sometimes it is also transformed into the percentage format, ranging from 0 to 100%. Value 0 means the ethnic group under examination is equally distributed over all OAs. For instance, if the ratio between w_i and b_i is constant across all OAs, the Index of Dissimilarity equals 0. In another extreme case, if the ethnic group under examination fully occupies each OA, the Index of Dissimilarity is maximised as 1 indicating completely segregated.

$$D = \frac{1}{2} \sum_{i=1}^{n} \left| \frac{w_i}{W} - \frac{b_i}{B} \right| \quad (5.1.)$$

Using Equation (5.1), pairwise dissimilarity indices for all of the ethnic groups are calculated from year 1998 onwards, aiming to examine the extent to which ethnic groups are evenly distributed across OAs of Britain. Results of selected ethnic groups are shown in Figure 5.6. The Index of Dissimilarity can be interpreted as the proportion of residents in the ethnic group under examination who would need to be moved to other OAs to achieve even distribution. First of all, the overall trend of residential segregation at the level of Great Britain is decreasing as Britain becomes more ethnically diverse at the same time. Obvious decline can be spotted from the temporal changes for most of the ethnic groups (Figure 5.6). However, the White British is an exception among other ethnic groups, with a slight rise of 1.4% in its dissimilarity index. Although there is an increase in the segregation level for the White British group, Catney (2015) interpreted this phenomenon in the context of new ethnic group mixing in less diverse locales. She argued that there would be an increase of unevenness whenever members of another ethnic group moved into a district where the White British group had a 100% perfectly even distribution.

The declining trend of dissimilarity indices for most minority ethnic groups suggests an increase in spatial integration among ethnic groups. Yet, the overall baseline levels of segregation differ considerably between groups, and three clusters of segregation can be identified (see Figure 5.6). The most segregated group of all, Bangladeshi, together with the Pakistani, Indian, Chinese and African groups, are highly segregated ethnic communities whose dissimilarity indices are around or above 70%. In contrast, the White British and Other White groups belong to the moderately segregated communities, whose dissimilarity indices are between 40% and 50%. The White Irish group stands out as the low segregation group whose dissimilarity index is below 30%. The Irish group has a long migration and settlement history in Britain and, if names have remained an indicator of ethnic identity, they appear to be more evenly distributed across Britain. The results also indicate that the White group, including the White British, White Irish, and Other White, is more spatially integrated across the whole of Britain than other ethnic minorities.

The above findings address the concern brought up at the beginning of this section as to whether Britain is becoming more residentially segregated or mixed. It leads to the conclusion that Britain has become more ethnically diverse and more residentially mixed at the national level. It should be noted, however, that segregation pattern is an outcome of not only selective residential mobility/ migration but also results from differential fertility and mortality rates among ethnic groups (Catney, 2015). Another demographic dynamic comes from international immigration during the past decade. According to the 2011 Census, 13% of the total population in England and Wales in 2011 were born outside the UK. There is a

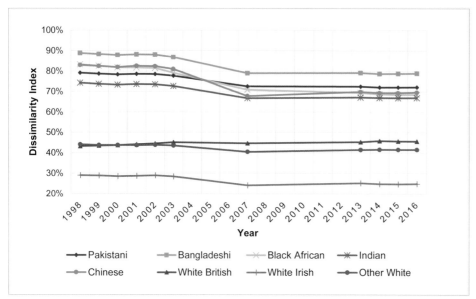

Figure 5.6
Changes of Index
of Dissimilarity for
selected ethnic
groups over time.

long history of immigrants into the UK. Initially they were drawn to the UK by labour shortages in particular areas, for example road-building in the early 20th century, health and transport services in the 1960s, the textile industry in the 1970s, and agriculture in the 2000s (Simpson, 2012). These particular migrant destinations, mostly major cities of the UK such as London, Manchester and Birmingham, served as 'gateway areas' (Catney, 2015) for immigration flows. International immigrants settled down in these gateway areas first and then some of them spread into other areas of the UK, which results in growing ethnic diversity and more even distributions of ethnic minorities.

Last but not least, it is nontrivial to investigate the cause for the dramatic drop starting from year 2003 shown in Figure 5.6. It has been noted earlier in this chapter that consumer data are compiled from multiple data sources. Consumer data are mainly derived from the public registers of electoral rolls before 2003. Afterwards, the consumer data are comprised of both electoral rolls and other commercial data sources. Therefore, it is necessary to justify whether the dramatic drop from 2003 is caused by the vagaries of data sources or by a demographic process. The best way is to filter out the consumer register part from the consumer data after 2003 so that the filtered consumer data solely consist of the public version of the electoral roll. The filtering can be done by using one attribute of each record that indicates the general source of the data. In order to examine whether the data source vagaries have an impact on the segregation indices, comparisons are made between dissimilarity indices calculated from the original consumer data and from the filtered consumer data.

Based on this strategy, the workflow in Figure 5.1 is repeated and the dissimilarity indices of ethnic groups from original consumer data and from filtered consumer data are compared respectively using different colours to represent different ethnic groups in Figure 5.7, where dashed lines represent the original consumer data while solid lines represent the filtered consumer data. Within each ethnic group, the segregation indices are relatively underestimated by the original consumer data after 2002 compared against the filtered consumer data. The most noticeable underestimation occurs in the Chinese

Figure 5.7
Dissimilarity indices
derived from original
consumer data (dashed
line) and from filtered
consumer data (solid line).

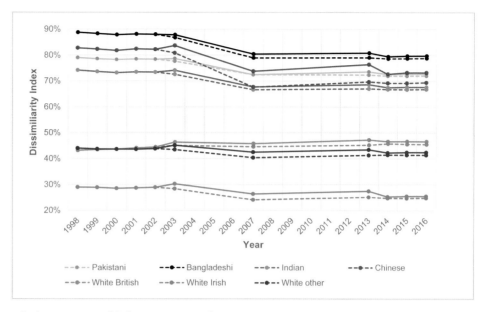

ethnic group, possibly because some of
them, for instance international students
from China, are not eligible to vote in any
election. Thus they are more under-
represented in the electoral registers than
in the consumer registers. In contrast, the
variations are not that large among some
native ethnic groups such as the White
British and White Irish, or some ethnic
communities from commonwealth
countries, for example the Indian,
Pakistani and Bangladeshi group,
or some of the Other White group from
EU countries, all of whom are allowed to
vote in at least some elections. Although
slightly underestimated, the dissimilarity
indices for all ethnic communities are still
decreasing and the overall patterns of high,
moderate and low segregation groups
still exist among these different ethnic
communities. It can be also concluded
that the dissimilarity indices for each
ethnic group prior to 2003 are
overestimated since fewer non-British
groups are included in the public electoral
roll before 2003. Afterwards, other
commercial data sources are compiled
into the consumer data to include as many
non-voters as possible. Changes in the data
source partly explain the strong decrease
in similarity indices observed from 2003

to 2007. However, they do not affect the
overall changing tendency of segregation
indices for individual ethnic groups. It is
likely because of a natural demographic
process, for example the increasing number
of immigrants and migrant dispersal,
which needs further evidence from the
Census migration data.

5.6
Conclusion

Contemporary Britain continues to
experience demographic changes in its
population, and these have accelerated in
recent years. Ethnic diversity at various
scales offers a key perspective on these
dynamics. Against this background, there
are concerns that a more diverse population
may become more segregated. By taking
the opportunity of the 2011 Census release,
numerous studies have been conducted into
these issues but are now beginning to look
outdated and possibly overtaken by events
as the Census data age. In addition, such
analyses are often limited to high levels
of spatial aggregation for reasons of
disclosure control. Thus, the use of
coded consumer data offers merit in
understanding changes over time at finer
spatial scales.

Our work in this area is just beginning, and there are very significant start-up costs in establishing the provenance and quality of consumer data as well as the veracity of the individual-level inference of ethnic group. The study contributes to the segregation debate with empirical findings from consumer data with finer-grained resolutions in both spatial and temporal dimensions. The results suggest that Britain is becoming more and more ethnically diverse over time with shrinking White British majorities and growing ethnic minorities. A decrease in the overall residential segregation in Britain can be identified from the changing of dissimilarity indices for most ethnic groups except for a small increase for the White British group. These findings reinforce the existing claims of a more mixed Britain in related studies in the literature with empirical evidence. It is believed that these changes are the consequence of a natural demographic process of fertility, mortality, migration and immigration of the population. The debate shows that there is a need to effectively assess ethnic geographies across a full range of spatial scales using data and methods that permit robust, timely and transparent assessments of residential segregation.

Consumer data appear to be an effective supplementary for census data; however several limitations should be noted. First, although achieving a relatively fine penetration rate of the population in the UK, consumer data are incomplete as they only record the adult population. The age limit depends on the eligible age for electing or applying for credit cards and loyalty cards. Second, due to the willingness and eligibility of election, different ethnic groups might be under-represented at different degrees (ethnic bias). Third, multiple data sources could have impact on the results of the analysis because it is only since 2003 that persons registered on the Electoral roll can opt out of inclusion in the derivative commercial dataset. Hence, since 2003, the consumer

registers have been further enhanced with other datasets. Although this might cause inconsistencies in trends between years, these seem to be limited based on the comparison between public electoral roll subset and the full consumer registers. Consequently, the Dissimilarity Indices likely underestimate segregation by the original consumer data to varying degrees, as found in the comparison between the original consumer data and the filtered consumer data (Figure 5.7). Considerations and precautions should be taken to understand the possible outcomes of these limitations with respect to the purpose of the analysis.

In this chapter, both opportunities and challenges of making use of consumer data are presented by re-visiting the ethnic diversity and segregation issues of contemporary Britain. It has been well demonstrated that it is feasible to address such social concern with novel data sources. By linking to other data sources, consumer data have even greater potential to address other micro demographics in a broader spectrum. For example, house price inflation and asset accumulation can be investigated by linking consumer data with Land Registry data. Other examples of possible application of consumer data could be issues such as changes in population density, household composition, and age structure. With more such new Big Data sources emerging, changes and dynamics of the contemporary population can be better understood in novel ways.

Further Reading

Casey, D. L. (2016). The Casey Review: A review into opportunity and integration. Online: https://www.gov.uk/government/publications/the-casey-review-a-review-into-opportunity-and-integration.

Catney, G. (2015). Exploring a decade of small area ethnic (de-)segregation in England and Wales. *Urban Studies*, 53(8), 1691-1709. doi:10.1177/0042098015576855

Catney, G. (2016). The Changing Geographies of Ethnic Diversity in England and Wales, 1991–2011. *Population, Space and Place*, 22(8), 750-765. doi:10.1002/psp.1954

Finney, N., and Simpson, L. (2009). *'Sleepwalking to segregation'? Challenging myths about race and migration*. Policy Press at the University of Bristol.

Mateos, P., Longley, P. A. and O'Sullivan, D. A. (2011). Ethnicity and Population Structure in Personal Naming Networks. *PLOS ONE*, 6(9). doi:10.1371/journal.pone.0022943

Massey, D. S., & Denton, N. A. (1988). The Dimensions of Residential Segregation. *Social Forces*, 67(2), 281-315. doi:10.2307/2579183

Openshaw, S. (1984). The modifiable areal unit problem. *Geobooks*. Norwich, England: University of East Anglia.

Peach, C. (2009). Slippery segregation: Discovering or manufacturing ghettos? *Journal of Ethnic and Migration Studies*, 35(9), 1381-1395. doi:10.1080/13691830903125885

Simpson, L. (2007). Ghettos of the mind: The empirical behaviour of indices of segregation and diversity. *Journal of the Royal Statistical Society: Series A (Statistics in Society)*, 170(2), 405-424. doi:10.1111/j.1467-985X.2007.00465.x

Simpson, L. (2012). More segregation or more mixing? Dynamics of diversity: Evidence from the 2011 Census. Online: http://hummedia.manchester.ac.uk/institutes/code/briefingsupdated/more-segregation-or-more-mixing.pdf

Simpson, L., Jivraj, S., and Warren, J. (2016). The stability of ethnic identity in England and Wales 2001–2011. *Journal of the Royal Statistical Society. Series A, (Statistics in Society)*, 179(4), 1025-1049. doi:10.1111/rssa.12175

Acknowledgements

The authors would like to thank CACI Ltd and DataTalk Research Ltd for providing the Consumer Register and Electoral Roll data under a special research licence to enable us to carry out this research. We would also like to thank Owen Abbott and Adriana Castaldo, Office for National Statistics, for their support in developing Ethnicity Estimator. The research was also funded by Engineering and Physical Science Research Council grant EP/M023483/1 and the Economic and Social Research Council grant ES/L013800/1.

Notes

1. http://ons.maps.arcgis.com/home/item.html?id=471e6948594540a3bccb2678e0cf50fe
2. www.ons.gov.uk/peoplepopulationandcommunity/
3. www.ordnancesurvey.co.uk/business-and-government/products/addressbase-products.html

6

Movements in Cities: Footfall and its Spatio-Temporal Distribution

Roberto Murcio, Balamurugan Soundararaj and Karlo Lugomer

6.1
Introduction

This chapter intends to address the problem of how to estimate human activities in retail centres by examining the WiFi probes in a SmartStreetSensors network at a fine spatial and temporal resolution. These sensors capture signals sent by WiFi-enabled devices present in their range. The data are then used as a proxy for estimating footfall at retail locations. An original methodology for cleaning and validating probe requests and then converting them into actual footfall counts is proposed and implemented. With these counts, a national level footfall index is proposed and, finally, the chapter concludes with a case study to use these data to characterise different retail locations.

The accurate measurement and estimation of human activity are one of the first steps towards understanding the structure of the urban environment (Louail et al, 2014). Human activities are highly granular and dynamic in both the spatial and temporal dimensions (Steenbruggen et al, 2013) and estimating them with confidence is crucial for decision-making in numerous applications such as urban management, retail, transport planning and emergency management. Traditionally insights into the distributions of such activities were gathered by studying the data available on night-time residence through population censuses and daytime estimates via various sample surveys such as traffic counts. The data generated by censuses, while being comprehensive, are only updated once a decade in countries such as the UK. In contrast, sample surveys and traffic counts get updated more frequently but are usually very specific. The key challenge has always been to capture and understand these dynamic and complex phenomena in detail efficiently and without compromising the privacy of those involved. This has led to a considerable volume of research in the last decade utilising various techniques and technologies. The proliferation of personal mobile devices has generated considerable interest for research in the past two decades by opening up unprecedented avenues in gathering detailed, granular information on people carrying these devices. The general technology landscape that supports this device ecosystem has also been constantly evolving and despite the increasing concern for privacy, it has been observed that the users show acceptance to the collection of their data at reasonable terms in return for incentives (Kobsa, 2014).

6.2
WiFi

There has been significant progress in employing novel technologies in measuring and analysing human activity patterns during the past two decades. A particular emphasis has been on the usage of mobile data and commonly associated technologies: cellular data, GPS (Vazquez-Prokopec et al, 2013), Bluetooth and, of course, WiFi (Schauer et al, 2014).

WiFi is a wireless network connection protocol standardised by IEEE in 2013. It is a distributed server-client based system where the client connects to access points (APs). Every device in the network has a unique hardware specific MAC address, which is transmitted between the device and AP before the connection is made. The key feature of WiFi infrastructure is that the network is distributed, i.e. the APs can be set up and operated by anyone locally unlike mobile networks. Since they are primarily used for Internet service provision, the protocol has priority for continuity of connectivity so the devices constantly scan for new and better connections using probe requests (detailed in later sections). WiFi, therefore, offers near complete coverage, is very resilient, and can encapsulate and reinforce civic space in cities (Torrens, 2008), while providing a middle ground between using infrastructure which is largely general purpose such as a cellular network and an

entirely special purpose infrastructure such as bespoke footfall counters.

Being a general network protocol designed to be used by mobile devices, WiFi devices relay a range of public signals - known as probe request frames - on regular intervals throughout its operation, for the purpose of connecting and maintaining a reliable and secure connection for the mobile device (Freudiger, 2015). These probe requests can be non-intrusively captured using inexpensive customised hardware and utilised in numerous applications. In addition to a uniquely identifiable MAC address, these probe requests include a range of other information that, when combined with the temporal signatures of the probe requests received, can help us understand the nature of, and identify, the devices generating these requests. Using the semantic information present in these probe requests it is possible to understand the nature of these users on a large scale.

Because of the security and privacy risks posed by the WiFi protocol's use of hardware based MAC addresses, various methods to strengthen the security have been introduced in mobile devices over the years. One such measure – randomisation of MAC addresses – has become more mainstream in mobile devices with its introduction as a default operating system behaviour in iOS 8 by Apple Inc.

6.3
The SmartStreetSensor project

The SmartStreetSensor project is one of the most comprehensive studies carried out on consumer volume and characteristics in retail areas across the UK. The project is a collaboration between Local Data Company (LDC) and the ESRC's Consumer Data Research Centre (CDRC). The data for the study are generated independently within the project through sensors installed at around 1,000 locations across Great Britain. It is the first comprehensive study into national footfall patterns using automated data collection.

As a first step, various locations for the study were identified by CDRC to ensure a geographical spread, different local demographic characteristics and range of retail centre profiles. A custom footfall counting technology using WiFi based sensors was developed by LDC and the sensors were installed in the identified locations. The sensor monitors and records signals sent by WiFi enabled mobile devices present in its range. In addition, pedestrians walking past the sensor were counted manually for short time periods during the installation. The project aims to combine these two sets of data to estimate footfall at these locations. The first sensor was installed in July 2015 and the network has grown to almost 789 total active sensors as of June 2017.

The primary aim of the project is to improve our understanding of the dynamics of high-street retailing in the UK. The key challenge in this area is the collection of data at the finest scales possible with minimal resources while not infringing on people's privacy. This challenge, when solved, can provide immense value to occupiers, landlords, local authorities, investors and consumers within the retail industry. The project aims to facilitate decision making by stakeholders in addition to the tremendous opportunities for academic research.

6.3.1
Hardware setup

The data are collected through a network of SmartStreetSensors: a WiFi based sensor that collects a specific type of packets (probe requests) relayed by mobile devices within the device's signal range. The sensor is usually installed in partnering retailer's shop windows so that its range covers the pavement in front of the shops. In a handful of cases (3%), the sensor is placed within a large shop to monitor internal footfall. Each device collects data

independently and uploads the collected data to a central container at 5-minute intervals through a dedicated 3G mobile data connection. The sensor hardware has been improved over the course of the project and currently has built-in failure prevention mechanisms such as backup battery for power failures, automatic reboot capabilities and in-device memory for holding data when the Internet is not available.

6.3.2
Data collection, data storage and data retrieval

The probe request frame is the signal sent by a WiFi capable device when it needs to obtain information from another WiFi device. For example, a smartphone would send a probe request to determine which WiFi access points are within range and suitable for connection. On receipt of a probe request, an access point sends a probe response frame that contains its capability information, supported data rates, etc. This 'request-response' interaction forms the first step in the connection process between these devices. The request frame has two parts, a MAC header part that identifies the source device, and the frame body that contains the information about the source device. As mentioned, the SmartStreetSensor collects some of the information available in the probe request frame relayed by the mobile devices, along with the time interval at which the request was collected and the number of such requests collected during that interval. The actual information present in the data collected by the SmartStreetSensor is shown in Table 6.1.

After the probe requests are collected, the MAC addresses in the data are hashed at the sensor level to preserve the privacy of the device owners and sent to LDC's cloud storage. From there, through a secure channel, they are sent to the CDRC secure servers, where the formal translation of a probe request to footfall data is completed.

Field	Description
MAC address	The MAC address of the source device with last two digits hashed
Date	Date of the data collection
Time interval	5-minute time interval in which the data was captured
Sensor	Unique ID of the sensor that captured data
Packets	Number of times the device sent packets to the sensor
Signal	The signal strength reported by the source device

6.3.3
Metadata

From July 2015 to May 2017, there were 652 operational sensors installed across Great Britain. During this time the sensors logged in the order of 2.6 billion probe requests at a rate of 6 million new requests per day. The geographical distribution of these sensors per region is shown in Table 6.2.

6.4
From probe request to footfall counts

The probe requests received by the sensor are not a direct measure of footfall, so, in order to extract a meaningful indicator for footfall, the information present in the requests are validated through a series of steps described in this section. The prime sources of information we use to accomplish this transformation from the probe requests to footfall are:

1) The hashed/anonymised MAC address of the mobile device.
2) The time interval at which the probe request was collected.
3) The Received Signal Strength Indicator (RSSI) present in the probe request.

We carry out the transformation both internally by looking at the patterns present in the data and externally by comparing it to data collected via field surveys. Before we validate the data we take into account the following:

Range of the sensor
Since the strength of the signal from a mobile device to the WiFi access point depends on various factors such as distance between them, the nature and size of obstructions between them, interference from other electromagnetic devices etc., the exact delineation of the range of the sensors is different for each and every sensor. We assume that the range of the sensor is equal in all directions and is linearly indicated by the RSSI reported by the mobile devices in range.

Probe request frequency
The frequency of probe requests generated by device varies widely based on the manufacturer, operating system, state of the device and the number of access points already known to the device (Freudiger, 2015). These requests are also generated in short bursts rather than at regular intervals. Moreover, Android devices send probe requests even when the WiFi is turned off. With the large number of different devices available, it is impossible to predict and create a general model for this probing behaviour. For simplicity, we assume that for a probe request received with a MAC address with a known Organisationally Unique Identifier (OUI), there is a corresponding device present within the range of the sensor at that time interval, irrespective of the number of such requests received in the mentioned interval. Essentially, we are just looking for unique MAC addresses within a time period rather than the total number of requests made by them.

Region	Sensors	Percentage (%)	May 2017 – Basic footfall counts	
			Average	Median
East Midlands	40	6.13	210,380	178,411
East of England	27	4.14	209,590	194,157
London	219	33.58	415,120	332,059
North East	16	2.45	271,600	246,210
North West	60	9.2	306,490	250,180
Scotland	78	11.96	196,120	138,935
South East	65	9.96	307,370	212,813
South West	54	8.28	171,440	149,400
Wales	13	1.99	275,740	332,414
West Midlands	22	3.37	367,840	271,200
Yorkshire and The Humber	58	8.89	248,100	212,282
Total	652	100.00	270,890	212,813

Table 6.2
Regional distribution of the installed sensors in Great Britain.

MAC address collisions

From the initial analysis, we have observed that there are a few instances of MAC address collisions reported where a device known to be in some place has been reported somewhere else. This might be occurring due to rogue MAC randomisation by certain devices and the hashing procedure done at two different stages. Due to the negligible volume of such collisions ($\sim$ 0.01%), for the purpose of this research, we ignore these collisions and treat all distinct hashed MAC addresses with known OUI to be the same device.

MAC address randomisation

A MAC address has two parts. The first part is the OUI, which identifies the manufacturer of the wireless card, and the second part belongs to the device, which, along with the OUI, was originally designed to uniquely identify the device at the hardware level. But with the introduction of randomisation, there is an increased use of 'unknown' or 'public' addresses that are not registered with IEEE. Once these uncertainties are addressed, the next step is to clean the data received to transform it into a consistent indicator for activity such as pedestrians at the location.

6.4.1
Internal validation

After the initial considerations we start transforming the data by standardising the time interval to 288 intervals of 5 minutes starting from 00:00. We do this by rounding-off the non-standard time intervals encountered, to the nearest 5 minutes. We then aggregate the number of probe requests by their unique MAC address. This results in a count reduction of approximately 85% (Figure 6.1).

After this aggregation, we investigate the occurrence of MAC addresses over the entire day. In this example, we see that around 15% of MAC addresses repeat for more than 5 minutes. Since we are interested in the pedestrian activity, we eliminate these long-dwelling MAC addresses and redo the count. The detailed account of the 5-minute interval count of probe requests collected through the day before and after cleaning is shown in Figure 6.1.

Finally, these devices randomly fail for short periods of time, leaving some intervals without any counts. At other times, retailers need to shut down the

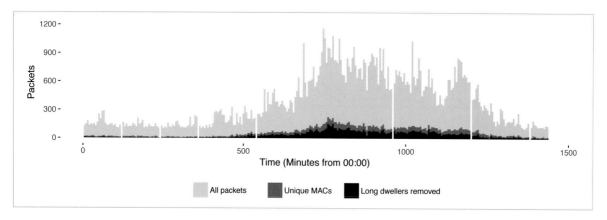

device, which also leads to periods of zero counts until the device is switched back on. If such intervals are short (no more than half an hour), we can safely interpolate the counts to have better aggregated estimations of the daily counts. In practice, the estimated count c, at time t, is obtained by a simple linear interpolation:

$$c = c_1 + m(t - t_1) \quad (6.1)$$

where m is the slope and c_1 are the counts at time t_1.

6.4.2
External validation

After addressing the aforementioned uncertainties and cleaning the data from the unwanted probe requests, some measurement error will still remain. The factors responsible for this difference are the various sources of measurement error which cause sensors to undercount. The stores in which the sensors are deployed have different layouts and walls built from construction materials with different physical properties and therefore result in different WiFi propagation characteristics. As a result, the sensors will be more effective in some stores than others. The demographic characteristics of passers-by are also relevant in this context since some population contingents – such as the elderly – are less likely to have WiFi enabled phones.

The previously internally validated data are externally validated against - and adjusted to - manual counts. The ratio between manual counts and internally validated (cleaned) sensor counts is known as adjustment factor α:

$$\alpha = \frac{M}{\psi} \quad (6.2)$$

Where α is the adjustment factor, though there are certain differences between weekdays and weekends, M is the number of the passers-by counted manually on the street and ψ is the number of the processed sensor counts.

Ideally, manual counts are taken in multiple periods throughout the day so an average adjustment factor for that particular location is derived. All the internally validated sensor counts are simply multiplied by α to provide the final estimate. This step is crucial in enabling the spatial comparability of flows measured at different locations.

Finally, it is important to mention that this method is quite sensitive to the way the manual counts are conducted, and it could lead to the omission of large groups of devices, potentially important for a wider type of application, like measures of flows or measures of local activity, beyond the retail domain.

Figure 6.1
The total number of probe requests collected every 5-min interval vs the number of unique MAC addresses collected in the same interval vs the final count for the same interval after cleaning long dwelling devices.

At this point, once we have translated probe requests into footfall counts with a sufficient degree of certainty, we can start a proper analysis of the particular patterns generated at each location to compare trends and define different functional areas across different parts of the country. An example of this is presented in Section 6.5.

6.5
UK footfall index

One of the first analyses conducted, based on the validated footfall counts, was to look at the shift in footfall figures nationwide to establish seasonal peaks and troughs and ensure they reflect known trends. For example, footfall tends to rise in the run up to Christmas but falls during the first months of the year.

Two different indexes were therefore defined: the first to track seasonal trends in footfall, taking a particular month as a base line and the second, to compare the change in footfall between two consecutive months. Both indexes try to detect major shifts and overall tendencies from one month to another at the national level, not to explain actual activity patterns.

For both, the counts were aggregated to each half-hour, removing those devices that were present for more than 5 minutes at every location and without applying any adjustment factor, as these indexes are more concerned with counting all the footfall activity around the sensors, and not only retail related activity.

Equation 6.3 measures the relative change in footfall from one month to another:

Footfall index (a,b) = ((b-a)/a)*100 (6.3)

where b = Total footfall at month M_b, a = Total footfall at base month M_a, $a{\neq}b$.

The major challenge was the actual construction of b and a, as, i) the number of sensors is not the same between any two

given months (at this stage of the project there are always more sensors in month M_b than in month M_a); ii) a single sensor could be measuring H hours in month M_a and K hours in month M_b, with $K{\neq}M$ and iii) some sensors can be considered just as white noise, because they may have only a few valid measures within a particular month. These discrepancies make, in principle, these two months incomparable with each other.

To solve this, we proceed as follows:

1) Define $S_{dM_{a,b}} = \sum_{i=1}^{H_{a,b}} h_{d_i}$

    where $H_{a,b}$ is the total number of half hours in months $M_{a,b}$, and M_{di} is the half hour aggregated footfall counts at sensor d at bin i. Put simply, $S_{dM_{a,b}}$

    is the sum of all the footfall in a single month at sensor d.

2) Calculate the theoretical probability distribution of all $S_{dM_{a,b}}$ in a month.

    a) Discard all sensors skewed to the left of the bulk of the distribution, i.e. those that are to the left of the standard deviation value. In other words, remove all sensors that didn't work properly during months $M_{a,b}$
    b) For sensors skewed to the right, i.e. those that are two times above the standard deviation value, we firstly verify if their behaviour is the same across the previous few months or if the month in question was an anomalous one. If it is the former, we remove the counts, otherwise they are kept in.

3) With the remaining sensors, we define a and b as follows:

$$a = \frac{\sum_{i=1}^{H_a} h_i}{S_a}, \quad b = \frac{\sum_{i=1}^{H_b} h_i}{S_b}, \quad (6.4)$$

where $H_{a,b}$ is the total number of hours in month $M_{a,b}$, h_i is the half an hour aggregated footfall counts at bin i and S_a and S_b are the total number of sensors left after step 2.

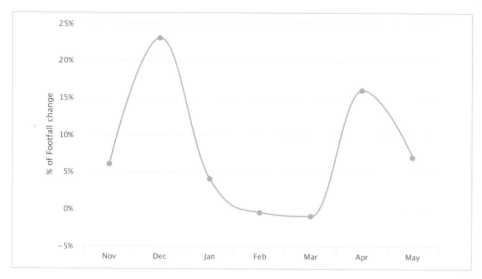

Figure 6.2
Percentage change in footfall over a 7-month period with October 2016 as the base month.

Equation 6.4 captures the weighted counts at each month, which standardises the measures, making both months comparable. In the next section, we present the results obtained when a single month is set as base month, in this case, October 2016. The second index, where we compare the change in footfall between two given months, is explained in detail in the online supplementary information.

6.5.1
Footfall trends over long time periods

Defining October 2016 (with a net footfall of approximately 131 million) as the base month, we explored the percentage change in footfall across a 7-month period (Figure 6.2). November shows a marginal increment of 6% while December increases by almost 25%, which is expected due to the festive season. After this peak, in the first trimester of the year, footfall returns to the October levels, then there is an unusual increase in April 2017 (17%) before finally returning to the base month level in May. The April increase could be related to the Easter holiday period, but this is something still to be investigated.

Although both indexes were presented at national level, they can be disaggregated to, for example, retail centre level, to

compare the corresponding flows between different retail areas.

6.5.2
Footfall trends over short time periods

In order to illustrate the differences in the volume of footfall across Central London, the validated sensor measurements were taken for the five-minute intervals of each day of the week over the period of ten weeks (9 January 2017 to 19 March 2017) for all the sensors for which data were available. The period was chosen to avoid holiday seasons (Christmas, Easter, summer) or the occurrence of Monday Bank Holidays which would have influenced the usual weekday footfall volumes. The spatial variation of overall average five-minute footfall during the weekdays between 7am and 7pm in Central London is shown on Figure 6.3.

Areas well known for their business are Soho (Central London) and Camden Town, as well as locations around some of the Tube and rail stations, with some notable examples labelled on the map (Victoria, Waterloo and Angel stations). The influence of station proximity is also seen on Edgware Road. Footfall around Edgware Road and Marble Arch Tube stations appears to be higher, while at the same

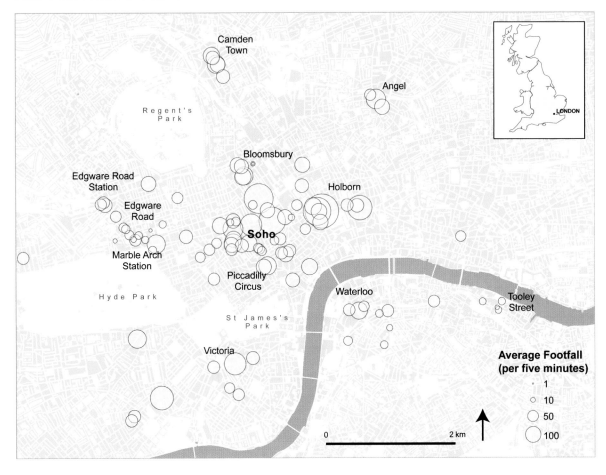

Figure 6.3
Average five-minute footfall in Central London during the working days (7am - 7pm) between 9 January and 19 March 2017. Source: Local Data Company (2017); Ordnance Survey Vector Map District (2017).

time sensors between them record lower and relatively consistent and spatially comparable footfall. On the other hand, stores situated in quieter side streets or less attractive areas show lower footfall, including areas that may be near main attractions but outside main corridors – Tooley Street being a good example, situated behind the far more crowded Thames path near Tower Bridge.

While very important, assessment of the overall footfall may fall short of detecting some other interesting patterns of human activity, for example how a certain area of the city is being used by its residents, workers and visitors during the characteristic time periods during the day and the week. In order to explore some of these differences in diurnal patterns, temporal profiles of three locations were constructed. Those locations were Holborn Station, Connaught Street (situated to the west of Edgware Road) and a pub in Tooley Street between London Bridge and Tower Bridge. Temporal patterns and volume of footfall differ among the three locations on multiple levels (Figure 6.4). First, overall volume is very high around Holborn Station and very low at the Connaught Street location. Second, general profiles differ, so that both Holborn and Tooley Street display three peaks (morning and afternoon rush hour and lunchtime), while Connaught Street has a less clear, noisier pattern, which could be owing to a low footfall. Finally, there are differences even between the profiles of Holborn and Tooley Street with the latter experiencing a relatively higher PM rush hour peak.

In addition to exploring the spatio-temporal variations of footfall throughout a single day, weekly patterns are also of interest. In this case, weekend activity patterns were compared to the weekday activity patterns by dividing the average five-minute footfall on Saturdays and Sundays between 7am and 7pm by the average five-minute footfall on weekdays between 7am and 7pm as follows:

$$l_w = \frac{F_{1(Sat\text{-}Sun,7\text{-}19)}}{F_{2(Mon\text{-}Fri,7\text{-}19)}} \; x \; 100 \quad (6.5)$$

where I_w is the index of relative weekend daytime activity, F_1 is the average five-minute weekend footfall between 7am and 7pm and F_2 is the average five-minute weekday footfall between 7am and 7pm.

This kind of index does not necessarily tell us which areas get busiest during the weekend daytimes, but rather which areas have more pronounced daytime weekend activity relative to their daytime weekday activity.

As Figure 6.5 shows, Soho, Camden Town and a location south of Hyde Park record higher footfall during the weekends than during the weekdays, which can be attributed to their reputation as highly attractive tourist and/or recreational areas. The results for Camden Town indirectly suggest where exactly the main attractions of the area (Inverness Street Market, Buck Street Market and Camden Lock Market further north) are located. Relative weekend activity is higher north of the Camden Town underground station and it diminishes in a southerly direction, i.e. away from the markets. On the other hand, many areas appear to be much busier during the weekdays (Victoria, Waterloo, Tooley Street, etc.), where there are concentrations of working places, including the universities in Bloomsbury.

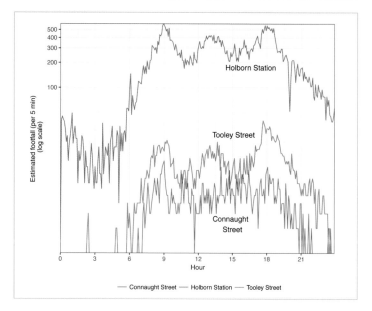

6.6
Conclusion

WiFi sensors are a very rich source of continuous and up-to-date data which can be used for a variety of purposes involving the importance of human mobility in the cities. These data are not free of measurement errors and associated issues and need to be handled by applying a complex validation methodology before making any pragmatic conclusions. However, despite those challenges, they provide a good estimate of the footfall around the area where the sensor is located and are therefore a useful estimate of the potential conversion rates and revenue, inevitable factors to be considered in the locational planning in many industries, especially retailing. One of the main advantages of WiFi sensors lies in their ability to measure flows of people on a rather fine scale, which in turn gives us the opportunity to assess the suitability of a microsite location for a particular business and its opening times. Case studies of spatio-temporal footfall patterns in Central London demonstrate that the impact of the microsite location is very significant and can be decisive, as some streets within otherwise busy areas may end up receiving relatively low footfall.

Figure 6.4
Temporal activity patterns at three locations in Central London on 16 January 2017.

Figure 6.5
Index of relative weekend
activity in Central London
between 9 January
and 19 March 2017. Source:
Local Data Company
(2017); Ordnance Survey
Vector Map District (2017).

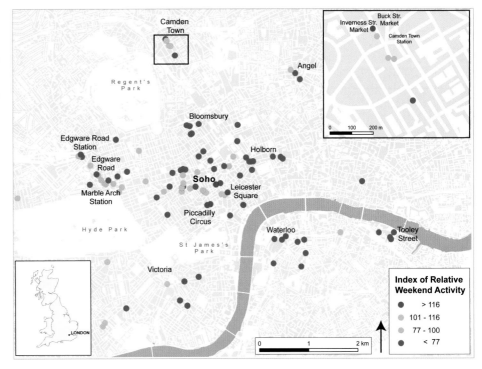

Further Reading

Barbera, M. V. et al. (2013). Signals from the crowd: Uncovering social relationships through smartphone probes. In *Proceedings of the 2013 Conference on Internet Measurement*. ACM (Association for Computing Machinery), pp. 265–276.

Cunche, M., Kaafar, M.-A. and Boreli, R. (2014). Linking wireless devices using information contained in Wi-Fi probe requests. *Pervasive and Mobile Computing*, 11, 56–69.

Freudiger, J. (2015). How talkative is your mobile device? An experimental study of Wi-Fi probe requests. In *Proceedings of the 8th ACM Conference on Security & Privacy in Wireless and Mobile Networks*. ACM, p. 8.

Hidalgo, C.A. and Rodriguez-Sickert, C. (2008). The dynamics of a mobile phone network. *Physica A: Statistical Mechanics and its Applications*, 387(12), 3017–3024.

Kobsa, A. (2014). User acceptance of footfall analytics with aggregated and anonymized mobile phone data. In *Lecture Notes in Computer Science* (Lecture Notes in Artificial Intelligence and Lecture Notes in Bioinformatics), pp. 168–179. Springer International Publishing Switzerland 2014

Louail, T. et al. (2014). From mobile phone data to the spatial structure of cities. *Scientific Reports*, 4, 1–14. doi:10.1038/srep05276

Schauer, L., Werner, M. and Marcus, P. (2014). Estimating crowd densities and pedestrian crowds using Wi-Fi and Bluetooth. *Proceedings of the 11th International Conference on Mobile and Ubiquitous Systems: Computing, Networking and Services*. ICST (Institute for Computer Sciences, Social Informatics and Telecommunications Engineering), pp. 171–177.

Steenbruggen, J. et al. (2013). Mobile phone data from GSM networks for traffic parameter and urban spatial pattern assessment: A review of applications and opportunities. *GeoJournal*, 78(2), 223–243.

Torrens, P. M. (2008). Wi-fi geographies. *Annals of the Association of American Geographers*, 98(1), 59–84.

Vazquez-Prokopec, G. M. et al. (2013). Using GPS technology to quantify human mobility, dynamic contacts and infectious disease dynamics in a resource-poor urban environment. *PloS one* 8(4), e58802.

Acknowledgements

The authors would like to thank Local Data Company Ltd, for providing, in partnership with CDRC, the SmartStreetSensor footfall data. The second and third authors' PhD research is sponsored by the Economic and Social Research Council through the UCL Doctoral Training Centre.

7

The Geography of Online Retail Behaviour

Alexandros Alexiou, Dean Riddlesden and Alex Singleton

7.1
Introduction

The advancements of information and communications technologies (ICTs) in the last 30 years have brought fundamental changes to the way in which populations can communicate, work and interact with services. Arguably, the most significant advancement has been the arrival of the Internet, giving disparate populations the ability to connect and interact with one another without the constraints of distance. Since its inception in the mid 1980s, the Internet has been used ubiquitously, engendering benefits for everyday life across multiple domains, such as communication, information access, education and entertainment.

Consumer behaviours have also changed as a result, with an increasing likelihood for Internet users to purchase online given the financial savings and added convenience it facilitates (Calderwood and Freathy, 2014; Beck and Rygl, 2015). The proliferation of online shopping has had a significant impact within the retail industry especially since many products such as newspapers, magazines and music are digitally rather than physically purchased. This has led to the demise or significant diversification of many retailers (Dholakia et al, 2010; Carlson et al, 2015; Verhoef et al, 2015). In terms of those products and services that cannot be digitised, widespread adoption of the Internet has increased competition, choice, access and reduced prices for the typical consumer.

The associated impact of the Internet on traditional retailers brought a significant shift from bricks and mortar retailing to omni-channel digital stores as a means of adaptation. The extent to which this increases resilience of physical stores to their online competitors has become a key theme in retail research (Wrigley and Dolega, 2011; Singleton and Dolega, 2015). Responses differ, but typically most large retailers will have invested in click-and-collect services to allow customers to order online and collect at their convenience, or enhanced home delivery services.

Nevertheless, not all retail activities are affected equally. For consumers, benefits to proximity still remain and clustering of economic activity prevails despite advances in ICTs (Nathan and Rosso, 2015). Furthermore, the importance of face-to-face communication is a considerable barrier constraining the use of the Internet in some circumstances (Kaufmann et al., 2003). Consumer demographics can also play an important role towards the impact of online shopping on retail geography. For example, the extent to which localised populations are engaged with the Internet could be considered as an influential factor in the attractiveness and success of traditional retail centres (Dolega et al, 2016). In this setting it is important to consider the changes in consumer behaviours in more detail as well as the extent to which these may vary geographically and across life cycles.

Any exploration of online retail behaviour should include not only factors that differentiate access to and engagement with the Internet, but also quality of infrastructure, local population characteristics and contextual geography. For instance, there are spatial disparities in fixed-line broadband services, particularly as a result of the urban-rural dichotomy. Population densities seem to play an important role in the quality of broadband services since commercial providers are more likely to develop network infrastructure in densely populated areas to facilitate increased demand. Moreover, attributes pertaining to, inter alia, age, education and professional occupation have been considered as having links to the levels of engagement.

These complex sets of input data can be combined using multivariate classification techniques to produce nested typologies at the small-area level. The methodology, outlined in the following sections, involves the creation of such a bespoke geodemographic classification system, using aggregate measures of Internet infrastructure, access, engagement and contextual information. This typology was created at the Lower Super Output Area (LSOA) Census geography level for England in the form of the Internet User Classification (IUC). The resulting classification is presented through a series of cluster summarisations and assessments, which describe the prevailing characteristics of each of the clusters identified. The IUC is currently openly available through the Consumer Data Research Centre (CDRC) data portal (data.cdrc.ac.uk/dataset/cdrc-2014-iuc-geodata-pack-england).

The IUC geodemographic system provides a basis of analysis regarding the characteristics of small area populations that can contribute to the wider field of research through the identification of socio-spatially differentiated patterns of Internet access and engagement. A use case of the IUC is presented here by examining the 'e-resilience' of retail centres in England. The analysis, detailed in Singleton et al (2016), evaluates the extent to which retail centres have spatially differentiated vulnerability to the impacts of online consumption. Retail centres are profiled by the IUC and demand factors are coupled with catchment models to create a composite index of exposure, engendering a remarkable geography of retail centres that are at high exposure to the effects of online retailing. Measures of exposure are then coupled with measures of supply vulnerability pertaining to the mix of stores within each retail catchment in order to create a composite e-resilience score.

7.2
Creating the Internet User Classification

Methodologically, building the IUC followed a conventional geodemographic approach, as presented in Harris et al (2005).

Domain	Description
Infrastructure	Fixed-line household infrastructure access and broadband Internet performance.
Mobile phones	Mobile access, connectivity and usage.
Perceptions	People's attitudes and perceptions about the use and utility of the Internet.
Access patterns	Information on Internet access patterns, e.g. only at home, while travelling, through a mobile, etc.
Commercial applications	Information on the use of commercial applications such as online shopping, online banking and online bill payments.
User population	Current Internet users, ex-users and non-users.
Demographics and attributes of contextual geography	Demographic attributes such as age, education and occupation and attributes of contextual geography such as rurality, population density, etc.

Table 7.1
Variable domains used in the IUC.

Generally, the steps required to create a classification include selecting the appropriate classification scale, selecting the input variables, preparing the data (e.g. variable transformations or weighting), applying a clustering method and finally interpreting results (clusters). Due to data availability, the IUC was built for England at the LSOA level. LSOA geography is the second most granular Census geography available, comprising 32,844 zones of between 1,000–3,000 people or 400–1,200 households. The majority of data under consideration were available at the Great Britain level, albeit that those datasets available for England were more robust. Furthermore, the nature of these geographies in Scotland and Wales varies significantly compared to England (e.g. in terms of the characteristics of rural areas) and so the decision was taken to exclude Scotland and Wales from the analysis.

Selecting the appropriate variables to be used in the classification, however, can be more challenging. The multi-dimensionality of the IUC is important; a wide range of spatially referenced input measures are essential to the success of the classification, similar to how geodemographics typically include a plethora of socio-economic attributes in order to represent neighbourhoods. If combined and summarised effectively, meaningful measures could represent a typology of Internet use and engagement. Broadly,

these datasets should cover several domains, such as those listed in Table 7.1.

An important source of data forming input to the IUC was the Oxford Internet Survey (OxIS), which was launched by the Oxford Internet Institute in 2003. The survey, conducted biannually, is carried out by interview using a probability sample of around 2,000 people in Great Britain, enabling comparisons over time (more details can be found on the OxIS website, available at: oxis.oii.ox.ac.uk/research/methodology/). For the creation of the IUC, the 2013 study was used. The OxIS covers a broad range of topics regarding people's perception of the Internet; given the vast number of questions that were available for analysis (there are over 500 potential lines of enquiry), it was necessary to identify a smaller subset of questions relating to key dimensions of Internet use, behaviours and attitudes.

The sample used for the 2013 OxIS is representative of the UK population, but its size is relatively small to capture the full breadth of the survey at higher geographic scales. As such, a method for synthetic data estimation was implemented to extrapolate the survey results to national small area coverage. Projection of the survey results was carried out using a Small Area Estimation (SAE) technique. SAE was applied to each question and generated a predicted response rate at the Output Area

(OA) Census geography. The estimations are 'indirect', in that they borrow strength by using values of the variables of interest from related areas through a model that provides that link using secondary data, such as Census counts and administrative records (Rao, 2003). In the most basic sense, it is possible to predict results for unsampled areas by using data from sampled areas. For instance, profiling the relationship between age structure and Internet usage and subsequently using the results to predict rates for an unsampled geography where no survey data are available, but the age structure is known (i.e. from a recent Census of population).

In practice, however, the process was more complex. Firstly, the required explanatory variables for each survey question should be identified. Predictor variables explored were based on those factors known to influence Internet use and behaviour that were identified in relevant literature, namely age (Rice and Katz, 2003; Warf, 2013), socio-economic status (Silver, 2014), ethnicity (Wilson et al., 2003), gender (Prieger and Hu, 2008); rurality (Warren, 2007), education (Helsper and Eynon, 2010) and Internet connectivity (Riddlesden and Singleton, 2014). There are a number of techniques that can be used to identify those attributes with the highest influence; in this case, a decision tree algorithm was implemented, specifically the Quick Unbiased Effective Statistical Tree (QUEST) algorithm, in order to identify the relationship of those external attributes to response rates. Decision tree algorithms are commonly used in data mining and seem to perform well compared to, e.g., ecological regression analysis, which in this case provided poor results.

In total, 42 OxIS questions were selected, covering each of the 171,372 OAs in England and Wales. The described model outputs a series of rates which were then fitted to OA geography by examining the distribution of these population sub-groups within each OA nationally. Essentially, an OA rate for each question is a weighted average derived from all the population sub-groups present within it.

Two tests were carried out in order to validate estimated results. One way was to compare the average deviation between mean rates of the estimated data at the national level, and mean rates of the original OxIS sample. The average difference was <0.1%, which suggests the estimated dataset is broadly representative, as national means are comparable to those of the original data. Furthermore, comparing distributions showed that the estimation method is not skewing the output such that it is unrepresentative of the sample it was built from. Vastly different average rates between the estimated and original data at this stage would have flagged potential problems with estimation methods.

The next stage in validation involved profiling responses geographically, to examine if variability pertained to patterns that would be expected. An external dataset was used for this purpose; each of the OA response estimates were profiled using the 2011 Output Area Classification (OAC), an open geodemographic system (available for download through the CDRC portal at: data.cdrc.ac.uk/dataset/cdrc-2011-oac-geodata-pack-uk), to ensure that the propensity for certain responses (e.g. engagement to online shopping) were in line with responses given to the general demographic profile of the clusters. For instance, the national average response rate of question QC30b: Buying Online for those who responded as 'frequently' (i.e. buying online at least monthly) is 53.5% of all Internet users. Figure 7.1 shows the deviation of frequent users from the national mean by OAC profiles.

Profiling response rates by OAC revealed significant correspondence between socio-spatial groups and prevailing levels of engagement with different domains of the Internet. In most cases, groups with

Figure 7.1
Deviation from the national average of response rates to the question QC30b: Engagement to Online Shopping, for those identified as 'frequent' users, by OAC Group.

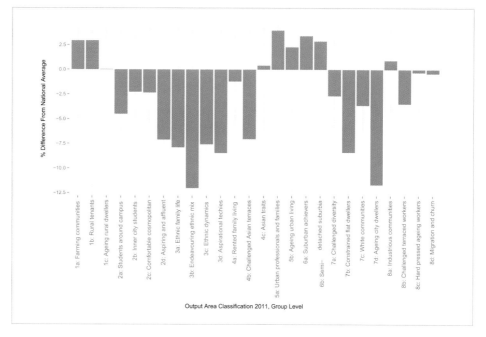

younger, urban populations and professional backgrounds displayed the highest levels of engagement with most aspects of the Internet. In contrast, those groups whose constituent populations are elderly, constrained by deprivation, or working in employment sectors that would not require significant exposure to ICT, were generally less engaged across multiple domains. Interestingly, rural constituencies displayed more mixed engagement characteristics, with higher engagement rates in some domains.

The next step of the analysis was to use estimated rates for the set of OxIS questions selected and aggregate them from OA to LSOA level. The 40 attributes provide small-area information about Internet users, information seeking, perception of the Internet, household and mobile access, access patterns and commercial applications. Finally, a range of socio-demographic indicators from the 2011 Census was collated, such as education level, employment sector, prevalence of full-time students, age structure and population density, in addition to attributes regarding local infrastructure. All the

variables considered as inputs to the classification were evaluated for their discrimination potential, and where possible, were limited to those without strong correlation, as such effects can overly influence cluster assignments.

A total of 75 measures were considered for the classification, which were compiled at the aggregate level of the LSOA geography for England and Wales (Table 7.2).

Once the dataset has been assembled, the next step of the analysis regards the consideration of transformation and normalisation procedures. In this case the classification was built using naturally observed attributes distributions; however values were transformed to z-scores, to ensure that all variables are ascribed equal weighting in the model. Alexiou and Singleton (2015) provide further details on the normalisation and standardisation techniques commonly used in geodemographic analysis.

After input measures were assembled, a geodemographic classification was created

Domain	Variables	Data Source
Age	15	Census 2011
Qualifications	7	Census 2011
Occupation	9	Census 2011
Density	1	Census 2011
HE Student	1	Census 2011
Commerce, Business and Retail	12	OxIS
Mobile Usage	8	OxIS
Engagement Attitude	7	OxIS
Access and Connectivity	13	OxIS
Infrastructure	2	Ofcom; Broadbandspeedchecker

Table 7.2
Number of variables per domain used in the IUC, and data sources.

using a clustering algorithm. A common clustering technique used in geodemographic analyses is the iterative allocation–reallocation algorithm, known as K-means. The algorithm aims to assign observations (in this case LSOAs) into a predetermined number of clusters, based on their similarity across the full range of input attributes. Results were evaluated in a number of ways before selecting the optimum number of clusters K. This was carried out through a combination of statistics regarding the sum of squared distances within each cluster, plots showing the configuration of clusters during iterations, mapping cluster

assignments and empirical testing. The classification procedure is firstly applied in order to create an initial 'coarse' tier referred to as 'Supergroups' and then re-applied within each cluster to form a second nested 'Group' level. The final classification formed a two-tier hierarchy of 4 Supergroups which are further classified into a total of 11 distinct Groups.

The final stage of the geodemographic analysis required the interpretation and labelling of cluster results. Interpretation includes looking at the cluster centres in order to identify the 'profile' of each cluster

Supergroup	Group
1: E-unengaged	1a: Too Old to Engage
	1b: E-marginals: Not a Necessity
	1c: E-marginals: Opt Out
2: E-professionals and students	2a: Next Generation Users
	2b: Totally Connected
	2c: Students Online
3: Typical trends	3a: Uncommitted and Casual Users
	3b: Young and Mobile
4: E-rural and fringe	4a: E-fringe
	4b: Constrained by Infrastructure
	4c: Low Density but High Connectivity

Table 7.3
The structure and class labels of the IUC.

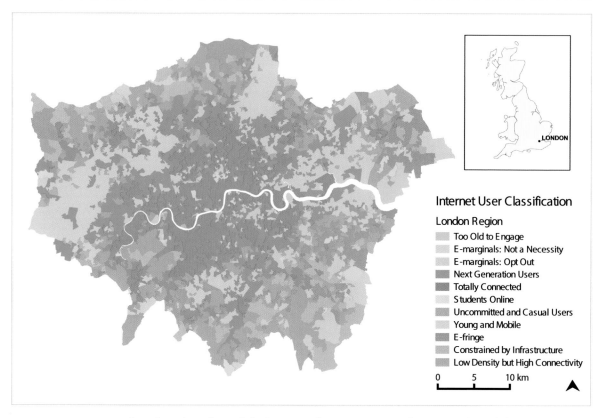

Figure 7.2
The Greater London
Region by IUC Group.

based on the values of the input attributes (usually through radial plots) and mapping results for visual analysis. These outputs informed the Supergroup and Group names (Table 7.3) as well as the 'Pen Portraits'. These describe the typical characteristics of the areas included in each of the clusters, while also considering their variability between clusters. The complete pen portraits can be found in Singleton et al (2016).

Along with pen portraits, a series of maps are essential in order to reveal the spatial structure that emerges from the classification. Figure 7.2 demonstrates the resulting Group typology for the Greater London Region. The map clearly shows the differentiation between central London and the periphery, with the centre occupied by the highly engaged Supergroup 2 classes, such as 2a: Next Generation Users and 2b: Totally Connected. Cluster 3b: Young and Mobile clearly forms several clusters to

East and West London, while the periphery is mostly identified by less engaged populations.

Potential uses of the IUC are broad, and fields of use may include data profiling, online survey stratification, targeted marketing, location planning, customer insight, and public policy formation and delivery. Such a classification is particularly useful in the commercial sector, as the IUC could be used in the profiling of existing customer databases to identify trends, assisting in the development of targeted marketing strategies. This may be valuable for businesses that operate online, or are interested in the aggregate Internet engagement characteristics of their customer base.

The IUC is an open product that is offered through the CDRC data portal (available for download at: data.cdrc.ac.uk/dataset/cdrc-2014-iuc-geodata-pack-england).

Furthermore, an interactive map of the classification is available on the CDRC website (maps.cdrc.ac.uk/#/geodemographics/iuc14/).

7.3
e-Resilience and the online geography of retail centres

Online shopping impacts upon retail centres in complex ways, often referred to in the literature as a 'slow burn' (Pendall et al, 2010). UK Government initiatives aimed at revitalisation of British high streets highlight the importance of digital technology in redefining traditional retail spaces (Digital High Street Advisory Board, 2015). In this framework, it is important to study the impacts that online shopping has on the structure of traditional high streets at a more granular level. For instance, in the UK a number of national retailers such as Borders, Zavvi, Jessops and Game have either entirely withdrawn or substantially limited their physical retail offerings within the past few years, while some other major retailers such as John Lewis, Next, Boots or Argos have successfully embraced new technologies through opening click-and-collect points, or by developing mobile applications (Turner and Gardner, 2014).

Despite evidence to suggest that factors impacting decisions about whether or not to shop online are linked to demographic and socioeconomic characteristics of populations (Longley and Singleton, 2009), there is limited knowledge about the geography of online sales (Forman et al, 2008). This study explored these challenges through a concept defined here as 'e-resilience', a concept that provided both the theoretical and methodological framework in assessing the vulnerability of retail centres to the effects of rapidly growing Internet sales, balancing characteristics of both supply and demand. E-resilience defines the vulnerability of retail centres to the effects of growing Internet sales, and estimates the likelihood that their existing infrastructure, functions and ownership will govern the extent to which they can adapt to or accommodate these changes. Essentially, e-resilience can be expressed as a balance between the propensity of localised populations to engage with online retailing and the physical retail provision and mix that might increase or constrain these effects, as not all retail categories would be equally impacted.

Measuring the vulnerability of competing retail destinations to consumers of differential Internet engagement characteristics requires an understanding of the location and geographic extent of retail centres, combined with some assessment of their composition and size. A nationally expansive record of the location, occupancy and facia of UK retail stores are generated by the Local Data Company (London, UK), a commercial organisation that employs a large survey team to collect these data on a rolling basis. A national extract for February 2014 was made available for this research, with each record comprising the location of a retail premise with latitude and longitude coordinates, retail category and details of the current occupier. The dataset is currently available through CDRC (data.cdrc.ac.uk/dataset/local-data-company-retail-unit-address-data) with permission.

Retail unit data were used to calculate a series of measures which were identified in relevant literature to influence propensity to online shopping, e.g. physical store attractiveness or retail category vulnerability, calculated as the level of risk of the main product switching from physical to online offering channels. A composite of these measures forms a 'supply vulnerability index'. Input measures to this index included the weighted percentage of anchor stores (Damian et al, 2011), i.e. the top 20 most attractive stores as presented by Wrigley and Dolega (2011), and leisure outlets (Reimers and Clulow, 2009), as opposed to the prevalence of 'digitalisation retail', such as newsagents, booksellers, computer

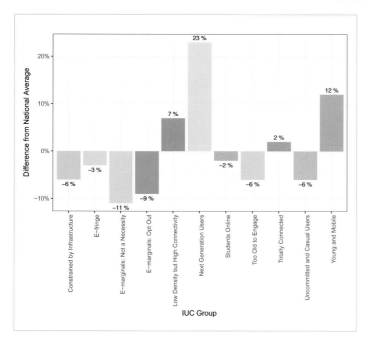

Figure 7.3
IUC profiles for the catchment area of Central Milton Keynes retail centre.

games and home entertainment, video and music stores etc.

As such, higher proportions of 'digitalisation retail' are associated with enhanced vulnerability of retail centres, whereas higher proportions of anchor store and leisure units indicated greater resilience. An index was then generated for each retail centre by creating a composite z-score for each variable, and computing an average for each centre. The final score, referred to as 'supply vulnerability index' was scaled between 1 (lowest vulnerability) and 100 (highest vulnerability).

While the above index portrays the impact of online retail on the supply side, there is still an impact that can be attributed to the demand side. For instance, retail clusters that are within close proximity of young, professional populations would be more vulnerable to the effects of online retail, as these populations have higher propensity to shop online; this kind of information can be obtained by means of the IUC.

Estimating the exposure of retail centres to populations who are active Internet users

as defined through the IUC required a method of modelling consumer flows to probable retail destinations. There is a long history of well-developed literature on the ways in which such supply and demand for retail centres can be reconciled through catchment area estimation (Birkin et al, 2002; Birkin et al, 2010; Wood and Reynolds, 2012). These techniques range in sophistication, from calculating the distances that consumers are willing to travel to a retail centre in a given time (Grewal et al, 2012), through to more complex mathematical models calibrated on the basis of how attractive different retail offerings are to proximal consumers (Newing et al, 2015).

This latter group of models was adopted, which typically makes assumptions that larger towns with more extensive retail and leisure offerings are more attractive, but these effects decay with distance. Specifically, catchments were estimated using a bespoke Huff model (Huff, 1964) which uses town centre composition and vacancy to produce allocated catchments through a distance decay function. The function was calibrated using road network distance and retail centre morphology.

Catchment areas were assigned using LSOAs as the spatial unit of analysis. Once catchments had been established, exposure to online shopping was calculated by overlaying the IUC group typology (presented earlier) and extracting their profiles based on the proportions of the IUC populations identified within. An example of a catchment profile for the Milton Keynes retail centre, located north of London, is shown in Figure 7.3.

Since each group has a different propensity for online shopping, the attribute mean of the OxIS variable 'Frequently Shopping for Products and Services Online' was extracted for every IUC Group. As such, the deviation of the catchment population's propensity to shop online compared to the national average (53%) was obtained. This score, calculated for each retail centre catchment and scaled between 1 and 100, formed the 'index of high exposure'. The index of high exposure indicates a rather distinct spatial pattern; secondary and tertiary retail centres located in more rural areas, including the satellite centres of more urbanised areas, have predominantly the greatest exposure to the impacts of online sales. This trend is reiterated for other parts of the country, although the majority of the highly exposed retail centres can be found within the South East. Moreover, based on those attractiveness scores that fed into the catchment model, it is worth noting that none of the highly exposed centres were drawn from the larger, most attractive centres, unlike the fortunes of many of the surrounding smaller towns and local shopping centres.

The index of high exposure and the supply vulnerability index were then combined to ascribe a measure of e-resilience to each individual retail centre. The indices were summed, and then the final score scaled into the range 1 and 100. The complete methodology for the creation of the e-resilience indicator can be simply represented by a flow diagram, as shown in Figure 7.4.

The following tables summarize the 10 most and least e-resilient retail centres. The most attractive retail centres, namely those in larger urban areas such as Greater London, Birmingham or Manchester, demonstrated the highest levels of e-resilience, followed by the small, local centres. Conversely, the least e-resilient centres were predominantly located in the suburban and rural areas of South East England, and to a lesser degree around other major conurbations of the country. Typically, these were the secondary and medium-sized centres, often referred to as 'Clone Towns' (Ryan-Collins et al, 2010). It could be argued that this is largely intertwined with the geography of Internet shopping, where customers in more remote

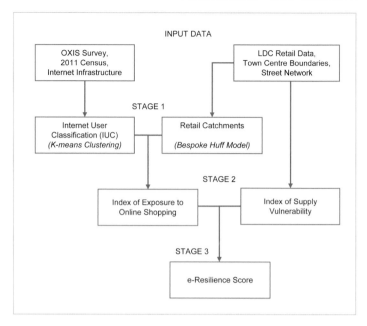

locations, typically faced with poorer retail provision, have displayed a higher propensity for online shopping.

These findings can be associated with a polarisation effect, implying that large and attractive centres function as hubs for higher volumes of comparison shopping and leisure, whereas the small local centres provide everyday convenience shopping. However, the mid-sized centres have a less clear function. Combining such effects with higher exposure to online sales due to the local population mix, these retailers may be increasingly faced with considerable challenges, such as how to diversify their store portfolio, downsize or move to other locations.

Figure 7.4
The model used to calculate e-resilience scores.

7.4
Conclusion

The growth of Internet sales is increasingly viewed as one of the most important forces currently shaping the evolving structure of retail centres (Wrigley and Lambiri, 2014; Hart and Laing, 2014). Although current research does not suggest a death of physical space, the consequences for traditional high streets remain unclear

Town centre	Region	e-Resilience Score
Boughton	East Midlands	100
Ravenside Retail Park, Bexhill-on-Sea	South East	97.58
Corbridge	North East	93.27
Torport	South West	71.61
Hersham	South East	70.29
Halton, Leeds	Yorkshire and the Humber	69.29
Cinderford	South West	68.51
Marsh Road, Luton	East of England	67.01
South Molton	South West	65.41
Parkgate Retail World	Yorkshire and the Humber	64.37

Table 7.4
The 10 most e-resilient town centres identified within England.

Town centre	Region	e-Resilience Score
Rochford	East of England	1
London Road, Leigh-on-Sea	East of England	15.61
North Seaton Industrial Estate	North East	16.86
Whalley	North West	17.2
Oxted	South East	17.25
Barnt Green	West Midlands	17.39
Eccleshall	West Midlands	17.39
Hurstpierpoint	South East	17.98
Botley Road, Oxford	South East	18.14
Woburn Sands	South East	18.52

Table 7.5
The 10 least e-resilient town centres identified within England.

as knowledge about the geography and drivers of Internet shopping are still limited. This study explores some aspects of online retail behaviour, particularly on the nature and impact that Internet user behaviour is having on retail centres nationally.

The analysis of the geography of online retail provides unique insights into the apparent diversity of population groups with regards to online shopping, and to the role and future of town centres at the national scale. Certainly, one of the most influencing factors is the behavioural component: whether or not to use the Internet for a given activity. The study highlighted that influencing such decisions are both demographic effects, mainly age and socioeconomic status, and local retail supply including 'softer' factors such as convenience and accessibility.

In this framework, the geography of online behaviour can be based on the IUC. The IUC is an open, freely available product that provides comprehensive summary measures of the complexities between behaviour, infrastructure and context at the small-area level. It can be viewed as a tool for both the private and public sector. For example, the 2021 Census in the UK will largely be completed online and so the IUC can assist in highlighting areas where low response rates are likely.

A further application of the IUC is its contribution to the e-resilience indicator. The distribution of e-resilience measures revealed a geography where attractive and large retail centres such as the inner cores of large metropolitan areas, along with smaller, specialised centres were highlighted as more resilient, while centres within many secondary and medium sized centres were identified as most vulnerable. One of the most defining contributions of this approach is that it provides a comprehensive classification of all retail centres based on their e-resilience levels, a resource that can be used by a wide range of stakeholders including academics, retailers and town centre managers, and inform policy decisions.

Futher Reading

Alexiou, A. and Singleton, A. D. (2015). Geodemographic analysis. In Singleton, A.D. and Brunsdon, C. (Eds.), *Geo computation: A practical primer*, pp. 137–151. London: Sage.

Beck, N. and Rygl, D. (2015). Categorization of multiple channel retailing in multi-, cross-, and omni-channel retailing for retailers and retailing. *Journal of Retailing and Consumer Services*, 27, 170–178.

Birkin, M., Clarke, G. and Clarke, M. (2002). *Retail Geography and Intelligent Network Planning*. Chichester, NY: Wiley.

Birkin, M., Clarke, G. and Clarke, M. (2010). Refining and operationalizing entropy-maximizing models for business applications. *Geographical Analysis*, 42(4), 422–445.

Calderwood, E. and Freathy, P. (2014). Consumer mobility in the Scottish isles: The impact of internet adoption upon retail travel patterns. *Transportation Research Part A: Policy and Practice*, 59: 192–203.

Carlson, J., O'Cass, A. and Ahrholdt, D. (2015). Assessing customers' perceived value of the online channel of multichannel retailers: A two country examination. *Journal of Retailing and Consumer Services*, 27, 90–102.

Damian, D., Curto, J. and Pinto, J. (2011). the impact of anchor stores on the performance of shopping centres: The case of Sonae Sierra. *International Journal of Retail & Distribution Management*, 39(6), 456–475.

Dholakia, U. M., Kahn, B. E., Reeves, R., Rindfleisch, A., Stewart, D. and Taylor, E. (2010). Consumer behavior in a multichannel, multimedia retailing environment. *Journal of Interactive Marketing*, 24(2), 86–95. Special Issue on Emerging Perspectives on Marketing in a Multichannel and Multimedia Retailing Environment.

Digital High Street Advisory Board (2015). Digital High Street 2020. thegreatbritishhighstreet.co.uk/digital-high-street-report-2020. Accessed 15 June 2015

Doherty, N. and Ellis-Chadwick, F. (2010). Internet retailing: The past the present and the future. *International Journal of Retail & Distribution Management*, 38(11/12), 943–965.

Dolega, L., Pavlis, M. and Singleton, A. (2016). Estimating attractiveness, hierarchy and catchment area extents for a national set of retail centre agglomerations. *Journal of Retailing and Consumer Service*, 28: 78–90.

Forman, C., Ghose, A. and Goldfarb, A. (2008). Competition between local and electronic markets: how the benefit of buying online depends on where you live. *Management Science*, 55(1), 47–57.

Grewal, D., Kopalle, P., Marmorstein, H. and Roggeveen, A. (2012). Does travel time to stores matter? The role of merchandise availability. *Journal of Retailing*, 88(3), 437–444.

Harris, R., Sleight, P. and Webber, R. (2005). *Geodemographics, GIS, and Neighbourhood Targeting.* Chichester: John Wiley and Sons.

Hart, C. and Laing, A. (2014). The consumer journey through the high street in the digital area. In *Evolving High Streets: Resilience and Reinvention – Perspectives from Social Science*, pp. 36–39. University of Southampton, Southampton.

Helsper, E. and Eynon, R. (2010). Digital natives: Where is the evidence? *British Educational Research Journal*, 36(3), 503–520.

Huff, D.L. (1964). Defining and estimating a trade area. *Journal of Marketing*, 28(3), 34–38.

Kaufmann, A., Lehner, P. and Todtling, F. (2003). Effects of the internet on the spatial structure of innovation networks. *Information Economics and Policy*, 15(3), 402–424.

Longley, P. A. and Singleton, A. D. (2009). Classification through consultation: Public views of the geography of the e-society. *International Journal of Geographical Information Science*, 23(6): 737–763.

Nathan, M. and Rosso, A. (2015). Mapping digital businesses with big data: Some early findings from the UK. *Research Policy*, 44(9), 1714 – 1733. The New Data Frontier.

Newing, A., Clarke, G. and Clarke, M. (2015). Developing and applying a disaggregated retail location model with extended retail demand estimations. *Geographical Analysis*, 47(3), 219–239.

Pendall, R., Foster, K. and Cowell, M. (2010). Resilience and regions: Building understanding of the metaphor. *Cambridge Journal of Regions Economy and Society*, 3(1), 71–84.

Prieger, J. E. and Hu, W. M. (2008). The broadband digital divide and the nexus of race, competition,and quality. *Information Economics and Policy*, 20(2), 150–167.

Rao, J. (2003). *Small Area Estimation.* Wiley series in survey methodology. Hoboken, NJ: John Wiley.

Reimers, V. and Clulow, V. (2009). Retail centres: It's time to make them convenient. *International Journal of Retail & Distribution Management*, 37(7), 541–562.

Rice, R. E. and Katz, J. E. (2003). Comparing internet and mobile phone usage: Digital divides of usage, adoption, and dropouts. *Telecommunications Policy*, 27(8), 597–623.

Riddlesden, D. and Singleton, A. D. (2014). Broadband speed equity: A new digital divide? *Applied Geography*, 52(0), 25–33.

Ryan-Collins, J., Cox, E., Potts, R., and Squires, P. (2010). *Re-imagining the High Street: Escape from Clone Town Britain.* London: New Economics Foundation.

Silver, M. (2014). Socio-economic status over the lifecourse and internet use in older adulthood. *Ageing and Society*, 34, 1019–1034.

Singleton, A. D. and Dolega, L. (2015). The e-resilience of UK town centres. In *Evolving High Streets: Resilience & Reinvention, Perspectives from Social Science*, pp. 40–43. Economic and Social Research Council.

Singleton, A. D., Dolega, D., Riddlesden, D. and Longley, P. A. (2016). Measuring the spatial vulnerability of retail centres to online consumption through a framework of e-resilience. *Geoforum*, 69(1), 5-18

Turner, J. and Gardner, T. (2014). Critical reflections on the decline of the UK high street: Exploratory conceptual research into the role of the service encounter. In *Handbook of Research on Retailer-Consumer Relationship Development*, pp. 127–151. Hershey, PA: IGI Global.

Verhoef, P. C., Kannan, P. and Inman, J. J. (2015). From multi-channel retailing to omni-channel retailing: Introduction to the special issue on multi-channel retailing. *Journal of Retailing*, 91(2), 174–181.

Warf, B. (2013). Contemporary digital divides in the United States. *Tijdschrift voor economischeen sociale geografie*, 104(1), 1–17.

Warren, M. (2007). The digital vicious cycle: Links between social disadvantage and digital exclusion in rural areas. *Telecommunications Policy*, 31(6-7), 374–388.

Wilson, K. R., Wallin, J. S. and Reiser, C. (2003). Social stratification and the digital divide. *Social Science Computer Review*, 21(2), 133–143.

Wood, S. and Reynolds, J. (2012). Leveraging locational insights within retail store development? Assessing the use of location planners' knowledge in retail marketing. *Geoforum*, 43(6), 1076–1087.

Wrigley, N. and Dolega, L. (2011). Resilience, fragility, and adaptation: New evidence on the performance of UK high streets during global economic crisis and its policy implications. *Environment and Planning A*, 43(10), 2337–2363.

Wrigley, N. and Lambiri, D. (2014). High Street Performance and Evolution: A Brief Guide to the Evidence. Technical report. Southampton: University of Southampton.

Acknowledgements

The authors would like to thank the Oxford Internet Institute for providing survey data and the Local Data Company Ltd for providing retail unit data for this research. The research was also funded by the Economic and Social Research Council, grant number ES/L003546/1.

Smart Card Data and Human Mobility

Nilufer Sari Aslam and Tao Cheng

8.1
Introduction

Prevailing models of urban mobility seek to establish an understanding of individual activity patterns using household travel demand surveys. These surveys, representative of a subset of the population, are used to create individual travel diaries for estimating projected travel demand. The whole model is not only time-consuming and costly, but is limited to partial snapshots of the overall dynamic needs of urban transportation. The advent of large data sources such as smart cards have created new opportunities for the understanding of urban mobility and behaviour research.

This chapter presents an overview of a heuristic model for the understanding of user mobility from smart card data. An understanding of individuals' mobility requires an appreciation of their key Points of Interest (POIs). Activities that originate around these key geographical locations are classified as either primary or secondary activities. Primary activities involve movement patterns that are regular in nature and comprise key user locations, for example work (for regular workers) or study (for students). The secondary activities are marked by unusual and infrequent activity patterns and involve movement between other POIs, for example theatres, stadiums, pubs or restaurants.

The results from the model have been validated against London Travel Demand Survey (LTDS) data. The ability for the model to accurately identify and analyse individual mobility patterns in major urban centres rests on the precise identification of these primary locations. This new activity-based modelling approach aims to provide a better understanding of human mobility for transport infrastructure planning.

8.2
Dynamic data and the analysis of human mobility

Developing an ever greater understanding of human mobility has clear benefits for the provision of transport. Traditional modelling systems have relied on information extracted from travel surveys, which, while they are designed to gather a wide range of travel use and socio-economic data from participants, are limited both in terms of the relatively short time spans they represent and their relative sample sizes. In recent years the data available regarding day-to-day movements of transport users has been greatly enriched by the transition away from paper tickets or single use tokens, towards smart card based systems whereby entries and exits are recorded as users tap their cards on readers. These systems build up detailed journey profiles per card (assumed to be a single user) that can form the basis for models to automatically generate 'travel diaries'. Such diaries can inform transport providers about typical user behaviour within their system and have the potential to markedly improve current survey-based approaches.

Whilst the primary motivation for the implementation of smart card payment systems within transportation networks is the streamlining of their revenue collection flows, the collected data has many auxiliary benefits such as long-term cost reduction, flexibility in pricing options, and the ability to share gathered information with other parties. Partially these benefits help explain the enthusiasm with which smart card automated fare collection systems are being extensively implemented around the world. In Europe, the use of smart cards is well advanced. Additionally, South America and over 15 cities in North America have currently implemented smart card transportation systems. The application of the smart card is also growing in Asia, for example Hong Kong has its 'Octopus' smart card, and

Singapore the 'EZ-Link' card (Pelletier et al, 2011); they also produce large quantities of very detailed data on onboard transactions. These data can be very useful to transit planners, from the day-to-day operation of the transit system to the strategic long-term planning of the network. This chapter covers several aspects of smart card data use in the public transit context. First, the technologies are presented: the hardware and information systems required to operate these tools; and privacy concerns and legal issues related to the dissemination of smart card data, data storage, and encryption are addressed. Then, the various uses of the data at three levels of management are described: strategic (long-term planning), tactical (service adjustments and network development), and operational (ridership statistics and performance indicators) (Pelletier et al, 2011).

As cards are associated with individual users, there emerges the possibility of uniquely logging each individual journey which can thus capture relatively detailed spatial and temporal attributes such as the location of origin, destination stations, and stay duration. The analysis of user behaviour can, therefore, be carried out by looking at the spatial patterns or the temporal pattern. The most comprehensive analysis would take into account the spatial and temporal aspects of the trip simultaneously.

8.3
Extracting meaning from Transport for London's Oyster card data

The focus of this chapter is an analysis of the Oyster card operated by Transport for London (TfL). The card is valid on all London public transport systems such as London Underground, the bus network, the Docklands Light Railway (DLR), London Overground, Tramline, some river boat services, and most National Rail services within the London Fare Zones.

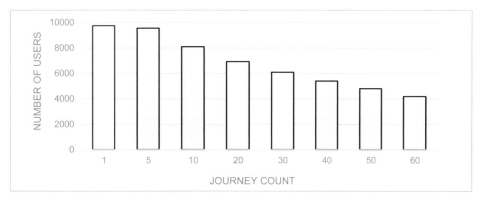

Figure 8.1
The frequency of journeys by number of users.

The volume of data from Oyster cards on the TfL network is extremely high; more than 80 percent of the 3 million journeys carried out each day on the network make use of Oyster cards (TfL, 2016). Although the Oyster card is used on multiple modes of transportation across London, 95% of all Oyster card usage is for London's Underground and bus journeys (Gordon, 2012). One of the limitations identified in the TfL dataset is the incomplete recording of trip information for bus journeys. As TfL do not currently capture the alighting information from its bus trips, bus journeys are often excluded from certain trip analysis. Such journeys, however, can be included with an enhancement of the model, where missing information is identified as a sub-step within the identification process.

In the following analysis, the sample data available comprised a total of 60 million journeys. Since the processing of such large volumes of data are so resource intensive, for the purpose of the study, the smart card records of 9,900 randomly selected TfL users were identified for further investigation. The sample contains a total of 1,823,906 complete journey records made by individual users for the months of October and November 2013.

8.3.1
Activity description

An understanding of human mobility requires the understanding of daily activities both at the individual and the aggregate level. The classification of this activity can be thought of as a two-step process. The first step is to use the temporal information within the commuting sequences to identify the periods of stay. A period of stay is characterised by two consecutive journeys to and from the same location. The time between these two journeys is significant as it is an indicator of the type of activity and can help discern activities from transit stops. The second step in the process is the classification of activities into predefined activity types. The activities are classified by means of their association with POI. Stay location, stay duration and time provide the spatial-temporal context of the activity. Also significant in the inference of the activity is the distance of POI to the transit station that is captured via smart card data. The combination of these factors could therefore explain the different characteristics of human movement. For example people travel to work on a daily basis but only go to watch a concert at specific times. Therefore a short stay near a concert venue can only be an indicator of the activity 'at the concert' if it matches the temporal attributes of POI. This chapter only discusses the identification of home and work locations along with the work related activities.

Commuting patterns provide the ability to identify regular activities such as work, once a stay location has been identified

Behaviour	Activities Classified	Activities Identified	Commute	Activity and locations
Regular	Primary Activities	Home (H) and Work (W) related activities	H to W W to H	Work, offices, universities, schools, college, etc.
	Secondary Activities	Before Work (W) Activities	H to X1 X1 to W	Dropping off child at school
		After Work (W) Activities	W to X2 X2 to H	Pub, dinner, shopping
		Midday/Work (W) Activities	W to X3 X3 to W	Lunch, shopping
Irregular	Unspecified	Unspecified	X4 to X5 X5 to X6	Unspecified location and activity

Table 8.1
A variety of travel-based activities can be identified.

with a certain degree of confidence. Therefore it is important to ensure the regularity of the usage prior to making inference about such activities.

Figure 8.1 shows that for 20% of the users, the available journey count (defined as a numeric parameter based on the regularity of usage) is less than 10 journeys, which is too low to carry out any meaningful analysis. The right balance is, therefore, required in the selection of threshold; a value too small will include a large number of irregular users in the dataset, and a threshold too high will be too restrictive and leave out regular users from the analysis (Hasan et al, 2012).

Table 8.1. provides examples of primary and secondary activities that are linked to work (W) and home (H) locations. It is assumed that an individual can have one or more locations classified as home locations if it fits the criteria defined for the home location identification. Similarly, one or more locations can be classified as work locations. Identification of secondary activities are not within the scope of this analysis.

Irregular activities are more challenging to model, so for the purpose of this chapter are defined as those activities that fall outside of a regular commuter journey's key user locations. User activities that are irregular in nature are more challenging to model. In such a scenario the spatial-temporal aspects of the trip alone do not provide significant insights into user behaviour. At the same time, spatial attributes of visited locations can provide clues for activity classification.

8.3.2
Individual mobility as a sequence of activities

Activities are representations of users' changing presence in both space and time. Some of the activities are captured by means of the smart card data whilst others lack a digital footprint. Importantly, the states that are visible provide clues about the states that are unobserved. Figure 8.2 illustrates a simple activity sequence for an Oyster card user. The individual carries out a morning commute between the hours of 08:00 to 09:00 from a home location to a work location. The same individual uses the network for their work to home commute between 17:00 to 18:00. Observed activities for this sequence are the journeys carried out by means of the Oyster card, whilst the hidden event is the work activity.

Figure 8.2
Sample activity sequence
(simple).

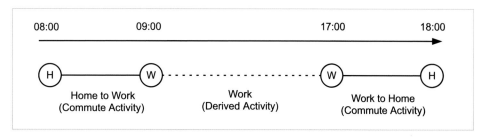

Figure 8.3
Sample activity sequence
(complex).

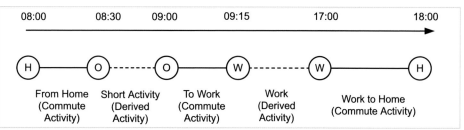

The methodology described in this work explains the identification and labelling of the activities based on POIs, for example home/work and variables such as stay duration and visit frequency.

Similarly, a more complex activity sequence is illustrated in Figure 8.3 where the home to work commute is interrupted by a short stay activity. Although the information captured within the smart card data are not sufficient to infer the exact nature of the short stay visit, the timing and location of the activities can be useful in assigning an appropriate description for such activities, for example day-care visit and school drop-offs.

8.3.3
Human mobility pattern identification

The heuristics described in this section consider the visit frequency (number of times a specific user visits a location) and stay duration (the duration between consecutive journeys) as parameters in the model to identify home and work locations. In order to explore mobility patterns of urban commuters, the data are grouped by frequency of use. An important characteristic of the temporal patterns of urban human mobility is the stay time duration. It describes the activities between

locations gathered from smart card data. It serves to identify the stay duration between consecutive journeys and enables the identification of work location.

8.3.3.1
Home location

The most frequently used station is a key marker in the identification of home stations. For a large majority of users, the station for the first and last journey of the day is an indicator of a home location. In this work, an algorithm has been devised based on the frequency of most frequently used stations coupled with the temporal information of the journey to classify home stations for users.

The origin station of the first journey of the day and the destination station of the last journey of the day is the POI-classified home location. Selected stations for the available number of the days are then further analysed, and if the selected station count fits the criteria required in the algorithm, the station is selected as a home location. It is possible to have more than one station classified as a user's home station if the station fits the criteria. The type of behaviour could be due to a number of reasons, such as a user having multiple home locations, service degradation on the

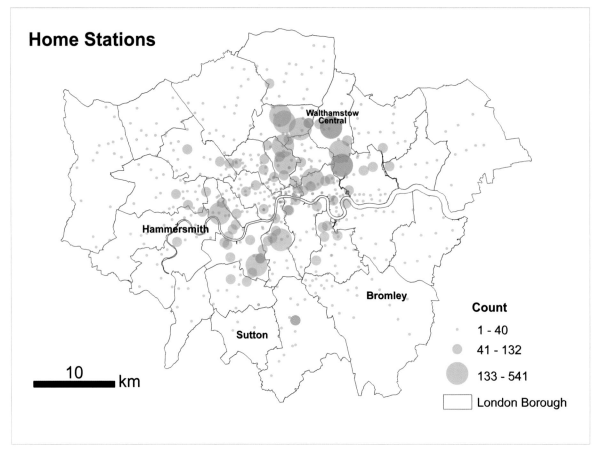

Home Stations

Count

· 1 - 40

● 41 - 132

⬤ 133 - 541

☐ London Borough

TfL network, or other personal journey choices. Similarly, it is also possible that the algorithm fails to highlight any station as home station if no location meets the expected criteria.

In Figure 8.4, home locations are spread evenly across London's outer boroughs with the City of London. Some commuter belt boroughs such as Sutton and Bromley are not well represented in the results. The users are still able to travel to and from these locations using National Rail infrastructure, but the journeys are not as accurately captured with Oyster cards. Therefore these stations do not feature significantly as major home locations.

Figure 8.4 also shows that outer London stations are represented by smaller points in comparison to the inner London stations.

This is representative of the high population density in the inner city. Similarly, some central London interchange stations such as Hammersmith, King's Cross and St Pancras station feature heavily as home locations in the results. This is because the final legs of many journeys to other cities and outer London stations are not captured by the Oyster network, hence the last station captured has been inaccurately marked as a home station. This is one significant limitation of the available data. To mitigate this, large transit stations can be excluded or additional rules for the identification of home locations can be devised. It is possible to add rules, such as frequency of weekend use, to the home location algorithm in order to identify such users.

Figure 8.4
The results of home locations around TfL and National Rail stations in London.

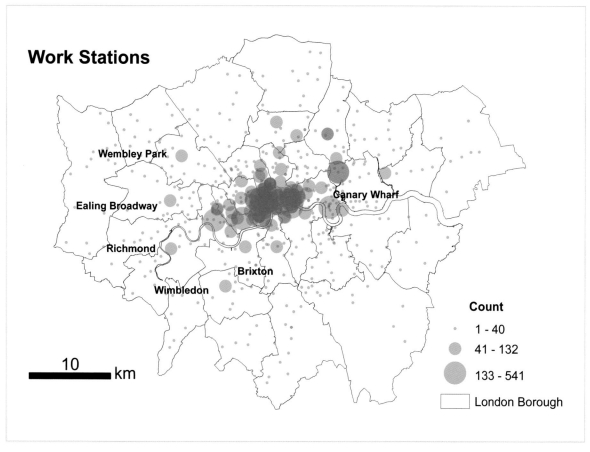

Work Stations

Wembley Park

Ealing Broadway

Richmond

Brixton

Wimbledon

Canary Wharf

10 ▬▬▬ km

Count
- 1 - 40
- 41 - 132
- 133 - 541
- London Borough

Figure 8.5
The results of work
locations around TfL
and National Rail stations
in London.

8.3.3.2
Work location

In order to estimate work locations, all weekday journeys are considered for the regular commuter. The identification of the POI work location is based on the assertion that for the majority of users with a regular commuting pattern, the most time spent away from home is the work location.

The work location identification can be based on the stay time/duration of the consecutive journeys for each user. This defines the work activity and location for the individual user. The destination station of the first journey in the pair and the origin station of the second journey for the journey pair are selected. This will give two stations for two consecutive journeys. These can be the same station or different stations.

If a station has been identified more than the defined threshold visit frequency, it is classified as a work station for that user. Based on this criterion, users can have one or more workstations. It is important to note the possibility that the algorithm fails to highlight any station as a work location if no location meets the expected criteria.

The examination of the characteristics of user journeys enabled the selection of the parameters of visit frequency and stay duration thresholds. Different values for the parameters provided a different outcome for the algorithms. The threshold for the parameters is based on the duration of data available and level of confidence required in the outcome.

Figure 8.5 presents the work locations identified, pointing to the centres of financial and commercial services around the City of London. This is due to the close proximity of these regions to the financial districts of the City of London and Canary Wharf.

Some locations such as Ealing Broadway, Wembley, Wimbledon, Richmond and Brixton outside of central London have also been identified as work locations. These locations are also an example of commercial centres outside of central London.

8.3.4
Validation

The results of identification of home and work locations were compared with the LTDS. LTDS data capture, among other attributes, information about home and work locations of the individuals (TfL, 2011). This makes LTDS data invaluable as it provides a source of validation for travel pattern algorithms.

The results were compared with the LTDS dataset, and 82% of home users were identified with the same location by the algorithm as LTDS data at the level of postcode district. For work locations, 60% were correctly identified.

The accuracy of the comparison relies heavily upon the correctness of the user data captured through the surveys. Any errors in the data gathering and entry would adversely impact the reliability of the comparison.

8.4
Prospects for understanding mobility

To present the complete picture of an individual's mobility, so-called 'secondary activities' need to be identified. In this context, secondary activities include all activities which last longer than the standard transit stops but are shorter than the presumed work activities. These are particularly challenging since they may not have obvious recurring travel patterns,

for example, a monthly theatre visit might fall into this category. With this in mind, approaches based on continuous learning from the data hold promise. For example, machine learning algorithms can recognise patterns in data and construct new rules dynamically (Ethem, 2004). Examples of machine learning in transportation include insurance premium calculations based on the driving patterns of individuals and tracking congestion. The most talked about of all the applications of machine learning in transportation is perhaps self-driving vehicles. Based on research by the Business Insider, there will be 10 million self-driving cars on the roads by 2020 (Gerage, 2017). The technology behind these relies upon sensors, which collect data from the surrounding environment and objects, such as size and speed. The task of machine learning algorithms is the continuous interpretation of this data in order to classify objects as pedestrians, cyclists or other cars and objects as well as the forecasting of their movements (Gates, 2017; Anil, 2017).

The identification of activities can be described as a classification problem in the context of machine learning. The activities that have been extracted based on the stay duration of individuals at a location need to be classified into one of the categories, for example, weekend social visits or weekday shopping trips. With respect to smart card data, one of the inherent challenges is the unavailability of labelled data that can be used to train the classifiers. In order to address this, a number of options can be considered to generate labelled datasets:

Expert labelling: This can be done with careful analysis of information, for example, the day of the week, time of the day, attributes of the locations (shopping centre, entertainment hub, residential area, and sports venue). Expert labelling of the activities relies on the intuition of the researcher to evaluate the available information about the activity and assign a suitable classification to the activity, e.g.

a two-hour activity on a Saturday evening in the vicinity of restaurants and bars is indicative of a weekend social activity.

App assisted labelling: In this approach, volunteers can be asked to install a mobile app that will record the GPS locations during the day, according to a predefined threshold (e.g. 1+ hours stay). Based on the stay locations observed during the day, each user will be prompted to answer 1-2 questions to label the activity captured, for example, two-hour stay near Piccadilly Circus was (1) socialising, (2) shopping, (3) other.

App assisted approaches have the potential to capture highly accurate information about the mobility of individual users, but they have some challenges including issues of development, fine tuning of the mobile app, and recruitment of volunteers. Labelled test data, combined with the individual user journey records from the smart card data, provide the two pieces of information necessary to classify the user activities.

8.5
Conclusion

Smart card data provide a rich and detailed window into activity patterns through their ability to capture vast quantities of information regarding daily journeys. This chapter presents a case for the usage of public transport smart card data for the characterisation of human mobility patterns. Activities of individuals and the identification of activity locations are discussed using data collected by Transport for London.

Home and work locations are important anchors since the majority of journey activities revolve around these. A better identification of these locations would provide a more effective classification of the activities of individual users. The heuristic approach to human mobility proposed in this chapter has the potential to improve our understanding of wider mobility patterns at an aggregate level. Therefore, an understanding of human mobility patterns plays an important role in addressing the problems of transportation and urban sustainability.

Further Reading

Anil, A. (2017). What kind of machine learning algorithms do the driverless cars use? *Quora*. Online: https://www.quora.com/What-kind-of-machine-learning-algorithms-do-the-driverless-cars-use.

Ethem, A. (2004). *Introduction to Machine Learning*. Cambridge, MA: MIT Press.

Gates, G. (2017). The race for self-driving cars. *The New York Times*. Online: www.nytimes.com/interactive/2016/12/14/technology/how-self-driving-cars-work.html.

Intelligence (2016). 10 million self-driving cars will be on the road by 2020. Online: http://uk.businessinsider.com/report-10-million-self-driving-cars-will-be-on-the-road-by-2020-2015-5-6

Gordon, J. B. (2012). Intermodal Passenger Flows on London's Public Transport Network. MIT Press.

Hasan, S. et al (2012). Spatiotemporal patterns of urban human mobility. *Journal of Statistical Physics*, 151, 304–318.

Pelletier, M.-P., Trépanier, M. & Morency, C. (2011). Smart card data use in public transit: A literature review. *Transportation Research Part C: Emerging Technologies*, 19(4), 557–568.

TfL (2011). *London Travel Demand Survey*. Online: www.clocs.org.uk/wp-content/uploads/2014/05/london-travel-demand-survey-2011.pdf.

TfL (2016). Oyster. Online: tfl.gov.uk/corporate/publications-and-reports/oyster-card.

Uniman, D. L. et al (2010). Service reliability measurement using automated fare card data. *Transportation Research Record: Journal of the Transportation Research Board*, 2143(1), 92–99. Online: trb.metapress.com/openurl.asp?genre=article&id=doi:10.3141/2143-12.

Acknowledgements

We are grateful to Transport for London (TfL) for provision of the experimental data for this research. The first author's PhD research is sponsored by the Economic and Social Research Council through the UCL Doctoral Training Centre.

Interpreting Smart Meter Data of UK Domestic Energy Consumers

Anastasia Ushakova and Roberto Murcio

9.1
Introduction

One of the recent innovations to domestic energy provision in Great Britain is the installation of smart meters. Given the immediate opportunities for reducing carbon emissions and helping customers who may struggle with energy bills, the government has incentivised energy providers to ensure that every home has a smart meter by 2020. Whilst the data from such meters present richness in both volume and granularity, there are a number of hurdles to overcome when understanding variability, bias and uncertainty in such datasets. Consequently, these challenges may affect the analytical strategies we consider for generating insight into the lifestyles and activities of a population. This chapter provides an overview of the CDRC dataset on gas and electricity smart meters, currently the largest collection of such data available for academic research in the UK.

There is a growing acknowledgement of the potential of commercial data for better understanding of consumer choices and behaviour at the level of the individual or household. In 2013, the UK government obligated the major domestic energy providers to roll out smart meter installation across the country. Such widespread installation of meters provides a particularly valuable resource for better understanding the geography of energy consumption. Smart meters provide continuous measures of consumption of electricity and gas and are central to a better understanding of energy consumption by suppliers and researchers alike. The data generated by smart meters are an example of the emergence of Big Data over the last decade, and characteristically provide detailed and disaggregate information without the need for routine survey collections.

As such, smart meter data are a new form of data that offers a temporal breakdown of energy consumption for both electricity and gas. Data are recorded automatically and offer real-time updates, typically aggregated to half hourly intervals. The data source can be considered large in volume since each household with dual fuel smart meters annually generates around 17,520 readings indicative of the correspondence between household characteristics and residential property attributes. There are thus immediate advantages to the use of smart meters in research with a focus upon consumer behaviour and energy policy. However, as these data are new to industry analysts and the research community alike, this chapter focuses on the interplay of issues of content and coverage of the data in the analysis.

Smart meters present novel opportunities for small-area population analysis when triangulated with the 2011 UK Census of Population (Anderson et al, 2017). In this chapter, we dedicate more attention to gas data as being a more direct indicator of household activities. Regardless, for understanding of behavioural patterns for both sources, be it gas/electricity energy expenditure or real-time energy consumption, these consumer data play a vital role for policy-making and regulation.

While offering greater precision in understanding the differences in behaviour over time by households, smart meter data also create further challenges when it comes to the generalisation of temporal profiles. How do we identify the average or expected energy consumption profile? Should this bring focus to the activity patterns of consuming households, their properties, or neighbourhood setting? 'Variability in residential consumption reported in the literature suggests that there is hardly a "typical" level of consumption for any energy end-use' (Lutzenhiser, 1993, 249). We address this by looking at both aggregate and disaggregated patterns of energy consumption.

We first provide a description of the available data within the context of the UK energy sector, briefly looking at the advantages and limitations posed by the introduction of smart meter data. We revise the methods for segmenting energy data with an example of the results. Finally, we build upon these preliminary investigations to set a research agenda for linking the smart meter data to other administrative and open datasets in order to better understand consumer behaviour in this domain. Using a case study of Bristol, we investigate the possibilities that may be available using UK Census data. The chapter is concluded with a concise discussion of issues for future research.

9.2
The UK energy sector and smart meter roll out

The UK energy sector is regulated by the Department for Business, Energy and Industrial Strategy (BEIS) and the Office of Gas and Electricity Markets (OFGEM). On the supply side, there are currently 12 large and 46 small energy companies. The market share is monitored by OFGEM and assessed on the basis of how many electricity meters are installed on the distributional network by a supplier. As of late 2016, British Gas was the largest provider with 23% share of the market, and Scottish and Southern Electricity (SSE) and e.ON the second and third largest providers with 15% and 14% share respectively.

The UK Government aims to ensure that by 2020 every domestic and non-domestic property will have been offered a smart meter. The regulatory environment encourages providers to roll out smart meters as quickly as possible to meet the obligation of complete installation by 2020. By the first quarter of 2017 there was a total of 6.78 million smart meters installed by energy suppliers across residential and business addresses in the UK of which six million had been installed in domestic properties by the 'Big Six' energy providers. Electricity meters account for more than half of the total of these installations due to wider availability over gas. BEIS (2017)

Type	Number of meters	Number of postcode sectors with at least 10 meters installed	Meters per Postcode sector	
			Mean	Median
Electricity	600,000	8,000	70	60
Gas	480,000	7,500	60	50

Table 9.1
Gas and electricity: the number of postcode sectors with at least 10 smart gas or electricity meters in Great Britain as of December 2015.

reports that despite an acceleration of smart meter rollout, most domestic properties nevertheless still have traditional meters.

It is unlikely to be the case that roll out by any energy company thus far has been to a random selection of addresses. For instance, some domestic properties are unsuitable for meter installation while the needs of disabled customers may pose challenges. The perceived wisdom is that there is a bias in successful installations towards elderly people or families. This is driven by the fact that when local installation campaigns are mounted, representatives are more likely to find households from these groups at home during normal working hours. It is also important to note that nationally, around 70% of households will have electricity and gas supplied by the same company, with 17% having duel supplier, meaning they will have a separate supplier for gas and electricity. The remaining 12% of households will be connected only to the electricity network.

9.3
Data

The national dataset of smart meter data that we use for the analysis in this chapter is held by the Consumer Data Research Centre (CDRC) and was sourced from one of the UK Big Six energy suppliers. The data contain details of around 1,080,000 electricity and gas domestic smart meters for the year 2015, which represents 43% of the 2.3 million smart meters installed by the end of December 2015 in the UK. The spatial granularity is at postcode sector. The broader figures are shown in Table 9.1 It is important to note that throughout this section, individual figures on numbers of smart meters and measures are rounded to the nearest hundred.

The number of energy users per month is not constant as the rollout of smart meters is increasing from one month to another. For example, in the case of electricity, 75% of the users were already present in the first quarter of 2015 meaning that these will be the customers' records with the full

Figure 9.1
Number of smart meters being rolled out at each quarter of 2015.

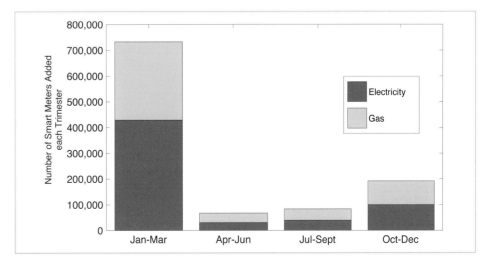

Estimate	Electricity	Gas
Mean	2,130 kWh	8,480 kWh
Median	1,820 kWh	7,105 kWh
Standard Deviation	1,680 kWh	6,510 kWh
BEIS 2015 Typical consumption median	3,148 kWh	13,202 kWh
BEIS 2015 Typical consumption mean	3,894 kWh	11,707 kWh

Table 9.2
The average annual
household energy
consumption compared
to BEIS 2015 national
estimates. As observed,
our estimates are slightly
lower than official
statistics. This may be
an indication of further
bias in our dataset.

Figure 9.2
Smart electricity and
gas meters by postcode
sector at the end of
December, 2015.
These maps show the
distribution of smart
meters across Great
Britain with the West
Midlands and North West
regions having the highest
frequencies of meters per
postcode sector.

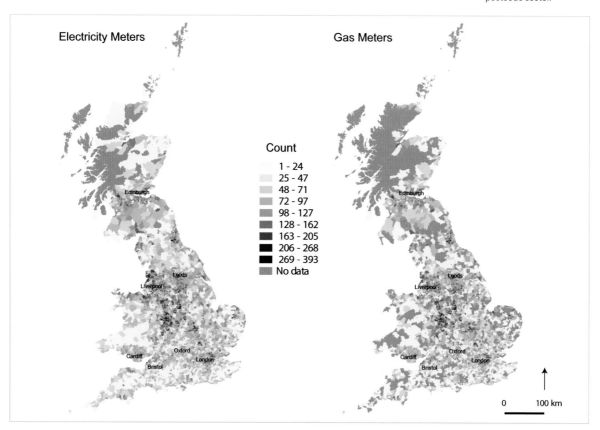

Region	Electricity meters (thousands)	% of all meters in the region in 2015	Gas meters (thousands)	% of all meters in the region in 2015
East Midlands	48.6	2.0%	40.3	2.0%
East of England	47.0	2.0%	38.0	2.0%
London	65.9	2.0%	54.6	2.0%
North East	24.7	2.0%	22.6	2.0%
North West	96.1	3.0%	76.0	3.0%
South East	57.1	1.3%	47.7	1.7%
South West	41.1	1.5%	31.6	2.2%
West Midlands	79.2	3.0%	64.8	4.0%
Yorkshire-Humber	58.0	2.0%	45.7	3.0%
Wales	28.1	1.8%	18.3	2.5%
Scotland	53.3	1.7%	40.4	2.6%
Total	**600.0**		**480.0**	
Percentage of total installed in Great Britain by all suppliers in Q4, 2015	69.0%		75.0%	
Percentage of all domestic meters in 2017 (smart and traditional)	2.0%		2.0%	

Table 9.3
Breakdown of smart gas
and electricity meters
by region.

year coverage (Figure 9.1). Between April and September, less than 5% of the total were enrolled. Finally, in December around 50,000 users were added bringing the total to 600,000 users with a smart meter. We may conclude that the rollout of the electricity meters is gathering momentum. This was also confirmed by BEIS (2017). A breakdown for the rollout by trimester is shown in Figure 9.1.

In 2015, 600,000 electricity smart meter users consumed 1,200 Gwh, representing just 1.1% of the total domestic electricity consumption in Great Britain for that year. For gas, 480,000 users consumed 4,000 Gwh, accounting for 1.3% of the total domestic gas consumption in Great Britain (2015). Basic centrality measures around individual consumption are shown in Table 9.2.

The geographical distribution of meters (Figure 9.2) is slightly biased towards the North West and West Midlands regions, for both electricity and gas, where almost

30% of the smart meters are installed. In contrast, Wales and North East regions are deeply under-represented, accounting for only 8% of the total of smart meters (Table 9.3).

The data for 2015 represent the early stages of smart meter roll out. One of the potential sources of bias associated with this, is the fact that the first properties to receive a smart meter were those with old energy meters. Another possible bias might arise from the fact that the first households to receive an installation were more likely to be at home during the campaign: this may skew the customer representativeness slightly towards the elderly and families. To test these ideas, we compare the distribution of property build period by region (generated by the Valuation Office Agency) with the total number of smart meters installed, particularly for the 1965 to 1972 period (Table 9.4). Although the North West region scores high in both measures and Wales scores low in both, this test is by no means conclusive and the

Region	Electricity Meters	Properties Built 1965 to 1972
South East	57,100	430,340
North West	96,100	330,780
East of England	47,000	314,640
West Midlands	79,200	292,610
South West	41,100	259,040
Yorkshire-Humber	58,000	238,860
London	65,900	224,600
East Midlands	48,600	211,720
Wales	28,100	135,900
North East	24,700	132,820
Scotland	53,300	NA

Table 9.4
Meters installed and properties built between 1965-1972. The correlation between number of meters installed and properties built in this period is 0.35, indicating a weak positive correlation.

correlation between both quantities is not particularly significant.

9.4
Comparison with the UK Census of population

To concentrate on how the data are representative of the British population we linked the dataset with the UK 2011 Census data on number of households that reside in each postcode sector. As smart meters are installed at address level, the number of households may be used as a proxy for the coverage of individuals represented in our data. We found that, in general, the percentage of households is no more than 3%, for both electricity and gas (Figure 9.3). This could imply that roll out of smart meters has started at the same time in each of the postcode sectors gradually, varying from 1 to 65 meters installed. It can also be observed that speed of installation may be greater in urban regions of the country.

In more than 80% of the postcode sectors, smart meters were installed at between 1% and 4.8% of the total number of households. The higher percentages can be found in the West Midlands, North West and the North of Wales. North West, in fact, is the second largest region by a number of all type meters present, while northern Wales is rather unusually over-represented in our sample. As in Figure 9.2, the brown areas represent the sectors with no available data.

9.5
Variability on energy consumption

Previous research on energy consumption (Huebner et al, 2015; McLoughlin et al, 2012) and energy expenditure (Druckman and Jackson, 2008) has considered aggregated consumption values at either annual or six month intervals. Previous analysis of smart meter data in the UK was performed primarily with Irish smart meter data (Silipo and Winters, 2013; Cao et al, 2013). A UK-wide national dataset may offer a more insightful approach when considering energy consumption. Previous work aimed to identify if there is any correspondence between property attributes and household characteristics that may explain variability in energy use. Huebner et al (2015) for instance found that building characteristics and socio-demographics can jointly explain only about 44% of energy use variation. Further work by Haben et al (2013) attempted to link profiled energy consumption patterns to socio-demographic classification and found little correspondence between temporal profiles and socio-economic groups. This suggested

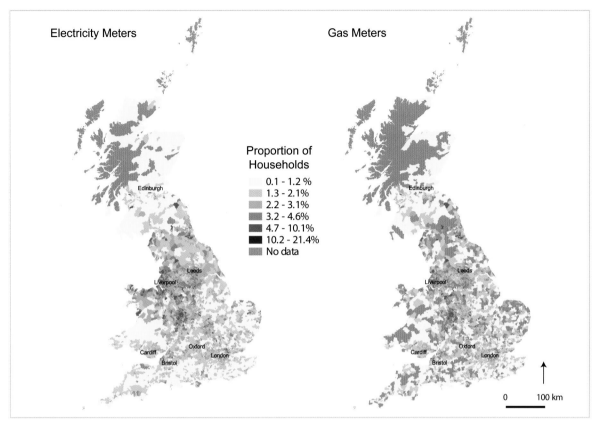

Figure 9.3
Proportion of electricity and gas meters relative to the total number of households by postcode sector.

that studying actual energy consumption at greater temporal breakdown may further inform us about behavioural patterns. For instance, variability in half hourly consumption can be used as an indicator of distinct consumption behaviours or lifestyles. As a response, we attempt to look not only at how much is consumed but where and when. Having the same total value for the day may, in fact, be associated with increased differentiation in customer profiles, which are based on the variation throughout the day and the region in which smart meter users reside. We address this by attempting to cluster temporal energy usage, to group customers not by their average total consumption, but rather with a combination of their consumption levels in and outside peak hours.

9.5.1
Classification methods and outlier detection

We accessed the suitability of some clustering methods for visualisation of variability in energy consumption profiles across postcode sectors. Potentially, this may be used for defining outlier groups of readings that represent slightly unusual behaviour compared to the majority of the sample. Several studies have attempted energy classification for electricity data. However, the samples tend to differ as well as the representations and additional features that are added to the smart meter readings. Further work may consider the clustering on a particular day or at a specific time; variation at such scales may be pre-determined by season or, even more narrowly, time of day that can be associated with different activities. The decision of whether these dimensions

Cluster name	% of total
Cluster 1	51%
Cluster 2	1%
Cluster 3	38%
Cluster 4	10%

Table 9.5
Resulting national clusters for annual half hour aggregates at postcode sector level.

can be considered simultaneously or sequentially underpins much of the CDRC research into these data.

To date, a number of methods has been developed for clustering consumer data. The majority are associated with a reliable performance on static data only, while disregarding the sequential links between variables. This poses further challenges if we are to consider spatial and temporal dimensions. One of the immediate solutions could be to transform dynamic data into static format. For example, we may calculate the mean for each of the individuals and create a numerical indicator that represents an estimate of average consumption for the individuals in our sample. The decision on the method is thus broadly driven by the data characteristics that include: discrete versus real values, uniformity of the sample,

univariate versus multivariate series, as well as lengths of time series considered for the analysis (Liao, 2005).

K-means clustering is the most popular approach due to its simplicity and fast minimisation of the similarities among the objects within each class centre. It may be suitable for datasets with static features. For highly variable temporal variables, the assignment of the cluster may be highly unstable as different customers will be assigned to a different cluster subject to the day and time.

Alternatively, a Gaussian Mixture Model based on a probabilistic setting for clustering may be proposed. Such a setting brings about the ability to handle diverse types of data, including dealing with missing or unobservable data that may have contributed to variation differences

Figure 9.4
Clusters derived from annual aggregates at postcode sector level. The whisker box plots represent the median energy consumption and the variation within four quantiles. Postcode sector differences in aggregated consumption are based mainly on the variation around expected morning and evening peaks consumption.

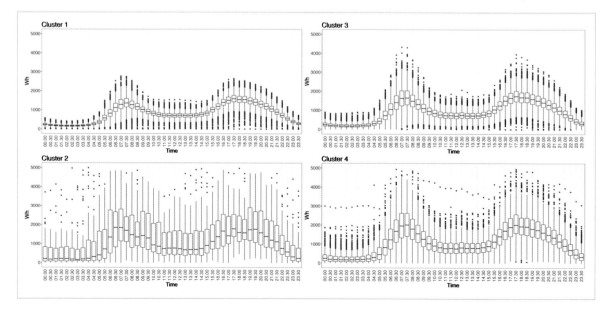

Table 9.6
Resulting national clusters for annual half hour aggregates at postcode sector level after exclusion of outlier group observations.

Cluster name	% of total
Cluster 1	30%
Cluster 2	13%
Cluster 3	7%
Cluster 4	1%
Cluster 5	2%
Cluster 6	3%
Cluster 7	19%
Cluster 8	18%
Cluster 9	7%

among segmented groups. This is achieved by assigning a probability measure to the cluster. Where uncertainty about the assignment is greater, additional variables may be introduced or the individual may be treated as an outlier or uncertain group. Unlike k-means, it produces stable results and selects the number of clusters using smoothing. This is also convenient for the matter of replication as clustering results remain the same regardless of how many times we run the algorithm. Further research may implement clustering by dynamics – for example, through grouping graphical models (please see further reading for more details).

Some immediate results of clustering for gas consumption are presented in Table 9.5 and Figure 9.4. As we note, cluster 2 represents very high and variable behaviour yet represents a very limited part of the sample. Cluster 1, in contrast, represents half of the national sample variation at aggregated level. We may conclude that, on average, gas energy consumption across Great Britain does not vary significantly and there is a tendency for highly stable consumption through the day with peak hours falling into intervals of 06:00 – 08:30 and 16:00 – 20:00. Customers in postcode sectors that fall in cluster 1 are more likely to consume during the peak hours with a lower tendency to consume at night in comparison with cluster 4, for example, where there is a greater propensity to use gas both overnight and throughout the day.

To look deeper into the variation in energy profiles across postcode sector we removed the data that fall into cluster 2, treating it as an outlier group. A number of factors may have contributed to the unusually high variation captured in this cluster: non-domestic properties may be mistakenly occurring in the sample, or multiple occupations may be associated with a single smart meter address (e.g. student halls). What we observe is that by excluding highly variable observations, the algorithm can differentiate more variability and after subtraction of these outliers gives rise to nine national clusters. From Table 9.6 and Figure 9.5 we observe once again that there is a clear tendency for morning and evening peaks to be similar across profiles. Additionally, on average the consumption levels stay at the limit of 2,500 kWh per half hour across the clustered profiles. However, what we are picking up is clusters of really low consumption (clusters 1 and 7) compared to high and variable groups (clusters 3,4,6) that are defined by the variability around night time consumption, early mornings and outside peak hours.

9.5.2
Usage during off-peak hours

As a further extension to this analysis we segment the temporal analysis of energy data in terms of peak hours as they have shown to be important for the definition of the clusters. Figure 9.5 suggests that

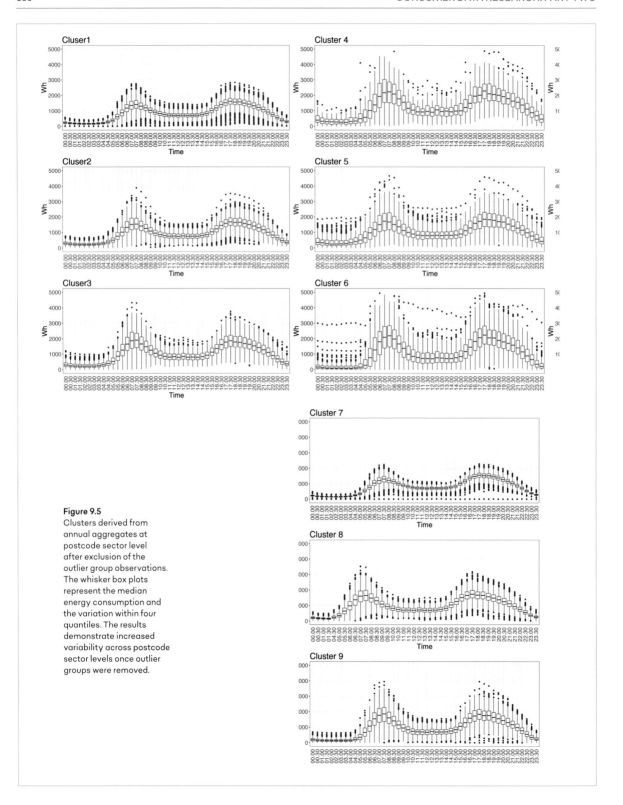

Figure 9.5
Clusters derived from annual aggregates at postcode sector level after exclusion of the outlier group observations. The whisker box plots represent the median energy consumption and the variation within four quantiles. The results demonstrate increased variability across postcode sector levels once outlier groups were removed.

Figure 9.6
Clustering of 'off-peak' hours data. Here we assess consumption levels that are represented as the times between 11:30 and 15:00. Note: Grey areas represent no data; data provided for areas with complete annual coverage only.

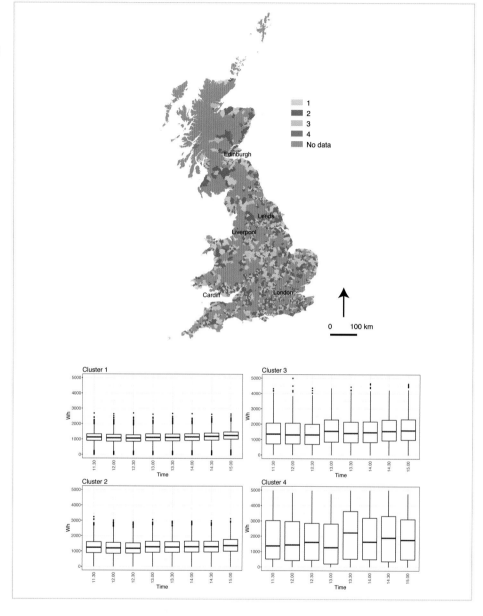

regardless of segmentation, there are quite similar patterns around morning and evening peak hours which vary in magnitude but are evident for each of the clusters. Examining peak and outside peak hours separately may tell us slightly more about a household's presence at home as well as particular habits or routine (i.e. waking up early for work, late nighters). We further show that for defining the

interactions between characteristics of people living in the area and energy, concentrating on specific time and location may reveal more information about energy consumption rather than when both time and space are aggregated. As may be observed in clusters 3 and 4 in Figure 9.6, consumption throughout the day is more frequent around the coastal regions and less in central England. Further investigation

Source	Name	Time Period	Geographical reference	Temporal Granularity	Description
UK Data Service (UKDS) and Department for Communities and Local Government (DCLG)	English Housing Survey (EHS)	2008-2015	Households/ Dwellings[1]	Annual Statistic	Updated each year and provides data on energy efficiency, insulation and tenure trend. Does not cover entire Great Britain. Sample of around 6-7,000 houses drawn randomly each year for an investigation. Sample for 2014/15 have slightly better coverage: 2,297 dwellings; 11,851 households. Similar surveys for other UK countries. www.ukdataservice.ac.uk
UKDS and BEIS	Energy Performance Certificates (EPC)	2005-2015	Region or address level	N/A	Sample is sufficiently large and covers over 15 million addresses in the UK. Data contain information on energy efficiency bands and variables such as age, type of property, floor area, annual gas and electricity consumption as fuel poverty indicators. Dates of records vary as according to regulations, assessments should be undertaken when conditions change, e.g., when a property is rented. epc.opendatacommunities.org
CDRC	House Ages and Prices	1989-2015	LSOA and MSOA	ONS (quarterly) and VOA (annual)	The data were collected originally by ONS and VOA. The dwelling age counts are at LSOA level and median house prices are at MSOA level. data.cdrc.ac.uk
Office for National Statistics (ONS)	Census 2011	2011	Census OA	Decennial statistic	These data offer a fairly detailed description of all households and properties in the UK. Useful variables could include household size, employment characteristics, dwelling age, country of origin and others. However, the data have no consideration for recent (<10 year) temporal variations and may contain missing data. www.ons.gov.uk/census/2011census
University of Southampton and ONS	Classification of Workplace Zones	2011	Census OA	NA	A geodemographic classification of the characteristics of Workplace Zones (WZs). The categorisation of WZs is based on the similarity measures derived from a range of variables from 2011 Census of England and Wales. Such a specific classification may be useful if we want to consider using energy consumption patterns to study the employment types of smart meter users (i.e. part-time vs full time, unemployment, retired). cowz.geodata.soton.ac.uk

Table 9.7
Openly-available
datasets that may aid the
understanding of variation
in energy consumption.

would be necessary as in general each cluster is scattered around the nation and may be well presented in each of the regions.

In this section we presented a preliminary analysis of smart meter segmentation and outlier detection by considering when and how people consume regardless of their location. One of the further research objectives is to look at how the profiles of customers are segmented geographically and whether their variational differences can be explained by characteristics of the areas where people live. This can be achieved with openly available adminstrative datasets.

9.5.3
Data linkage

Various datasets available for linkage with energy consumption are presented in Table 9.7 where we list the sources of additional data, the geographical and temporal references and time period that these datasets cover. A number of limitations should be addressed when considering these data sources. Firstly, the vast majority of data on the population are only available in aggregate geographic units. However, some data are available at the household level which will enable us to link them to specific trends identified by individual smart meters. One such example is the Energy Performance Certificate (EPC) data which contains energy performance related variables for over 15.6 million households.

9.5.4
Bristol energy consumption and UK Census Output Area Classification

In this section, we present an analysis of the region around Bristol where energy consumption in 2014 is linked to Census Output Area (OA) geography. We tested the ability of some common predictors of energy consumption, such as property size and life-stage of energy customers combined in a single indicator, Census Output Area Classification (OAC). Based

on previous research that looked at the forecasting of energy consumption, the main factor for consumption dynamics was considered to be the weather (Swan and Ugursal, 2009). Nevertheless, as more data were added to smart meter analysis what has become clearer is that a response to the weather is affected by the type of property, tenure, house size, life stage, income group, and other customer characteristics (McLoughlin et al, 2012). A further, and perhaps no less obvious point, is that of economics and the relationship between income variables and energy consumption at both national and individual level. As we might expect, those who are wealthier tend to consume more energy as they are likely to live in more spacious properties.

Before looking at links between socio-demographic characteristics and consumption, we clustered temporal profiles in Bristol in a similar fashion as we did for the national dataset; the only difference is we are now looking at a much finer OA level geography. The resulting clusters are presented in Table 9.8 and Figure 9.7. The number of distinct clusters is smaller than that of the national dataset. Nevertheless, some immediate correspondence with the clusters that we defined previously can be noted for clusters 1 and 2. The consumption in Bristol is observed to be differentiated by both peak hours and throughout the day patterns. Most of the OA aggregates are associated with very low or no consumption during night time. This may suggest that the variability of energy consumption at a finer geographical level may not necessarily be less representative as in the large sample. Further to this, it may help us in filling the gaps where data are missing by defining some common energy behavioural patterns that are more frequent in each of the areas in Great Britain, or as we call them, typical profiles.

Despite defining some clear relationships between household characteristics and

Cluster name	% of total
Cluster 1	27%
Cluster 2	38%
Cluster 3	35%

Table 9.8
Clusters derived from annual aggregates at OA level, Bristol.

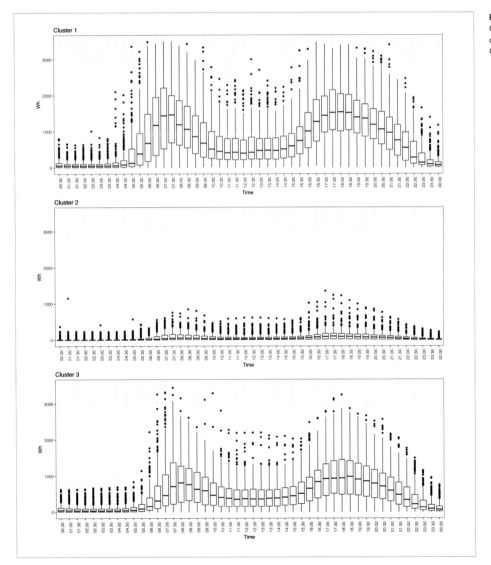

Figure 9.7
Clusters derived from annual aggregates at OA level for Bristol.

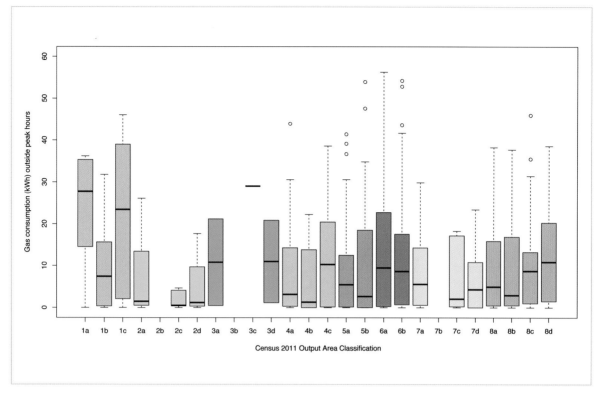

Figure 9.8
An attempt to use the 2011 Census Output Area Classification (OAC) to explain the variation outside peak hours on a regular winter's day on a sample of 1,105 meters in Bristol. Note: Interestingly, even while the number of meters representing each group is relatively small, we can identify students, rural tenants, families and the elderly as those most likely to consume outside peak hours.

energy use, the current research suggests that over recent years energy consumption has tended to be shaped more significantly by consumer habits and lifestyle, than by household size or dwelling type. Capturing this is challenging, yet the behaviour patterns clustered together perhaps may give us more direction in quantifying the lifestyles of energy customers.

Figure 9.8 presents some preliminary results using OAC to define the links between household characteristics and energy consumption outside peak hours as a potential proxy for households staying at home. It is important to note that the roll out of the smart meter as outlined earlier may bias these results as it was suggested that in 2014–2015 people who were likely to be present at home were among the first to receive a smart meter. In the case of Bristol, we observe that around 20% of the sample falls into the category of 'Urban Professionals and Families' which is quite contrary to the suggestion that composition

of smart meter data may be skewed towards elderly people. Besides, a number of factors may be associated with consumption outside peak hours that need further validation. To name but a few, the households present at home may be those who work from home, are retired or are carers.

9.6
Conclusion

Research domains that investigate energy consumption range from engineering and informatics to economics and political science. The complexities of investigating energy consumption motivate the development of new research methodologies to cope with the diversity of energy data available. The method we considered in this chapter, the Gaussian Mixture Model, tends to work in a quite stable fashion for the different set of data, meaning that no matter how many times we implement an algorithm the result will hold. Further research should consider a more thorough design of energy consumption process-generation. We primarily used the gas data as little attention was given to it in previous research. The ability to use smart meter data to group and identify customers can help to improve energy efficiency through better utilisation of data to target interventions and policies. A more targeted policy framework may thus be designed to address simultaneously the issues of carbon emission reduction and affordability of energy.

We suggest that subsamples of the smart meter data may be taken in order to bring focus to the analysis of variability in consumption, possibly also stratified according to the study area. In this chapter, we presented work the largest sample of smart meter data ever available for Great Britain. On this geographically extensive scale, greater heterogeneity is observed, both over time and space. In an effort to identify potential sources of bias in our dataset we compared the data to official sources. In our case, further limitations may also be posed by the specific customer base of our data provider and issues that may prevent households in receiving a smart meter (e.g. low priority house type or condition during the early stages of roll out). We further identified that clustering may be useful for visualisations of Big Data from smart meters and provide a ground for identification of the outliers or unusual behaviours.

The substantial variety in energy usage across Great Britain, and the acknowledgement that what can be true for one household may not necessarily always tell us about the residential area, provide immediate opportunities for further research. As we observed in our results, around 50% of our sample tend to follow quite typical gas consumption patterns with morning and evening peaks and relatively lower consumption outside peak hours. However, the amount of residential variation that would not meet the criteria of the 'expected' or 'typical' temporal profile remains ambiguous, unexplained and in need of further inter-disciplinary research — analysis that could integrate spatial, temporal and social components. Addressing the validation processes for investigations that attempt to infer the causes of energy consumption variation remains an important aspect for anyone who is interested in smart meter data exploration. Further to this, one of our conclusions is that perhaps, 'smaller is better', meaning that reducing Big Data generated by smart meters to Small Data may lead to more insightful results. Researchers with a smaller sample but more data available on household characteristics or property attributes may use this national dataset to define how representative the profiles obtained on a smaller sample are of wider British trends in behaviour and lifestyle. Such analysis could further help us to define what the acceptable sample size is that can be used to study energy consumption such that the results can be acceptably generalised for the whole of the UK.

While there are many challenges surrounding smart meter data for both energy company analysts and researchers, undoubtedly these are also great possibilities to see the study of consumption behaviour in a new light. As suggested by Swan and Ugursal (2009), previous research that analysed energy consumption had tended to place a focus on private sector actors that have greater incentives and expertise for consumption reduction, as well as the need to adhere to tougher regulatory requirements. Academic research can complement such work and unlock the further potential of smart meter data, for instance to generate new insights about people's consumption patterns, which in turn would give us a better knowledge about the areas and activities across the country and inform public policy decision-making.

Further Reading

Anderson, B., Lin, S., Newing, A., Bahaj, A. and James, P. (2017). Electricity consumption and household characteristics: Implications for census-taking in a smart metered future. *Computers, Environment and Urban Systems*, 63, 58-67.

BEIS. (2016). Sub-National Electricity and Gas Consumption Statistics. Regional, Local Authority, Middle and Lower Layer Super Output Area. Report, December 2016.

BEIS (2017). Smart meters, Great Britain. Quarterly report, March 2017.

Cao, H.-A., Beckel, C. and Staake, T. (2013). Are domestic load profiles stable over time? An attempt to identify target households for demand side management campaigns. In *Industrial Electronics Society, IECON 2013 - 39th Annual Conference of the IEEE*. IEEE, pp.4733–4738.

Chicco, G. (2012). Overview and performance assessment of the clustering methods for electrical load pattern grouping. *Energy*, 42(1), 68–80.

DECC (2015). Smart meters, Great Britain. Quarterly report, December 2015.

Druckman, A. and Jackson, T. (2008). Household energy consumption in the UK: A highly geographically and socio-economically disaggregated model. *Energy Policy*, 36(8), 3177-3192.

Haben, S., Rowe, M., Greetham, D. V., Grindrod, P., Holderbaum, W., Potter, B. and Singleton, C. (2013). Mathematical solutions for electricity networks in a low carbon future. In *22nd International Conference and Exhibition on Electricity Distribution* (CIRED 2013) pp. 1-4.

Holderbaum, W., Potter, B. and Singleton, C. (2013). Mathematical solutions for electricity networks in a low carbon future. In *22nd International Conference and Exhibition on Electricity Distribution* (CIRED 2013).

Huebner, G. M., Hamilton, I., Chalabi, Z., Shipworth, D. and Oreszczyn, T. (2015). Explaining domestic energy consumption: The comparative contribution of building factors, socio-demographics, behaviours and attitudes. *Applied Energy*, 159, 589-600.

Liao, T. W. (2005). Clustering of time series data – a survey. *Pattern Recognition*, 38(11), 1857–1874.

Lutzenhiser, L. (1993). Social and behavioral aspects of energy use. *Annual Review of Energy and the Environment*, 18(1), 247–289.

McLoughlin, F., Duffy, A. and Conlon, M. (2012). Characterizing domestic electricity consumption patterns by dwelling and occupant socio-economic variables: An Irish case study. *Energy and Buildings*, 48, 240–248.

Silipo, R., and Winters, P. (2013). Big data, smart energy, and predictive analytics. *Time Series Prediction of Smart Energy Data*, 1, 37.

Swan, L. G. and Ugursal, V. I. (2009). Modeling of end-use energy consumption in the residential sector: A review of modeling techniques. *Renewable and Sustainable Energy Reviews*. 13(8), 1819–1835.

Acknowledgements

The authors are grateful to the 'Domestic Energy Provider', for providing smart meter data for this research. The first author's PhD research is sponsored by the Economic and Social Research Council through the UCL Doctoral Training Centre.

PART THREE

NEW APPLICATIONS AND DATA LINKAGE

10

Geovisualisation of Consumer Data

Oliver O'Brien and James Cheshire

10.1
Introduction

As the volume and variety of spatially-referenced consumer data continues to grow there is an unprecedented need for their curation, analysis and communication. Consumers like to be informed about what their data says about them, retailers are keen to exploit data to drive sales and researchers see great potential in such data for deriving insights into social processes. Interactive maps are a proven tool in facilitating data access across these groups. They communicate insights, in addition to providing an interface through which subsets of large and complex databases can be downloaded for further analysis.

This chapter will share insights from a decade of research into the creation of web-mapping tools for a variety of consumer and government datasets. It will detail the developments that underpin the creation of three innovative mapping platforms before signposting a series of research priorities for more informative geovisualisation of consumer datasets, and population data more broadly.

10.1.1
Background

Central to the field of geographical information science has been the need to handle large and complex datasets. Without developments in this and associated fields there would, for example, be no efficient means of combining demographic data to its respective locations: essential procedures in the analysis of consumer data.

What's more we are in an era of unprecedented change in the nature of, funding for and access to social, economic and demographic datasets. It is a pressing concern that the full potential of consumer data is realised as government-funded datasets become a diminished part of the data landscape. Such data offer the possibility of investigating new research issues in unprecedented spatiotemporal detail, but their effective concatenation, conflation and synthesis are far from unproblematic. There is also the potential and need for more sophisticated visualisation, in the form of visual analytics, of these kinds of data both for exploratory analysis and also for the communication of results. This provides the chapter's focus.

During the past decade the acceleration in the development and uptake of web-mapping technologies has led to a proliferation of highly advanced mapping interfaces. These are now routinely accessed across a full range of platforms – from mobile phones to desktop computers – and have expanded from navigational devices to key forms of information visualisation. A trend facilitated by a move away from serving image tiles to users and towards the use of vector tiles where the web browser effectively performs the geographic information system (GIS) operations previously undertaken on the website's servers at source. Such tiles have the advantage of being generated as and when required, which enables the inclusion of real-time data or rapid updates.

As the technology and data for map creation become more complex, a dichotomy is emerging in the skillsets required by potential users. Web maps can now be immediately accessed and utilised with limited prior experience, but the data used to create them require more programming skills as spreadsheets give way to databases. This bifurcation, in part, fuels the data science industry as it seeks to meet the increasing demand for innovative visualisations of new data to be served to a large number of non-specialist users. Companies such as Mapbox and CARTO all offer demographic data maps, alongside Esri, the leader in this sector for the past three decades.

The Consumer Data Research Centre (CDRC) is an academic initiative that has entered this space and developed a bespoke mapping platform called CDRC Maps. Users can access maps generated from millions of data points depicting a range of data from deprivation through to Internet usage with links to the raw data for use in their own analysis. A key motivation for creating the platform was the desire to share data from the CDRC and a recognition that online data repositories have limited effectiveness with users seeking to browse datasets or for raising awareness of particular data. As will be discussed below, CDRC Maps is coupled with the centre's portal CDRC Data in order that users can download the raw data they have seen mapped if they wish to undertake more in-depth analysis. This has proved very useful to analysts in local and national government in addition to the commercial and third sector which lack the budget and skills to produce their own maps from complex data but also wish to explore relevant subsets of larger datasets.

10.2
Web mapping

The earliest web maps were created in 1993 and became more ubiquitous in the early 2000s when the growth of real-time geographic services such as mapping, routing and location-based advertising really took off, most notably in 2005 with Google's release of Google Maps. First-generation applications provided only unidirectional flows of data and information from websites to their user bases. Over time, this system evolved into services that facilitate bi-directional collaboration between users and sites, the outcome of which is that information is collated and made available to others. The two main technologies that stimulated this development were Asynchronous JavaScript And XML (AJAX) and Application Programming Interfaces (APIs). AJAX enabled the development of websites that retain the look and feel of desktop applications, while APIs defined and documented consistent ways of accessing assets and tools created by other projects.

They have improved the usability of Web mapping significantly by enabling direct manipulation of map data where user interactions (such as 'click and drag') are visualised instantaneously.

Early versions of web maps were detached from the underlying data used to create them since in all cases the developer was required to pre-render the maps before loading onto the server – users were given access to images only. As web browsers have become more powerful and base-mapping data has become freely available through initiatives such as OpenStreetMap and government open data platforms, for example the London Data Store, image tiles have been superseded by vector-based systems. These offer the key advantage that the maps are rendered on demand, that is they are generated at the time they need to be viewed, from data served via a series of database requests. As we demonstrate below, this enables a much greater amount of flexibility both in terms of reported statistics and the cartographic representation. In addition maps can act as platforms for data download to the point that they can now be thought of as data services rather than simply static representations of a single dataset.

10.2.1
CensusProfiler

One of the first comprehensive web maps of population data was constructed from the UK's 2001 Census data and called CensusProfiler. It was one of the first to offer panning and zooming controls, a revolution in comparison to the pre-2005 standard of clicking around a map's edge to visualise the 'next page'. The user interface had three key layers: a basemap showing context such as roads and rivers, the 2001 Census data, and a number of moveable toolbars that controlled the data shown and colour palettes. In the simplest sense CensusProfiler was a series of choropleth maps. This style of mapping is widely used for demographic data and typically colours a statistical unit area according to the proportion of the population within it that has a particular attribute, for example the proportion of the working-age population that are in full-time employment.

Choropleth colour ramps are usually scaled from the lowest to the highest proportions across all the areas and may be evenly banded (stepped/graduated, i.e. discrete) or use a continuous ramp. Alternatively, other methods of banding may be applied, such as Jenks, natural breaks (Jenks, 1967). To serve the choropleth map to the user it is partitioned into square images, or tiles, that are created only when needed on a server, following a request made by the user's browser – the 'client'. Because of the enormous number of possible combinations, each resulting in a unique map tile that could therefore be viewed, it is essential to be able to create the map tiles 'on demand' in an efficient and timely manner, as opposed to pre-rendering these maps and storing all the tiles on a server. Therefore, CensusProfiler had a system that efficiently created custom-made maps. The website architecture also employed limited 'caching' of the most popular map views, to avoid repeated server-intensive spatial operations on the database and accelerate response time, but for the great majority of queries these were created at the time of the query. This development was one of the key drivers behind the creation of CensusProfiler's successor: the DataShine platform.

10.2.2
DataShine (datashine.org.uk)

DataShine visualises and provides access to the UK's 2011 Census aggregated datasets; users can access and map nearly 2,000 variables across a quarter of a million statistical unit areas. It marks a significant advancement on the technologies deployed by its predecessor by enabling more advanced cartography and map customisation, rescaling of the data on demand and data download functions.

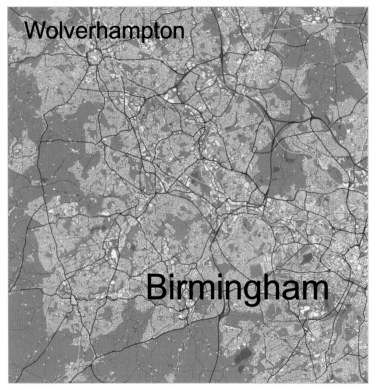

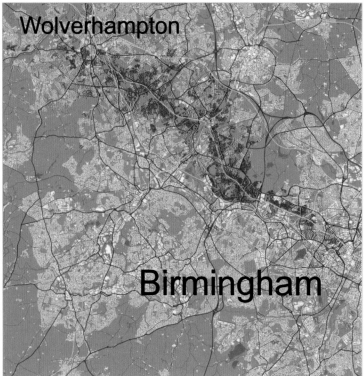

Figure 10.1
Impact of rescaling the colour ramp based on the local values, shown for metro use in north-west Birmingham. Top: Nationally scaled colour ramp. Bottom: Locally scaled colour ramp. The rescaling allows the variations in the low (relative to national use) but still significant (in local terms) usage to be viewed.

One of the most useful functions that exploits the dynamic rendering of map tiles from the underlying database is the ability to recalculate the values for the colour breaks used in the display of the data. This feature was designed to address the challenge of showing change over local areas when global values have been used in the colour binning calculation. For example, a user may be in a region where a particular demographic has very low (or high) values compared to the national average but these become under/over saturated and show a single colour. DataShine therefore has the option to take the average percentage and the corresponding standard deviation using only data from the area shown in the extent of the web browser. This can result in the binning strategy changing, for local areas that are significantly divergent from global averages. For example, the popularity of London's underground network with its large population, means that, for other cities with metros or trams, their usage is harder to pick out from the census. So, in Birmingham, the Midland Metro can be hard to spot (see Figure 10.1). Upon rescaling, just the local results are used when calculating the average and standard deviation, allowing usage variations, in this case along the route of the railway, to be more clearly seen. For transport planners in Birmingham this results in a much more useful map.

DataShine is also a data service that enables users to download the data behind the map in a CSV format for further analysis – something not possible if the website had been built exclusively from image tiles. This gives users the chance to source only the data they need without the arduous process of navigating the myriad of large and complex tables provided as the standard statistical release. In practice this has meant that students can download census data for their local area and utilise it within seconds – a feature that has become particularly popular with secondary schools and universities.

10.2.3
CDRC Maps (maps.cdrc.ac.uk)

DataShine has demonstrated the value of maps for facilitating data access and sharing insights. These are core aims of the CDRC and therefore a mapping platform was considered a crucial aspect of the initiative. CDRC Maps features a range of socioeconomic data for the United Kingdom, such as population density, broadband speeds and relative deprivation levels. Currently around 50 maps are available on the platform.

A layered tiling approach is taken with the creation and display of the maps on the CDRC Maps platform. A label layer lies on top, along with an invisible lower-resolution gridded vector layer that provides information about the choropleth value, current statistical area ID and name, and other useful information. A common mantra in web development is that every click required to view a page results in a halving of the audience. It is therefore essential to present geodemographic and choropleth maps as simply and as attractively as possible, minimising the clicks needed to retrieve the data or view. The JQuery framework and its JQueryUI extensions used in CDRC Maps achieve this. Every choropleth map can be accessed in just three clicks. All other map customisations are selected in a single click on the appropriate buttons. Further buttons are available to jump to key cities in the UK.

As with its predecessor websites, the map itself is the dominant feature, with user interface controls and additional data display occupying only a small part of the design, and not always displayed. As CDRC Data displays data from a range of sources, rather than just census data, a number of design simplifications are necessary in order to retain a single user interface. The available maps are split into three categories, with the corresponding key for each map displayed in a different way, and a different range of metadata values shown, for each category.

There is the additional UI requirement for more context and information to be shown around some of the maps. For example, some maps show composite indicators that partition areas into specific categories that need further explanation. This is provided in a series of pop-ups with links to more detailed guidance. This, again, adds to the potential complexity of the user interface that needs to be managed.

As part of broadening access to the CDRC's data holdings, we were keen to include a series of eye-catching and easily interpretable layers to CDRC Maps to drive traffic to the platform from our user groups. To this end we feature a series of single-metric maps, showing how the metric value varies from low to high, typically using a fixed-hue colour ramp. It also shows example geodemographic maps, where areas are assigned a category based on the clustering of multiple metrics. As the relationship between each category is not normally directly quantifiable, qualitative colour palettes (changing hue for each category) are typically used. Finally, a hybrid type of map is also included. Known as 'Top Metric Maps', these show, for each area, the top category for a single qualitative metric, for example the most common industry type or the most popular mode used to travel to work. As the categories are qualitative, hue-varying colour palettes are used. Whilst they have proved popular with our users, we are aware that top metric maps have to be used cautiously, as they may not be representative of the wider population in each area, particularly if the category break-downs are not carefully calibrated.

The entire geostack used in CDRC Maps – namely Mapnik and PostGIS for data storage and creation; and OpenLayers, JQuery and JQueryUI for display - is open source, and the datasets mapped are generally themselves derived from, or simple aggregations of, open data, with the data being available at CDRC Data, the aforementioned complementary site

to CDRC Maps that acts as a data repository and viewer. CDRC Maps therefore both raises awareness of data and facilitates access to it.

10.3
Developments in web mapping

Techniques for showing maps of data on the web continue to evolve rapidly, as the geostack technology continues to be in active development. Technologists are looking to pure-vector based maps, as client-computer browsers become more sophisticated at rendering content themselves. However, the traditional raster approach can still lead to rich and effective mapping that cannot yet easily be replaced with a vector pathway. Digital cartographers are starting to consider augmenting the basic approach of displaying the data with colour variations, by incorporating other kinds of symbology, such as texturing, still best served as raster tiles.

The following section considers some of the possible advances in this area. It will first discuss prototypes to display of levels uncertainty in a dataset. The second example is the use of colour compositing of multiple datasets, each represented in different hues, on an automated, rule-based basis, to generate new ways of looking at multivariate data. Finally, we consider an alternative approach to the 'building mask' technique of DataShine and CDRC Maps (discussed above), by using colour to emphasise the population's location.

10.3.1
Uncertainty

Consumer datasets are often inputs into, or augmented by, indicators such as geodemographic classifications. These are also subject to a quantifiable degree of uncertainty that is rarely mapped, but that can have important implications for analysis and interpretation. Here we take one such indicator, the UK Output Area Classification (OAC), and demonstrate

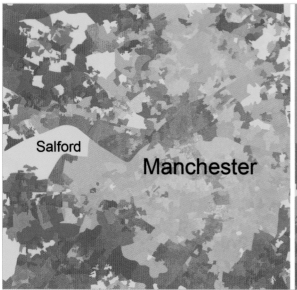 

Figure 10.2
Left: Manchester's urban core, showing sharp divisions. Right: Halifax (south part of map) and Bradford (north part of map) where different demographics are manifest as differences in how well the central zone is defined. Both maps are aligned with north upwards.

how the uncertainty inherent to it can be mapped. Unlike its commercial counterparts, this free-to-use classification benefits from an open-source methodology that facilitates the calculation of a range of uncertainty measures. Here we use the 2011 OAC developed by geographers at UCL in collaboration with the UK's Office for National Statistics.

It is now possible to apply textures to web-based choropleth. We try two such approaches in this work; the first is applying an image file of noise and the second is to apply hatching. The level of distortion is controlled by an uncertainty measure in the 2011 OAC known as the 'standard equalised distance' (SED) that offers an indication of how close to the centre of each cluster a single output area (OA) falls. The smaller the SED, the more certain we can be that the bulk of an OA's population fits its assigned 'supergroup' (category). The smallest SED to each supergroup, for each area, becomes that area's designated supergroup classification, but the SED to the other supergroups are retained. Both the absolute SED values and the relative SED between the 'winning' (referred to as primary) and 'runner-up' (secondary, tertiary etc.) supergroups are

used when visualising the uncertainty of classification of each area.

With each approach we offer an example of the insights it can provide into the success, or otherwise, of 2011 OAC. Across the entire OAC 2011 supergroup dataset, the OA average SED for the dominant supergroup is 0.913, with a population standard deviation of 0.239. We apply a screen compositing operation that lightens the supergroup colour in a spatially randomised way by combining it with a 'grain' texture supplied by a source JPEG file. The grain effect has an opacity set based on the absolute SED score, from 0 (i.e. no compositing effect) for SED less than 0.6, increasing linearly to 1.0 (i.e. compositing the texture fully) for SED greater than 2.4.

On examining a version of the OAC 2011 map with the textured noise applied, untextured area boundaries show strongly on the choropleth map while boundaries between two areas both with a high SED are much less distinguishable. The former case often occurs if there is a linear feature that forms a physical barrier (e.g. a river or major highway) separating the two areas. The identification of such transitions is aided by the use of texture as well as lightness. As coarseness increases with SED score the blocks of colour will appear to fade whilst evidence of the original colour allocation – and therefore geodemographic group – will remain. In addition to the visual impact of fading and intensity, this increased coarseness also serves to highlight poorer quality data. Two examples are shown in Figure 10.2. In Manchester's case, the sharp changes in colour to the west of the city centre suggest a physical barrier, in this case the Manchester Ship Canal. Other areas, such as the south and north, are less geographically constrained and so the supergroups 'merge' into noise and only then switch to another colour. Halifax and Bradford show contrasts despite having similarly sized 'Cosmopolitan' zones (red colours). Halifax's zone is more sharply defined, with a more obvious transition to other colours. The amount of texturing in this city is relatively low, showing a good individual fit for many areas to a single supergroup.

We add white diagonal stripes of various densities to show varying SEDs. We use four different tileable images, ranging from ¼ density (i.e. 25% white lines, 75% underlying classification colour) for SED greater than 1.6, to 1/32 density for SED greater than 1.0 but less than 1.2. SEDs less than 1.0 were considered to be so good a match that it was not necessary to indicate any uncertainty on the map for such areas. These SED thresholds can be changed to increase or decrease the impact of uncertainty on the visualisation. Figure 10.3 demonstrates the impact that the different densities of stripes have on the perception of the classification across a wide area - Scotland shows a noticeably higher absolute SED for rural areas, resulting in more diagonal stripes appearing once moving north across the border. The noticeable transition across the border suggests a poorer fit to the idealised 'rural residents' classification shown in green, in the Scottish context.

10.3.2
Multivariate choropleth displays

In addition to showing uncertainty it is also now possible to combine multiple variables in a single map. The effect can be thought of as a simple visual index with similar areas securing similar colours in the mixing process.

For example, combining red and blues, separately showing metrics about an area produces a hue somewhere between blue and red, typically purple if both metrics have large values, but tending towards one or the other otherwise. This is already a popular approach to mapping election results – particularly in the USA – where the maps can indicate the size of the winning result for each area. The hue mixing effect can be easily achieved using colour compositing operations that are available in some web mapping frameworks, such as Mapnik, along with careful layering of the component metrics.

This technique requires careful implementation since interpretation can quickly become difficult, particularly as many people may not be familiar with typical colour combinations, and because different colour compositing operations (e.g. 'darken', 'lighten', 'difference') will result in different results when combining the same two or more colours together. The problem can be partly minimised by supplying an interactive key that adapts as different hue-based layers are viewed, and shows all the possible combinations of colours and the underlying metric values.

Here we show the potential for this technique with a number of simple socioeconomic variables, using composites of multiple hues that were created as part of a prototype website. The technique proved to be powerful in showing areas with similar characteristics across multiple variables (similar to more sophisticated geodemographic cluster classifications); however the hue variations were

Figure 10.3
Variations in SED across the border between Scotland and England, which runs diagonally, approximately through the middle of the image from the bottom left to top right.

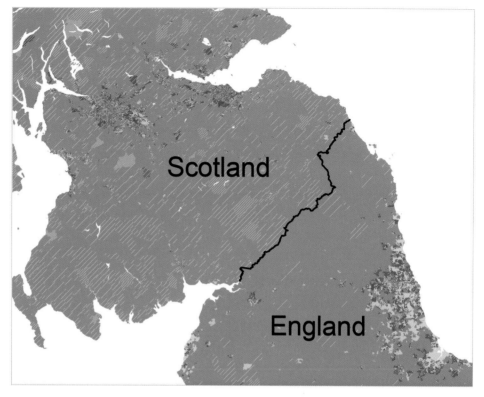

continuous rather than discrete as in a classification. Basic user tests suggested it was difficult to interpret the result, particularly since creating a key that was flexible enough to show all combinations proved problematic. The map therefore largely relies on the user knowing what hues are formed by combining the component hues together and knowing the compositing operation. The effect is shown in Figure 10.4, with a 'lighten' compositing operation and green, purple and red source hues. For all three source hues, grey represents the low value and the full-intensity hue represents the highest value. Roughly, high red and high green areas show as yellow; high red and high purple areas show as magenta; and high purple and high green colours show as turquoise. Combining all three together shows as white, as the three source hues are well separated from each other on a standard RGB colour wheel.

The approach highlights areas of similarity and difference and can therefore aid in initial exploratory data analysis. Users can then access the underlying data to undertake more conventional quantitative analyses as they wish.

10.3.3
Population density colour palettes

One final area of active development is exploration of the most effective means of accounting for variations in population density. As discussed above, choropleth maps of population-related statistics tend to fill areas of low and high population density with equally strong, distinct colours, even though the statistic is likely only relevant to where the underlying population is actually located. Various techniques can correct this and focus the map on the population location. CDRC Maps takes a clipping approach, where only areas occupied by buildings receive the colour of the choropleth. Dot density maps are

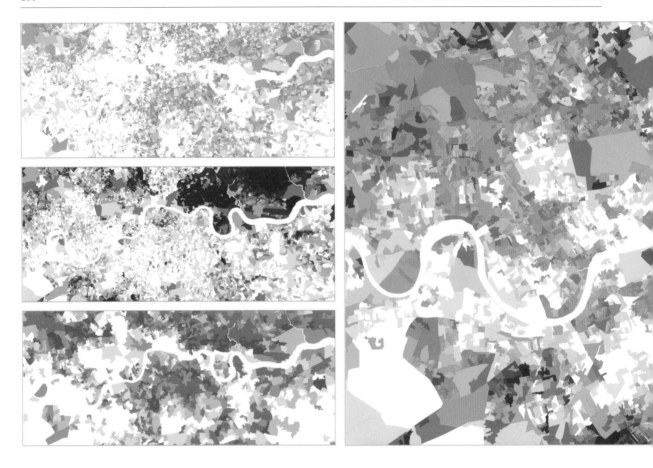

another technique; these assign population units to a random or weighted location within each statistical unit area. However, these maps are fundamentally different from choropleth maps and are more computationally intensive to produce and not as easily interpretable since they introduce a large degree of false precision.

An alternative approach, assuming that the statistical variation in the choropleth is shown by varying the hue and/or lightness, is to vary the other colour variable (saturation in the case of the HSL colour space described here). By fading the choropleth colour in sparsely populated areas, and oversaturating it in areas of relatively high population density, the eye is drawn naturally to the latter areas on the map, regardless of the other properties of the colour shown. An appropriate key showing the hue or lightness variations for different metric values, superimposed across a number of different saturations, can help emphasise this. Care should be taken however to ensure that large variations in saturation don't dominate the overall visual appearance of the map, at the expense of showing the variation in the main population metric that is being mapped. This technique is used in maps.cdrc.ac.uk/#/metrics/ruralurban/ where the hue shows the category of settlement classification – the main metric being mapped – and lightness is used to show the variation in population density.

Figure 10.4
Combining different hues to show relative high values of unemployment (green), South Asian ethnicity (purple) and deprivation (red) in central London, alongside the River Thames. The three hue-based maps (above left) are overlaid to show the three socioeconomic variables on the single map (above).

10.4
Conclusion

This chapter has demonstrated the progress made in using web maps to both communicate and provide access to large and complex datasets. As these data become more prevalent, and arguably complex, thanks to their generation in both the public and private sectors, so too must the maps continue to develop in order to keep pace. The chapter discusses a range of possible development areas, in particular for the visualisation of uncertainty and multiple variables. There is more work to do, but in the coming years further important technological innovations can be expected.

Further Reading

Jenks, G. F. (1967). The Data Model Concept in Statistical Mapping. International Yearbook of Cartography 7: 186–190.

11

Geotemporal Twitter Demographics

Alistair Leak and Guy Lansley

11.1
Introduction

The study and application of demographic data are widespread in both industry and academia, with applications ranging from demographic profiling to supply and demand modelling. Yet, while there exist numerous applications, in recent years demographics has seen few major developments. This may in part reflect continuing dependence on traditional population data, such as the UK Census of Population. Given these limitations, there is an increased interest in the potential of new forms of data such as are collected from online social networks or by utilities companies. Here, we demonstrate how, given sufficient consideration, Twitter data may be employed as an effective source of population insight.

Since their inception, geodemographics has evolved at a rapid pace seeking to describe the population in ever increasing levels of detail. While the earliest classifications, such as those of Charles Booth, depicted the population on a single ordinal scale, classifications have increasingly sought to split the population into ever more precise groups. In the UK, the ability to perform such nuanced classification has been facilitated by the regular collection of detailed population data which are made available in the public domain. A prime example of such data is the UK Census of Population. Collected on a decennial basis, the UK Census presents a snapshot of the UK population across a broad range of themes including employment, education and demographics. Using such data, analysts are able to partition the population into parsimonious groups which exhibit generally homogenous characteristics. Such classifications are, however, clearly not without significant limitations. These limitations include the regular adoption of a 'one size fits all applications' methodology, the focus on residential setting, the reliance upon infrequently published datasets and the 'black box' nature of many commercial products.

This said, it may be argued that the progress has been made in the commercial sectors, with private entities such as CACI Ltd and Experian Ltd incorporating multiple novel data sources into their classifications. As with any commercial classification, there are issues for academic users that centre upon transparency or reproducibility, as well as licencing and access arrangements.

The advent of social media and other new forms of data are now bringing focus to the creation of new demographic insight, and indeed this is a central motivation of the Consumer Data Research Centre (CDRC). The term 'new forms of data' is particularly broad and includes data ranging from those that are gleaned from social media, data that are published as open-data and data that are generated by consumer-facing organisations. In each case, the data offer a new and novel gateway through which human behaviour may be observed. However, such data are often beset with their own unique limitations. The OECD (2013) report 'New Data for Understanding the Human Condition' cites accessibility, provenance, permanence, comparability, legality, ethics, linkage and data structure as nascent concerns. On top of this, one must also be conscious of the representativeness of such data versus the population for which it is to be employed.

In this chapter, we focus on geo-tagged Tweets harvested in real-time via the Twitter online social network. Launched in 2006, Twitter has grown rapidly with an estimated 328 million active users.[1] Twitter enables users to post short 140 character messages which may contain URLs, pictures and personal or topical tags. Users are able to 'follow' the accounts of others as in most social networks, although there is no requirement for reciprocal connections. Further, where users so choose, a location may be recorded in the form of latitude and longitude. Beyond providing a social platform, Twitter makes user data generated by its service available to third parties via an Application Programming Interface (API). The API provides both free and paid-for options, though, for many applications, the free

Figure 11.1
Map showing a random sample of 1 million geo-tagged Tweets collected between December 2012 and January 2014. Each Tweet is depicted by a single blue point.

service is often sufficient. The availability of such data and the ease in which they may be accessed have led to an explosion in the publication of academic literature demonstrating the potential insight that may be drawn ranging in themes from crime and security to health and mobility. However, while significant volumes of literature have been published touting the potential of Twitter data, it is often the case that only lip service is paid to the limitations of the data source – specifically with respect to the demographic of those individuals who are users of the service versus those of the population at large. Unlike traditional demographic data, those individuals who are users of Twitter are a self-selecting sample which is further

limited to those who choose to disclose their location. While various anecdotal evidence exists in regards to the demographic bias present, there are limited means by which said bias may be quantified. The reason for this being that users of the service are not explicitly required to provide any identifying information as part of the registration process.

Given this lack of demographic specificity, it is necessary that key markers are modelled such that they may be assessed against existing data or be employed in the study of demographics. In seeking to achieve this goal, individual screen names may be employed in the interference of key demographic markers whilst the location information encoded within Tweets may be used to infer individuals' places of residence, work and travel. In the remainder of this chapter, we discuss how key demographic markers may be inferred based on the novel analysis of individuals' personal names, and how such insight may facilitate the establishment of the data's representativeness versus the usually resident population of the United Kingdom. The latter half of the chapter will develop a case study demonstrating the potential of demographically attributed Twitter data for the observation of stocks and flows of human populations, showcasing both the recreation of traditional demographic insight and also various new insight facilitated by the data's rich attribution.

11.2
Data

For this analysis, the dataset employed is a corpus of geo-tagged Tweets composed of 1.4 billion unique messages submitted between December 2012 and January 2014. Illustrated in Figure 11.1, the data are global in coverage, though, as may be observed, are clearly not consistent with the global distribution of population. The data were harvested in real-time using the Twitter Filtered Streaming API and stored within a PostgreSQL database. It should be noted that the free Streaming API is limited such that only data, equivalent to 1% of the total throughput at any given time, may be collected. While this may initially appear a limiting factor, in practice only around 1% of Tweets are attributed with location. Thus, it may be presumed that the majority of geo-tagged Tweets are successfully obtained. The representativeness of the sample stream versus the full stream, referred to as the 'Firehose', has previously been established by Morstatter et al (2013). While Morstatter et al confirmed the completeness of the geo-tagged Tweets, they also found that the non-spatial sample was not representative of the equivalent data from the Firehose.

11.2.1
Data enrichment

As previously noted, the raw Twitter data are devoid of any demographic markers necessitating that such attribution be modelled. The key to such inference is the assumption that individuals' personal names are a statement of aspects of their identities. Not only does an individual's name provide a means of identification, analysed in a suitable manner, a name may provide an indicator of gender, age and cultural, ethnic and linguistic identity. Such an approach is in effect the automation of the human process of social perception. Before these techniques may be applied, it is necessary that individuals' personal names are extracted. By default, users' screen names are a single character string with no defined structure. Individuals' name tokens are extracted based on the western-naming order in which forenames typically precede surnames. Individuals' forenames are employed in the inference of their ages and genders using a forenames database built from birth certificate records and consumer data (see Lansley and Longley, 2016a). Further, individuals' full names are processed using the Onomap (www. onomap.org) classification tool for the inference of their ethnicities. Note that prior to the application of the various heuristics, it is necessary that the nationality of those users being analysed is determined. While the association between names, genders and ethnicities is relatively stable, the association between names and ages tend to exhibit national tendencies. We determine individuals' nationalities and regions of residence based on the analysis of the location inherent in each user's Tweets. The rule applied to assigning nationality is that a user must have 50% of their total Tweets and five or more Tweets in the area to which they are assigned. The key premise in such an analysis is that an individual will tweet most frequently within the region and country with which they are likely resident.

In the UK, this approach results in 273,000 Twitter users being identified as being residents.

11.3
Benchmarking

Prior to performing any analysis, it is imperative that the nature of the sample being studied is understood. Such consideration, given existing anecdotal evidence, suggests that demographic bias in the Twitter data will be particularly important where the phenomenon being studied bears an identifiable correspondence with age, gender or ethnicity. For example, in the UK, political views are known to relate to age with younger people having a greater affinity to Labour and those who are older leaning towards the Conservative party. Given that the Twitter users are

believed to generally be younger, this may lead to a left-wing bias being present in any data being analysed. Failure to account for such bias may adversely affect interpretation and, by effect, the conclusions drawn. In possession of demographically attributed data, however, it is possible that an assessment of the data's representativeness may be obtained. In the following, benchmarking of age, gender, ethnicity and geographic distribution are reported.

For the purpose of benchmarking, two reference datasets are employed: the 2013 Consumer Register produced by CACI Ltd and the 2011 UK Census of Population. The Consumer Register is an augmented version of the publicly available Electoral Register which substitutes names from other commercial sources.

Figure 11.2
Population pyramid of Twitter users in the UK versus the equivalent Office for National Statistics data for 2011. The ONS data are illustrated in grey.

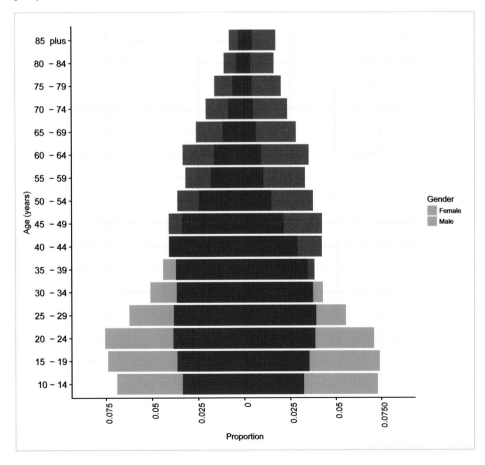

Ethnicity Group	Twitter %	Consumer Register %	Quotient
White – All – Gypsy- Traveller – Irish Traveller	93.36	87.20	1.07
Asian – Asian British – Indian	1.36	2.30	0.59
Asian – Asian British – Pakistani	1.11	1.90	0.58
Black – African – Caribbean – Black British	0.75	3.00	0.25
Asian – Asian British – Other Asian	0.77	1.40	0.55
Asian – Asian British – Bangladeshi	0.23	0.70	0.33
Asian – Asian British – Chinese	0.54	0.70	0.77
Mixed – Multiple Ethnic Groups	0.0006	2.00	0.00
Other Ethnic Groups	1.88	0.90	2.09

11.3.1
Age and gender

As a first step in understanding the demographic composition of users, a comparison is performed between the age and gender of Twitter users as determined by the forenames database (as described in Lansley and Longley, 2016a) and the equivalent data from the 2011 UK Census of Population.

The population pyramid shown in Figure 11.2 confirms the anecdotal belief that Twitter is predominantly used by a younger proportion of the population. However, having differentiated the data by gender it is evident that differences exist. While female users are more prevalent in the 10 to 19 bands, males become increasingly dominant beyond this age. Beyond the 20 -24 age bracket, the proportion of male users increases significantly suggesting that it is older males who have chosen to adopt the platform.

11.3.2
Ethnicity

As with age and gender, it is well recognised that ethnicity may play a role in individuals' social attitudes, health and wellbeing. In seeking to quantify the degree to which each ethnic group is represented, we applied the Onomap tool to both the UK Twitter population inventory and likewise

to the 2013 Consumer Register. The decision to benchmark against the Consumer Register as opposed to the 2011 Census was designed to minimise the impact of bias/ uncertainty in ethnic classification that may be manifest within the Onomap classification tool.

Table 11.1 presents a comparison between the ethnic composition of Twitter and the Consumer Register as estimated by Onomap. This highlights population segments in which Twitter users are likely to be more or less well represented relative to the usual resident population of the UK. Clearly evident is that the combined White Group is over-represented whilst the Asian and Black groups are systematically under-represented. The Mixed group (arguably the hardest to identify using our chosen data classification techniques) is the most under-represented. Thus, in seeking to draw general inference regarding population behaviour based on Twitter it must be recognised that the minority groups are likely to be under-represented within the sample.

11.3.3
Geographic distribution

Geographic distribution is examined using the Location Quotient (LQ) measure. The LQ may be considered as the quotient of the proportion of Twitter users in a specific geographic area versus the corresponding

Table 11.1
Ethnicity breakdown comparison between the UK Twitter population and the 2013 Consumer Register. The quotient indicates the relative difference between the expected and observed ethnicity proportions.

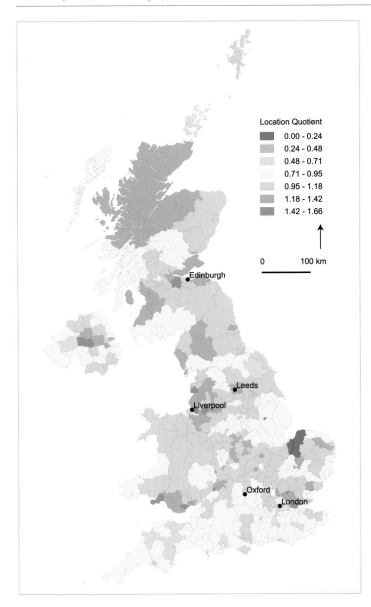

Figure 11.3
Location Quotient map
showing the geographic
distribution of Twitter
users in the UK versus
the resident population.

proportion of the observable population to be resident in the same region. A value of 1.0 indicates the expected proportion of the population. A value of < 1.0 indicates fewer Twitter users than expected and a value of >1.0 indicates a greater than expected volume of Twitter users.

Figure 11.3 illustrates the difference in the observed versus expected Twitter population at local authority and district level in the UK. Clearly evident is a south to north progression with Scotland exhibiting the highest proportion of Twitter users relative to the normally residential population. A second trend is the high proportions in areas which have large student populations. An example of such an area is Swansea in the south of Wales. While not discussed here, it must be recognised that the uptake of Twitter varies on a global scale within and between countries.

11.3.4
Demographic summary

Through the application of a range of novel data mining techniques the data collected via Twitter have been significantly enriched. In possession of such knowledge, it becomes increasingly possible that Twitter may be employed in the observation and modelling of the stocks and flows of population. The key considerations which must be recognised is the importance of performing analysis in a data rich environment and second, that suitable consideration must be given to the unit and scale of analysis. Concerning the first point, where possible, all data by users within the study areas should be sourced. Such data facilitate the identification of critical attribution concerning nationality and region of residence. Concerning the second point, it is important to consider whether one wishes to analyse either the Tweet or the user. For example, when analysing sentiment, we clearly want to examine individuals' Tweets in time and space. Conversely, when performing an

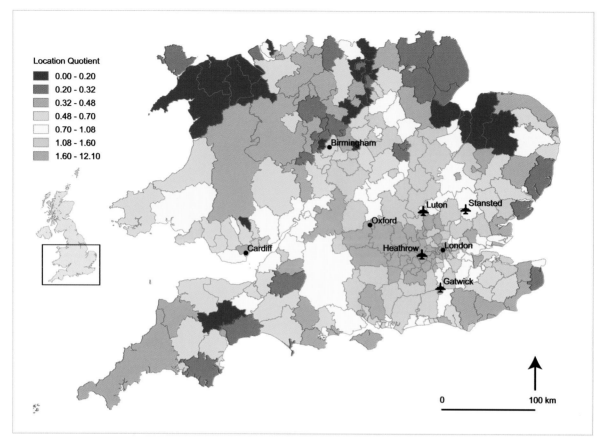

Figure 11.4
Map showing the LQ of residential locations of those UK-based Twitter users observed within the Heathrow extent.

assessment of demographics structure, we need to focus on individual users. Failure to consider the appropriate unit of analysis can result in the generation of invalid results or distorts insight.

11.4
Application

Having established a means by which the representativeness of Twitter data may be ascertained, the focus is shifted to that of applications. Applications are considered here in two parts: the recreation of conventional population insight using the demographically attributed Twitter data and second, new insight not previously possible. We demonstrate the identification of airport catchments based on the analysis of Tweets and also the potential of text-based mining as a means to draw out previously unobtainable insight. In both cases, the analysis is performed using data collected from London's Heathrow Airport. The largest of London's six airports, Heathrow handled 72 million passengers in 2013. There are various motivations for understanding the behaviour of those individuals travelling through the airport. At the national scale there is a desire to understand the functional catchments of the airport and at the local level there is a need to understand how people move within the airport complex. Traditionally, such analysis has been performed using a selection of manual counting and survey techniques; however, such techniques are often expensive or laborious. Further, much of the data collected are unavailable in the public domain. Here, we demonstrate how such insight may be generated at zero cost in a manner that may be readily applied in a range of other contexts.

11.4.1
Airport catchments

Typically, an airport catchment comprises the region from within which the majority of domestic travellers originate from. Various approaches exist to the identification of such regions ranging from the collection of passenger surveys to the modelling of activity based on probable travel time. In the first instance, there is a requirement to perform large-scale surveys; in the second, the analysis is based on assumption rather than observation of existing behaviour. Here, we seek to replicate the approach based on passenger surveys; however, we recreate the analysis using solely spatial Tweets by those individuals recorded within the Heathrow Airport extent. We identify the probable residential location of the UK users that use the Twitter service within the airport.

Figure 11.4 highlights the functional catchment of Heathrow Airport based solely on those Twitter users identified within the Heathrow extent. Around Heathrow a clear pattern may be observed permeating out from the airport. While shown for Heathrow, it is important in such analysis to consider the interaction between other airports. This could potentially be examined. Such approaches are not without their own limitations. Of particular note is the challenge of differentiating between those individuals who are employed within the airport and those who are travelling. However, while these limitations exist, the benefits of such an approach far exceed the drawbacks.

11.4.2
Text mining

While the first application demonstrated the recreation of traditional demographic analysis, this exploits just some of the Twitter data's facets. Beyond space and time, a key feature of the data is the availability of rich textual content. It is possible to harness useful spatio-temporal information from the contents of Twitter posts on a very large scale using text mining techniques. Spatial and temporal trends in what is tweeted about within a given location could also be informative for local service planners and the marketing industry. In the context of Heathrow, the quantitative analysis of social media data could be used to track complaints and disruptions, and harvest users' interests to improve their service delivery and dynamic advertising portfolios. Following a methodology outlined in Lansley and Longley (2016b), we will use an unsupervised model to segment the textual data into distinctive topics and observe key trends.

The content of Twitter data is notoriously difficult to quantify due to the short length of documents and use of informal language (Andrienko et al, 2013). Consequently, there have been relatively few attempts to generate the typical trends in social media usage for a given time and location. Most textual work has focused on unusual events, often utilising given lists of key words or methods that detect anomalies (e.g. Chae et al, 2012). However, as demonstrated above and in our own previous research, with appropriate data cleaning techniques it is possible to identify 'typical' topics from large samples of Tweets (Lansley and Longley, 2016b). Lansley and Longley modelled Tweets from an extensive area with the intention of identifying the 'typical' geography of topics across the given urban extent, in that case, Inner London. Each of the topics were distinctive in terms of content, and most also conveyed temporal or spatial patterns across the city; often these trends could be linked to known activities. However, this study will focus exclusively on Tweets from Heathrow Airport. Therefore, the popular topics devised by the model will be particular to the individuals passing through Heathrow and their activities.

	Topic	Frequency	Percentage
1	Destinations	3,547	8.03
2	Anger	5,183	11.73
3	Thoughts	3,597	8.14
4	Anticipation	5,031	11.39
5	Conversations	3,951	8.94
6	England	5,792	13.11
7	Travel	5,779	13.08
8	Consumers	2,975	6.73
9	Media	3,021	6.84
10	Other	5,312	12.02

Table 11.2
Frequencies of Tweets by topic as determined in the LDA analysis.

Using the same sample of Tweets from Heathrow as described in the preceding sections, the Tweet messages were first cleaned in order to ensure the topic model returned valid and coherent segmentations of documents. We removed duplicated Tweets under the assumption that these rarely reflect original content, also often these can be automatically generated messages. We then removed stop words, punctuation and non-Latin characters. We also removed very short Tweets with less than three words as it would be difficult to generate significant topics from very short documents. It was also necessary to remove all Tweets with uncertain coordinates. Following the data cleaning, 48,188 of the original 56,417 Tweets from Heathrow were deemed to be appropriate for topic modelling. We used Latent Dirichlet Allocation (LDA) to generate probabilistic topics from the Twitter documents. LDA creates semantic groups from large collections of documents (Blei et al, 2003). Each word (or value) is assigned a score for each topic. It is, therefore, possible to view the topics for each Tweet by looking up the scores for each of their words.

Although LDA is an unsupervised model, the researcher does need to select the number of topics (k) to be generated (see Table 11.2). As this study is intended to demonstrate the utility of topic modelling Tweets, we have produced just 10 groups.

Of course, a higher number would allow more specific and intricate topics to be generated, although these would represent fewer Tweets. The results of the model were then appended to each Tweet in the data so we could detect trends. In this case, we simply allocated each Tweet to its most probable topic based on its total probability scores. The group sizes are relatively well balanced; the smallest group represents over 6.7% of all the Tweets in our final sample.

The topics are presented as a word cloud in Figure 11.5. Only the most common words from the Tweets are shown, which have been partitioned by the topics they are most commonly found in. Labels have been given to each of the topics and were manually derived from interpreting the top words and via observing a random selection of Tweets. Each of the topics is sufficiently distinctive. Whilst a small number of topics are perhaps typical of general social media usage in the UK, many of the topics are probably particular to airport activities. The group labelled *Travel* predominantly describes travelling. These messages range from complaints about queues and delays within the airport to flights and transport links to central London. The *England* topic contains many messages about people saying their farewells to the country, notably including complaints about the English weather. The group also includes comments from those who have arrived at the airport, both

Figure 11.5
Comparative word cloud illustrating the most common terms observed in each of the 10 groups.

tourists looking forward to their holiday and people happy to return home. The topic we labelled *Consumers* largely represents comments about retail and hospitality services; it is probable that a substantial proportion of these messages refer to purchases within the departure lounges. Lastly, the *Other* group comprises Tweets that could not be allocated into the other categories; almost all of the Tweets from this group are written in foreign languages. With more data, it would be viable to split these groups into unique subgroups.

It is also possible that each of the groups has distinctive temporal and spatial patterns, and these may resonate more so in groups that describe particular activities that are usually restricted to particular routines or locations. For example, the

Tweets in the *Consumers* topic are more likely to be found in locations across Heathrow where the services are provided. Figure 11.6 illustrates the distribution of the *Consumers* Tweets (red) and the rest of the Tweets from the sample (blue). It can be observed that Tweets from the *Consumers* topic are very densely concentrated between a handful of locations across the site. These are departure and arrivals lounges where retail and catering facilities are located which correspond with much of the activities discussed.

The classification we present here is fairly rudimentary as it was built with a relatively small number of Tweets and was restricted to just 10 topics. However, it is a valid demonstration of the types of trends that can be determined from unstructured

social media data. It is also inferred that what is spoken about on social media can often be associated with activities that may have distinctive geographies. Therefore, it is possible that harnessing Twitter data can be useful in identifying activity trends across time and space. These can range from unusual delays to feedback on retail offerings. Looking forwards, analysts can use the probability scores for our database of words to model future data into the pre-existing topic categories in order to identify trends on the fly.

11.5
Conclusion

At the outset, the objective of this chapter was to showcase the potential of Twitter data in the study of demography and

highlight key considerations for the effective use of such data as part of the analysis process. It has been demonstrated how, through the novel analysis of personal names, key identity markers may be inferred and, subsequently, how such data may facilitate the assessment of representativeness. Using said data, it has been possible to estimate the degree to which Twitter is representative of the UK's residential population.

Beyond illustrating potential techniques for data enrichment, we have sought to showcase the potential of Twitter in the study of demography. Using the example of London Heathrow Airport, it has been shown how one may recreate conventional forms of analysis and, further, how the richness of the data may be exploited

Figure 11.6
Map of Heathrow Airport showing the distribution of Tweets relating to consumer activity (red) versus all Tweets submitted within the airport extent. Basemap supplied by Stamen.

to extract levels of insight that previously would have been unobtainable. In particular, we have demonstrated the use of text mining as a means to exploit the textual content of the Tweets. In appreciating the above, it must be recognised that the methods employed are both repeatable and transferable. Further, unlike many different new forms of data, the ease with which the raw data may be sourced makes Twitter data the ideal starting point for the development and presentation of novel population insight.

However, for the effective use of Twitter data in the generation of actionable population insight it is necessary that the analyst remains conscious of the limitations manifest within the data. In particular, one must consider the population for whom the data are representative and, arguably more importantly, for whom they are not. We may thus conclude on a positive note. While the demographic insight generated from Twitter is by no means a perfect replacement for conventional data and methods, it does provide an exciting insight into the future of demography and population studies.

Further Reading

Andrienko, G., Andrienko, N., Bosch, H., Ertl, T., Fuchs, G., Jankowski, P. and Thom, D. (2013). Thematic patterns in georeferenced tweets through space-time visual analytics. *Computing in Science & Engineering*, 15(3), 72–82.

Blei, D. M., Ng, A. Y. and Jordan, M. I. (2003). Latent Dirichlet Allocation. *Journal of Machine Learning Research*, 3(Jan), 993–1022.

Chae, J., Thom, D., Bosch, H., Jang, Y., Maciejewski, R., Ebert, D. S. and Ertl, T. (2012), October. Spatiotemporal social media analytics for abnormal event detection and examination using seasonal-trend decomposition. In *Visual Analytics Science and Technology (VAST), 2012 IEEE Conference on* (pp. 143–152). IEEE.

Global Science Forum (2013). New Data for Understanding the Human Condition: International Perspectives: OECD Global Science Forum Report on Data and Research Infrastructure for the Social Sciences.

Lansley, G. and Longley, P. (2016a). Deriving age and gender from forenames for consumer analytics. *Journal of Retailing and Consumer Services*, 30, 271–278.

Lansley, G. and Longley, P. (2016b). The geography of Twitter topics in London. *Computers, Environment and Urban Systems*, 58, 85–96.

Morstatter, F., Pfeffer, J., Liu, H. and Carley, K. M. (2013), June. Is the sample good enough? Comparing data from Twitter's Streaming API with Twitter's Firehose. In *Proceedings of the 7th International Conference on Weblogs and Social Media*, ICWSM 2013.

Acknowledgements

The first author would like to thank the Defence Science and Technology Laboratory (DSTL) for supporting this research (DSTL Grant No. 12/13NatPhD_61).

Note

1. An active user is considered as an individual who has used the service at least once in the preceding month. Statistic accessed via Statistica for Q1 2017.

12

Developing Indicators for Measuring Health-Related Features of Neighbourhoods

Konstantinos Daras, Alec Davies, Mark A Green and Alex Singleton

12.1
Introduction

Geographical inequalities in health outcomes have long been observed. For example, in 1842 social reformer Edwin Chadwick identified that male life expectancy of labourers (i.e. low occupational group) in Rutland (38) was higher than that of professional tradesmen (high occupational group) in Liverpool (35). Fast forward 175 years and male life expectancy in Rutland is 81.4 compared to 76.4 in Liverpool. These spatial patterns peaked interest into the extent that living in particular locations influence our health. The differences that Chadwick observed were due to urban-rural disparities, such as the presence of slum housing, outbreaks of infectious diseases and overall air quality. Today, many of these issues are no longer present and the environments we live in are very different. Therefore, it is important to be able to measure certain features of neighbourhoods and to be able to answer questions about whether they are important for our health or not.

This study details the creation of a series of national open source low-level geographical measures of accessibility to health-related features of the environment. There are three main domains across the indicators: the retail environment, the provision of health care and the physical environment.

12.2
Retail environment

Unhealthy foods, smoking and alcohol misuse represent important determinants for ill health. A common shared feature across each of these very different harms is that they each require purchasing from retail outlets. As such, our opportunities to consume such items may be shaped by the built environment surrounding us. Accessibility to retail outlets selling these products is therefore of interest for understanding whether they influence (and how much) our way of consuming such items.

We developed indicators of accessibility to 'fast food outlets', 'pubs, bars and nightclubs', 'off-licences' and 'tobacconists'. Fast food outlets typically sell foods that are energy dense and nutritionally poor, and the consumption of such foods are associated with increased risk of obesity. We have two measures of accessibility to alcohol. Pubs, bars and nightclubs represent outlets that sell alcohol on-trade (i.e. alcohol is purchased and consumed on site) and off-licences are stores that primarily sell alcohol as off-trade (i.e. alcohol is purchased on site but consumed off site). These have different harms, with access to on-trade outlets typically associated with acute alcohol-related harms and off-trade outlets with chronic harms. Finally, tobacconists are specialist stores which sell primarily tobacco-related products such as cigarettes, cigars and loose form tobacco.

We also include access to 'gambling outlets'. These represent slightly different harms compared to our other indicators. Gambling outlets represent the potential for economic losses which are indirectly related to health. Individuals who use them have also been shown to be associated with poorer mental health.

Local governments in the UK (and beyond) have sought to regulate aspects of the built environment in attempts to address the access and supply of unhealthy amenities. Planning regulations have been introduced to limit the density of fast food outlets, pubs/bars and off-licences. There is also similar interest in reducing access to gambling outlets. Therefore, the interest in such metrics is not purely academic, but has important policy relevance.

12.3
Provision of health care

Health care services provide important point of care amenities for the diagnosis, treatment and maintenance of health. One of the founding principles of the UK's National Health Service (NHS) was that the provision of these services should be made available to all. One area of interest in implementing such a policy has been the equitable access to services with the aim of minimising geographical barriers. However, health services are not always equally spread throughout the population and there has been considerable interest in whether geographical barriers prevent the utilisation of such services.

We include measures of accessibility to features of primary and secondary health care. These include 'General Practices (GPs)' which are the first point of care for patients, 'pharmacies' which sell medicines, 'dentists' which provide oral health care, and finally 'hospitals with accident and emergency (A&E) departments' which provide more serious care. We also include accessibility to leisure services that while they are not health services, offer individuals the opportunity to exercise, which is important for promoting healthy lifestyles.

12.4
Physical environment

There has been longer interest in understanding how features of the physical environment impact health compared to other domains. We focus on two important aspects of the physical domain: green space and air quality.

Green space refers to areas of natural environments including grassland, woodland, parks and other areas of vegetation. It has been demonstrated to be an important determinant of physical and mental health. Parks offer opportunities for physical activity, as well as social interactions with friends and family. Individuals residing in 'greener' environments also tend to have improved mental wellbeing.

Air quality is an important determinant of respiratory health and is viewed as one of the most important determinants of ill health globally. Ideally air should be clean and free of pollutants to allow healthy respiration; however this is often not the case. Levels of air pollution receive extensive policy interest particularly in urban areas with busy road networks, airports and industry. We focus on levels of three important pollutants which have each been independently shown to be associated with health outcomes: Particulate Matter (PM_{10}), Sulphur Dioxide (SO_2) and Nitrogen Dioxide (NO_2).

12.5
Opening up data

It is clear that geographic context matters for both understanding health patterns and for delivering policy strategies aimed at improving health. However, there are several issues that have limited our ability to measure these features. Firstly, processing these data types at low spatial resolutions requires heavy data manipulation. Researchers and policy officials often don't have the expertise available to them to process such data readily. Secondly, accessibility to these data can be restricted and often consumer data on retail outlets are either not available or must be paid for. Finally, where these previous issues have been overcome, data are often not available for all locations at a small spatial scale. The majority of studies that have explored the role of these environmental features have been undertaken in local contexts that may not be generalisable to the national level. Where they are available at the national level, this is often only for large geographical zones, which are not always useful. Our project aims to open up geographic data on health indicators at a low-level spatial resolution for Great Britain that will address each of these barriers.

We also build on prior research using these health indicators to develop a new descriptive tool. One limitation common to the majority of research investigating the

role of environmental factors on health is that they are often considered in isolation. However, this is a false representation of reality as they each co-exist and interact. Developing indicators to measure the multidimensional features for how geography may influence health is important for informing future research and policy applications. Similar approaches have been useful for measuring poverty and deprivation (e.g. the Index of Multiple Deprivation).

12.6
Methodology

Firstly, we acquired data on the retail environment. Data on about half a million retail businesses throughout Great Britain were provided by the Local Data Company (LDC)[1] using the Consumer Data Research Centre (CDRC) services. The LDC dataset aims to include records for every operating retail business including a hierarchical classification of retail types (39 categories and 370 subcategories) and the address of the store. We used this dataset as it is regularly updated and therefore more accurate compared to other common sources (e.g. Ordnance Survey's Points of Interest database) used for measuring neighbourhood features. Table 12.1 presents the categories selected for developing the retail environment indicators, including the number of retail businesses assigned to each category.

Our health services domain integrated data from multiple sources, including openly available data on the location of health services (GP practices, hospitals with A&E departments, pharmacies and dentists) from NHS Digital[2] (England and Wales); and the Information Services Division (ISD)[3] in NHS Scotland. These data were supplemented with the location of leisure sport centres from the LDC data.

Finally, in order to provide context to the physical environment, we integrated two sources of data. As a measure of air quality,

Indicator	LDC Category / Subcategory	Business Addresses
Accessibility to Fast Food outlets	Chinese Fast Food Takeaway	2,855
	Fast Food Delivery	1,049
	Fast Food Takeaway	11,115
	Fish & Chip Shops	3,829
	Indian Takeaway	1,256
	Pizza Takeaway	2,835
	Sandwich Delivery Service	342
	Take Away Food Shops	8,449
Accessibility to Gambling outlets	Casino Clubs	156
	Bookmakers	8,379
Accessibility to Off-licences	Off Licences	2,770
Accessibility to Tobacconists	Tobacconists	1,948
Accessibility to Pubs, bars and nightclubs	Night Clubs	1,172
	Bars	4,520
	Public Houses & Inns	18,775

we used modelled estimates from Department for Environment, Food and Rural Affairs (DEFRA) for a series of air pollutants with known health implications (NO_2, PM_{10} and SO_2). The air pollution data are modelled under DEFRA's Modelling of Ambient Air Quality contract to provide policy support and are created at a 1x1 km resolution. Model estimates are derived from a mixture of data collected from monitoring sites and estimated levels based on the location of industry and road networks. Additionally, we acquired information on 'green' spaces available for use by the public from the Open Street Map (OSM) through selecting areas with the following tags: cemetery, common, dog park, scrub, fell, forest, garden, greenfield, golf course, grass, grassland, heath, meadow, nature reserve, orchard, park, pitch, recreation ground, village green, vineyard and wood. Accessibility to each of our indicators (other than the indicators of physical environment domain) were created using the Routino[4] open source software. Routino is an application for finding a route between two points using the OSM road network, and takes into account

restrictions on roads as well as tagged speed limits and barriers. We measured the network distance between the centroid of each postcode in the National Statistics Postcode Lookup (NSPL) (a database containing all postcodes for Great Britain) and the coordinates of the nearest service (e.g. a postcode centroid for GP practice). However, the overall process for calculating network distances for about 2 million postcodes in Great Britain is CPU-intensive and the Routino tool computes distances sequentially. To address both these issues, we implemented a parallelisation framework using 10 Docker[5] containers that run Routino instances in parallel for subsets of 200,000 GB postcodes. In this way, we achieved a significant decrease in processing time from roughly eight days to about eight hours per indicator!

The indicators for the physical environment domain required a different approach. For measuring access to green space, we defined accessibility as a measure of the overall area of green space available to each postcode that falls within a 900 metres buffer zone. We selected this

Table 12.1
LDC categories and subcategories selected for each indicator of the Retail environment domain.

Domain	Indicator	Health promoting	
		Low value	High value
Retail Environment	Accessibility to Fast food outlets	-	+
	Accessibility to Gambling outlets	-	+
	Accessibility to Off-licences	-	+
	Accessibility to Tobacconists	-	+
	Accessibility to Pubs, bars and nightclubs	-	+
Health Services	Accessibility to GP practices	+	-
	Accessibility to A&E hospitals	+	-
	Accessibility to Pharmacies	+	-
	Accessibility to Dentist practices	+	-
	Accessibility to Leisure services	+	-
Physical Environment	Accessibility to Green spaces	-	+
	Nitrogen Dioxide (NO_2)	+	-
	PM_{10} Particles	+	-
	Sulphur Dioxide (SO_2)	+	-

Table 12.2
Indicator weights and direction for each indicator of the Access to Healthy Assets and Hazards (AHAH) index.

measure following the recommendation of the European Environment Agency which argues that each person should have access to green space no further than 900 metres (or a 15 min walk) from their home (Stanners and Bourdeau, 1995). We additionally performed sensitivity testing of additional buffer sizes; however the results did not significantly alter. We did not measure access to our air pollution measures but used their modelled values from DEFRA and aggregated them at the LSOA level.

Measured network distances for each indicator were aggregated from postcode into an aggregate geography. For England and Wales, these were Lower Super Output Area (LSOA), and in Scotland, Data Zones. We selected these geographies since they are relatively small zones which are regularly used in research, local government or health, and could be easily aggregated to other statistical geographies if required. To give an idea of scale, LSOAs contain a mean population size of 1,500 people with a minimum of 1,000 and maximum of 3,000 people per LSOA. For Scotland, we used 'Data Zones', which are the equivalent geographical scale

(we refer to these as LSOAs for simplicity in the rest of the chapter) although they are slightly smaller with population sizes between 500 and 1,000 people.

Each indicator was then individually standardised by ranking LSOAs from best to worst. The direction of each variable was dictated by the literature (e.g. accessibility to fast food outlets were identified as health negating, whereas accessibility to GP practices were health promoting; see Table 12.2). Each variable was then transformed to the standard normal distribution. The indicators within each domain were combined with equal weights forming an overall domain score. We chose to equally weight each indicator since there was no clear justification for different weightings, which otherwise would emphasise the relative importance of the composite score versus those others considered.

To calculate our overall index (and domain-specific values), we followed an aspect of the methodology from the 2015 English Index of Multiple Deprivation (Smith et al, 2015). We ranked each domain R and scaled it to the range [0,1]. R=1/N was defined as

Domain	Indicator	Great Britain - LSOAs			England - LSOAs			
		All	Urban	Rural	All	Urban	Rural	
Retail Environment	Accessibility to Fast Food outlets (km)	1.30	1.08	7.41	1.22	1.03	5.36	
	Accessibility to Gambling outlets (km)	1.21	1.02	5.85	1.19	1.02	5.98	
	Accessibility to Off-licences (km)	2.58	2.02	9.55	2.24	1.85	8.34	
	Accessibility to Tobacconists (km)	3.08	2.48	10.90	2.89	2.43	10.01	
	Accessibility to Pubs, bars and nightclubs (km)	1.12	0.96	3.70	1.03	0.92	3.24	
Health Services	Accessibility to GP practices (km)	1.05	0.93	2.92	0.99	0.89	3.02	
	Accessibility to A&E hospitals (km)	7.45	6.06	18.61	7.12	6.04	17.62	
	Accessibility to Pharmacies (km)	0.85	0.77	2.25	0.83	0.76	2.70	
	Accessibility to Dentist practices (km)	1.05	0.92	3.65	1.00	0.90	3.78	
	Accessibility to Leisure services (km)	2.45	1.98	8.92	2.23	1.88	8.09	
Physical Environment	Accessibility to Green spaces (km^2)	0.55	0.58	0.42	0.53	0.56	0.37	
	Nitrogen Dioxide (NO_2) ($\mu g\ m^{-3}$)	10.60	11.55	7.23	11.44	12.20	8.23	
	PM_{10} Particles ($\mu g\ m^{-3}$)	12.74	12.99	11.76	13.36	13.48	12.82	
	Sulphur Dioxide (SO_2) ($\mu g\ m{-3}$)	1.15	1.19	0.97	1.21	1.23	1.07	

Table 12.3
Median values of each indicator for LSOAs by urban/rural status.

the most 'health promoting' LSOA and R=N/N for the least promoting (N is the number of LSOAs in Great Britain). Exponential transformation of the ranked domain scores was then applied to LSOA values to reduce '*cancellation effects*' (Smith et al, 2015). So, for example, high levels of accessibility in one domain are not completely cancelled out by low levels of accessibility in a different domain. The exponential transformation applied also puts more emphasis on the LSOAs at the end of the health demoting side of the distribution and so facilitates identification of the neighbourhoods with the worst health promoting aspects. The exponential transformed indicator score X is given by:

$$X = -\,23\,ln\,(1-\,R(1-\,exp^{-100/23}))$$

where 'ln' denotes natural logarithm and 'exp' the exponential transformation.

The main domains across our indicators: retail environment, health services and the physical environment then were combined to form an overall index of 'Access to Healthy Assets & Hazards' (AHAH).

12.7
Results

Table 12.3 presents descriptive statistics for each of our indicators. These reveal for the first time low-level differences in access to various health-related features for the whole of Great Britain. Many features of the retail environment are located on average within less than 1.5 km of the population. Pubs, bars and nightclubs were the most accessible. This was followed by gambling and fast food outlets which both demonstrated high accessibility. Off-licences and tobacconists were the least accessible premises in the retail environment, particularly in Scotland

	Scotland - LSOAs			Wales - LSOAs		
	All	Urban	Rural	All	Urban	Rural
	1.63	1.25	5.83	2.14	1.55	6.68
	1.26	0.99	4.73	1.57	1.21	6.59
	4.89	3.14	14.25	6.61	3.86	13.15
	4.08	2.69	15.19	4.61	2.98	12.74
	1.64	1.29	5.57	1.48	1.15	4.60
	1.32	1.16	2.57	1.23	1.06	2.99
	8.66	5.64	22.00	12.15	9.51	20.20
	0.93	0.82	1.49	1.05	0.89	2.04
	1.20	1.00	2.99	1.40	1.18	4.14
	3.45	2.46	12.37	5.25	3.23	12.34
	0.66	0.68	0.59	0.48	0.48	0.47
	7.18	8.44	4.27	7.31	8.26	4.73
	9.02	9.18	8.34	11.43	11.75	10.17
	0.76	0.80	0.61	1.32	1.41	1.00

and Wales. Each of these services were more accessible in urban compared to rural areas, partly as these amenities cluster within settings where there are greater populations and demand. Pubs, bars and nightclubs had the smallest difference between urban and rural areas, with each of the other amenities fairly uncommon in rural areas.

Each of the primary health services (GPs, dentists and pharmacies) demonstrated high access and were more accessible than any feature of the retail environment. While access in rural areas was poorer than urban areas, average distances were not large. Access to hospitals with A&E departments was poor in rural areas of Great Britain, and they were the least accessible of any of our indicators. In particular, the Scottish and the Welsh population in rural areas had to travel an extra 3-5 kilometres to get access to an A&E hospital.

Finally, each of our measures of the physical environment promoted healthier locations in rural versus urban areas. This makes sense since the main sources of pollution (e.g. industrial sites) are located in urban areas, and rural areas are 'greener'. In Scotland and Wales physical environment indicators such as the NO_2 and the PM_{10} show a less polluted environment compared to the indicators of England (Table 12.3). We next mapped each of the domain scores and explored their geographic distributions (Figure 12.1). The physical environment domain (Figure 12.1a) demonstrates better physical environments in rural areas (as supported by Table 12.3). There are vast expanses of areas grouped in the 'best' quintile across Scotland, Cumbria and North Yorkshire, Wales, Devon and Cornwall. Smaller areas can also be detected on the map representing the locations of national parks, such as the Peak District or the South Downs, which vividly stick out from the surrounding urbanised areas which perform poorly. Considering the domain indicators, this is to be expected as these areas feature both good accessibility to green spaces whilst also having legislation against development protecting these areas from the pollution associated with urbanisation.

The worse locations identified through our physical environment domain are clearly outlined urban areas. The largest expanse tracks from Humberside and follows the M1 motorway past Doncaster and Sheffield to Nottingham. This M1 corridor features a large number of power stations alongside large industrial sites. Other industrialised areas can be clearly picked out, such as Newcastle, Liverpool, Manchester and Leeds. Birmingham and London are the two largest conurbations with poorest physical environments outside of the expanse in the East Midlands, and Southampton is another clearly defined area. A more rural area that exhibits a poor environment is that encompassing Boston and Peterborough around the Wash, where land use is predominantly large-scale agriculture. Although this area features

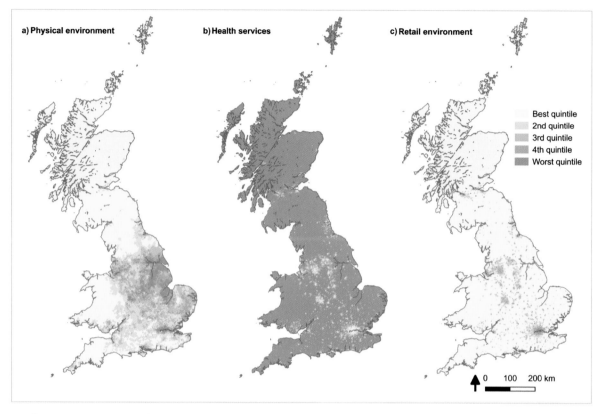

a) Physical environment   b) Health services   c) Retail environment

Best quintile
2nd quintile
3rd quintile
4th quintile
Worst quintile

0   100   200 km

Figure 12.1
Quintiles of accessibility in GB: a) Physical environment domain, b) Health services domain, c) Retail environment domain.

good green space accessibility it also has high scores for the indicators of SO_2 and PM_{10} from the farming process.

The health services domain (Figure 12.1.b) has a contrasting pattern to that seen in the physical environment (Figure 12.1.a). Rural areas have poorer accessibility to health services than urban areas (as shown in Table 12.3). Urban areas are more clearly defined in Figure 12.1.b, which is expected due to the distinct differences in infrastructure provision and population density. Plotting quintiles hides some variation between areas particularly in rural areas where remote regions in Wales and Scotland have very poor access to health services.

The retail services domain is very similar to the health domain, with urban areas once again clearly defined. Though the relationships are reversed, urban areas have higher accessibility to health negating retail features in contrast to health services. On the contrary, rural areas have poorer access to these retail outlets in comparison with urban areas.

Figure 12.2 shows our overall index of 'Access to Healthy Assets & Hazards' (AHAH). The figure shows that the most remote rural areas are identified as 'unhealthy' areas in terms of accessibility in our measure. While they typically performed well on our physical environment and retail domains (although not always, e.g. Lincolnshire), they perform poorly on accessibility to health services, due to their remoteness and being sparsely populated. By contrast, most urban cores of cities such as central London, central Birmingham, and the city centres of areas such as Liverpool, Leeds and Manchester also perform poorly on our index. These urban centres have high volumes of health services, but have poor accessibility due to the high number of 'unhealthy' services

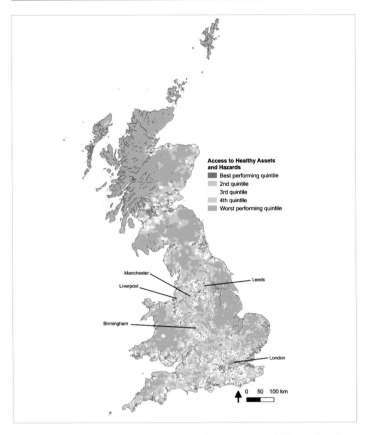

Figure 12.2
Quintiles of Access to
Healthy Assets & Hazards
in GB.

from the retail indicator and higher levels of air pollution.

The LSOA identified by the index that performed the worst was 'Camden 037B'. The LSOA is located in Holborn, Camden and incorporates Hatton Garden and Farringdon station. The LSOA scored highly on the retail and environment domains, due to its high levels of pollution and high accessibility to most of the retail outlets we measure (e.g. on average individuals were only 0.11 km from their nearest fast food outlet). Each of the other LSOAs within the top 10 unhealthiest environments were also located in Inner London.

The areas that were identified as the most health promoting through our index are typically smaller towns and suburban areas on the outskirts of cities. These areas perform well since they were generally located near to health services and green

spaces, but further away from polluted environments or retail services that were unhealthy. The LSOA that performed the best on our overall index was 'Torridge 006B'. The area comprises 'Great Torrington' which is a small town in north Devon in the South West of England. It has low levels of pollution, good access to parks and green space, few retail outlets that may encourage poor health-related behaviours, and good access to health services, in particular, with a hospital located in the centre of the town. Only two of the top ten best areas were not located in Scotland (with the other one being the Isle of Portland near Weymouth in the South West of England). The Scottish areas were mainly small towns and villages in rural areas located across the Central and Lowlands areas of Scotland, with two of them being located in the Greater Glasgow region.

Figures 12.3 and 12.4 move away from the national level and look at more local distributions of the index and domains (Liverpool and London respectively). Figure 12.3.a shows AHAH for Liverpool and demonstrates distinct geographical patterns. There is a clear region that performs poorly on our index in the city centre and north west of the city. Figures 12.3.b, 12.3.c and 12.3.d help to provide explanation for this. Figure 12.3.b shows the environment domain is worse in the city centre due to heavy traffic flow and in the northern docklands up towards Bootle, which is the old industrial area of the city. For retail services (Figure 12.3.d) the city centre has the best accessibility because of the volume of infrastructure; however this also extends into the north west of the city. These patterns exist despite good access to health services (Figure 12.3.c).

The two best performing areas of the city are Sefton Park and Aigburth, south west of the city centre, and Croxteth in the north east. These regions seem to perform well across each of the domains, particularly the Croxteth region. South Liverpool also performs well overall, given the particular performance on the physical environment and health services domains.

Our indicators also pick out more fine scale patterns. Figure 12.3.b demonstrates an area of poor physical environment in the east of the city. This region covers where the M62 motorway enters the city, and combined with a major train junction, represents the main arterial flow of traffic into Liverpool. Figure 12.3.a also demonstrates a small area that is poor performing just south of the city centre adjacent to the Sefton Park area which performs well. This is the Smithdown Road area which attracts Liverpool's student population, and has a high concentration of pubs, bars and fast food outlets. Out-of-town shopping centres and other high streets can be clearly seen in Figure 12.3.d as well as they represent areas of greater access to unhealthy aspects of the retail environment outside of the city centre.

A second local focus is that of London shown in Figure 12.4. Much like Liverpool, the inner core and central region of London exhibits the lowest access to healthy choices (Figure 12.4.a). These higher values are driven by the high level of air pollution (as represented by the poor scores on the physical environment domain; Figure 12.4.b) and high access to the unhealthy aspects of the retail environment (Figure 12.4.d). By contrast, the area does have good access to health services (Figure 12.4.c).

The areas that perform poorly are not restricted to just the urban core but also extend out to the east and west. In the east, areas in the lowest quintile extend along the River Thames representing the location of industry and river traffic. The west is characterised by Heathrow Airport which has high levels of pollution and poor access to health services.

The areas that perform best on AHAH can be found in the periphery/outskirts of the city. These areas are characterised by good access to health services and high

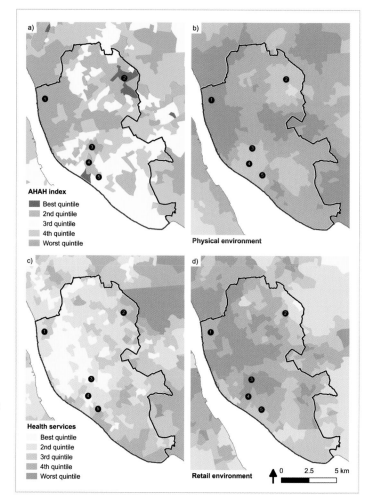

quality physical environments. They do not perform well on the retail environment domain; however this is common across London due to the high density of infrastructure and people. Outside of the Greater London metropolitan area, accessibility to retail outlets is by contrast poorer (i.e. further away) since these areas are predominantly more rural / less densely populated. There is one area within Inner London that does perform well on AHAH despite being surrounded by areas that do not perform well. This is Richmond Park and Wimbledon Common, two large expenses of green space and parkland. This area performs best on the physical environment domain (and to a lesser extent on the retail environment domain).

Figure 12.3
Quintiles of accessibility in Liverpool: 1) Bootle area, 2) Croxteth area, 3) Smithdown area, 4) Sefton Park and 5) Aigburth area.

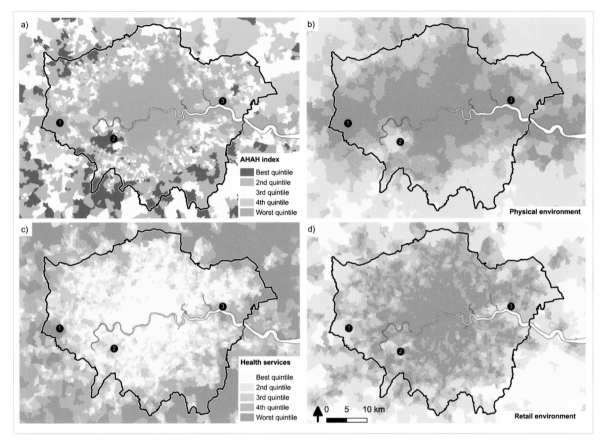

Figure 12.4
Quintiles of accessibility in London: 1) Heathrow Airport, 2) Richmond Park & Wimbledon Common and 3) East London.

12.8
Conclusion

Our study details the creation of a series of national open source low-level geographical measures on the accessibility to health-related features of the environment. These measures are combined to create an index of 'healthiness' for areas ('*Access to Healthy Assets & Hazards*') and help to summarise the complex geographical patterns demonstrated across our indicators. The data are available at indicators.cdrc.ac.uk/health where they can be viewed and downloaded. The website will be updated over time with new indicators that we develop or update.

Further Reading

Smith, T., Noble, M., Noble, S., Wright, G., McLennan, D. and Plunkett, E. (2015). *The English Indices of Deprivation 2015*, Department for Communities and Local Government. Online: https://www.gov.uk/government/publications/english-indices-of-deprivation-2015-technical-report [Accessed 10 Dec 2016]

Stanners, D. and Bourdeau, P., (1995). The urban environment. In Stanners, D. and Bourdeau, P. (Eds.), *Europe's Environment: The Dobris Assessment. European Environment Agency*, Copenhagen, pp. 261–296.

Notes

1. data.cdrc.ac.uk/product/local-data-company-retail-data
2. digital.nhs.uk/
3. www.isdscotland.org/
4. www.routino.org/
5. www.docker.com/what-docker

Acknowledgements

The authors would like to thank the Local Data Company Ltd for providing the retail unit data, the NHS of England, Wales and Scotland and the DEFRA for providing the health data and the air pollution data respectively under the OGL license and the OpenStreetMap Foundation (OSMF) for providing the GB network data under the Open Data Commons Open Database License. The second author's PhD research is sponsored by the Economic and Social Research Council through the North West Doctoral Training Centre.

13

Consumers in their Built Environment Context

Alexandros Alexiou and Alex Singleton

13.1
Introduction

Within consumer analytics, geodemographic classifications imbued with a variety of data are used widely as one of the most powerful discriminators of consumer behaviour (Graham, 2005). These divide customers into homogenous groups and have a long lineage as a basic strategy of marketing, often in order to identify population types and their correlation to a product uptake (neighbourhood targeting). The advantages of such approaches were identified very early on, for example the analysis carried out by Green and colleagues (1967) examining the relationships between newspaper circulation and city type.

Identifying socio-spatial patterns through geodemographic classification has proven utility over a range of disciplines. While most of these spatial classification systems include a plethora of socio-economic attributes, there is arguably little to no input regarding attributes of the built environment or physical space, and their relationship to socio-economic profiles within this context have not been evaluated in any systematic way. There is, however, an abundance of variables that might be collected on the built forms and relative locations that underpin neighbourhood differentiation.

The rationale for this research drew upon strong evidence that residential preference holds a significant relationship to the form of the built environment, suggesting that there is an important dimension to residential differentiation beyond a desire to live in areas that contain other people we deem 'like us'. Proximity to certain amenities is important to residential decisions, for example, transport nodes, parks, retail or healthcare facilities, and such attributes may have varying importance between different segments of the population. For instance, families with children often favour greenspace and recreational opportunities nearby, while those without, may prefer smaller residences closer to the city centre. As a result, consumption patterns can be inferred by the characteristics of residential location. Although geodemographic frameworks can incorporate a variety of input attributes, built and physical environment variables are typically limited to housing conditions or types. As such, this chapter presents the results of a project that explores the generation of a neighbourhood typology with focus on such characteristics of urban morphology, through integration of a range of spatial data from open sources.

13.2
Data sources

Currently, there are several providers of built and physical environment data in the UK. One of the main providers of geographical data for England and Wales is the national mapping agency Ordnance Survey (OS), and there are many datasets available within their repository, with varying degrees of granularity, depending on whether they are publicly accessible or available for purchase. As this research focuses on Open Data sources, a variety of open vector data sources that can be used directly or supplementary, such as *OpenStreetMap* (www.openstreetmap.org), were considered. Nevertheless, in order to maintain a consistent level of accuracy, the *OS Open Map - Local* product was used, the most recent and detailed open OS vector data product currently available (Ordnance Survey, 2015). This particular vector data product provides a variety of information, including outlines of buildings, street network with hierarchy, railways, woodland areas, surface water and important functional sites.

While the OS Open Map – Local provides the main source of these data, there were a few other sources within England and Wales deemed useful. These included data about listed buildings and historic parks and gardens supplied by the *Historic England*

Archive (services.historicengland.org.uk/ NMRDataDownload/) that is regularly updated (November 2015 update used here) and also under Open Data License. For Wales, the corresponding provider is the *Cadw* heritage organisation (available through the *UK Data Service*: data.gov.uk/ dataset/listed-buildings-in-wales-gis-point-dataset), although the data are slightly outdated (September 2011). Commercial buildings for local retail centres were identified using data from the *Local Data Company*, an Open version of which is available through the *ESRC Consumer Data Retail Centre* (CDRC) (available at: data.cdrc.ac.uk/dataset/ cdrc-maps-retail-centre-locations).

Finally, the selected datasets include aggregated data on housing type from the 2011 Census supplied by the Office for National Statistics. Unfortunately, there are currently no Open Data available on building age or height. The *UK Environmental Agency* has recently started providing raw LIDAR datasets that can offer such possibilities (data.gov.uk/publisher/ environment-agency), but still do not offer complete coverage. Future updates of this classification product may include more attributes such as roof types, car parks, delineated retail clusters and Energy Efficiency Certificate (EPC) data.

Table 13.1 summarises the range of inputs used to derive measures featured in this analysis.

The selection of the Output Area (OA) zonal level offers advantage over other administrative units in England and Wales since many other socio-economic classifications are offered at the OA level, such as the 2011 Output Area Classification (OAC), thus making comparisons possible. Additionally, such geography allows the incorporation of Census data which are distributed for these units. However, for the range of the derived measures that are described in the remainder of this section, there are problems with this approach (and

Dataset Name	Dataset Description	Source
D1: OA Boundaries	181,408 Output Area (OA) boundaries, as defined by the 2011 Census. All other data were spatially joined with respective OAs that they fall into (data features were split when falling into more than one OA).	Ordnance Survey
D1: Building Units	12,878,666 Building objects represented as polygons. Note that these areas do not represent individual households.	Ordnance Survey
D2: Road Network	Road network is represented as line segments, approximate to the road centre. The categories include 'Motorway', 'Primary Road', 'A Road', 'B Road', 'Minor Road', 'Pedestrianised Street', 'Local Street' and 'Private Road Publicly Accessible', as well as their 'Collapsed Dual Carriageway' counterparts.	Ordnance Survey
D3: Woodland	Areas of trees represented as polygons, described as coniferous and non-coniferous.	Ordnance Survey
D4: Functional Sites / Important Buildings	Functional sites comprised of 120,677 building polygons. They are categorised into themes such as 'Air Transport', 'Education', 'Medical Care', 'Road Transport' and 'Water Transport', which are further classified into more discrete classes.	Ordnance Survey
D5: Railway Stations and Tracks	Railway tracks and tunnels represented as lines and railway stations represented as points.	Ordnance Survey
D6: Surface water	Polygons of surface water. Small rivers and streams are represented as lines and are not included in the dataset. The dataset was also supplemented with a polygon for 'sea water', derived from the country's coastline.	Ordnance Survey
D7: Registered Historic Buildings	406,496 listed historic buildings defined as points, which were geolocated.	Historic England Archive; Cadw
D8: Registered Parks and Gardens	2,007 Polygon features with extents of the parks / gardens, classified as I, II*, or II, from most to least important. For Wales, the 372 sites were identified from points from a 'Named Places' dataset and given an approximate 200m radius.	Historic England Archive; Cadw
D9: Retail Centres	1,312 Retail Centres across England and Wales. There is no recent update for this dataset which dates back to 2004. The centres are only depicted as points and have no typology attached. We assumed an average radius of 200m to convert them to areas.	Local Data Company (CDRC)
D10: Housing Type	Percentage of households that are classified by the Census as 'Detached', 'Semi-detached', 'Terraced' or 'Flat'.	Office for National Statistics
D11: Population	Population of total persons per OA.	Office for National Statistics

Table 13.1
Description of the spatial dataset compiled.

as a matter of fact, any other Census geography). OA borders were designed to minimise within-zone homogeneity in population characteristics (population normalisation), without regard to the geographical features of the area (Martin et al, 2001; see Figure 13.1). As such, for proximity based inputs there were

challenges about how such measures might be calculated, and to which area they should be attributed.

To facilitate these methodological shortcomings, three different types of attribute measures are introduced for each OA that related to either two types of

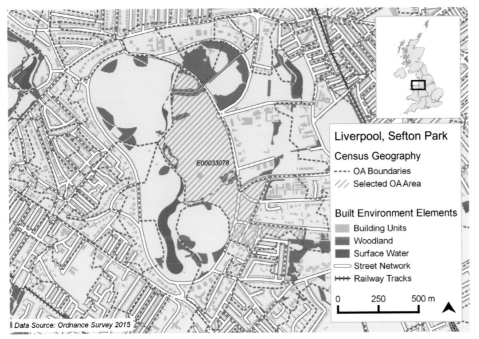

Figure 13.1
Map looking at the un-generalised OA borders (blue lines) in the Sefton Park area, Liverpool. Notice how the area of the park is divided arbitrarily between proximal OAs (pink hashed line pattern). Moreover, OA borders usually coincide with the street network, making any street network-to-area measurements impracticable.

proximity measures including adjacency effects or intermediate effects; and additionally direct measures. The lattermost of these are simply attributes captured at the OA level, while the first two assume buildings as the initial unit of analysis which are then later assigned to OAs. Building polygon features serve as observations in this input dataset, and represent homogenous built-up areas which can include one or more households. A graphical representation of the model is described in Figure 13.2.

For both types of proximity measures, a series of spatial queries were used that identified buildings that fulfil certain criteria, for instance, 'Which buildings are within a set distance of a major street?'. The surface of the buildings that met each criterion were then aggregated per OA and calculated as a ratio to the total building surface. Thus, within each OA, a ratio of the area of buildings meeting the criteria relative to the total built area was calculated for each of the attributes considered in the analysis.

This research defined *adjacency effects* to features measured within 100m linear distance, as commonly used in the literature on negative externality effects of built environment features, such as noise or pollution from roads (Rijnders et al, 2001). For *intermediate effects* a distance of 600m was used, on the basis of various western international definitions of 'within walking distance'. The distance figure generally varies depending on the context of analysis, but distances between 300m and 900m are considered appropriate for urban features (Hui et al, 2007; Barbosa et al, 2007).

Outside of these distances, it is assumed there are no effects. The delineation of *adjacency effects* or *intermediate effects* brings additional practical considerations which relate to the overall density of the built environment features being considered. In common with practice when creating inputs to multidimensional classifications, preference should be for those attributes which in addition to theoretical rationale, also provide useful differentiation between areas (Spielman

Figure 13.2
The spatial data model used to process data and produce OA zonal inputs to the classification.

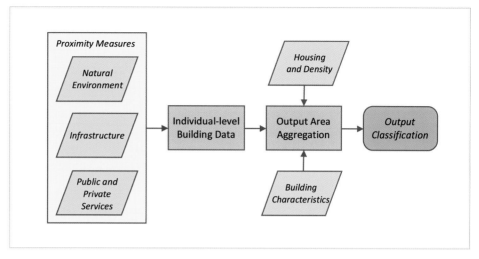

and Singleton, 2015). For example, in this application, when 600m buffers were used for major roads, this resulted in more than 50% of buildings meeting this criterion, providing a weak differentiation. These tasks were computationally expensive, as the complete dataset contained more than 12.8 million observations (building polygons). Therefore, the database was processed within the *R* coding language.

Finally, there were two further types of *direct* measure: those that were derived from building-level geographic features, and those that were simple inputs from secondary data. The derived direct measures included listed buildings (Figure 13.3) and cul-de-sacs. The latter were defined geocomputationally as the end of a line segment that did not intersect with any other such segment. A sensitivity of 10m was applied to this criterion in order to avoid topological errors and intermittent street segments. Results show that such measures can capture specific urban morphologies even at the small-area level.

For the other non-derived direct measures, the variables were simply aggregated directly at the OA level, such as housing

Figure 13.3
The total surface area of listed (registered) buildings (ha) per OA within the Greater Manchester metropolitan area.

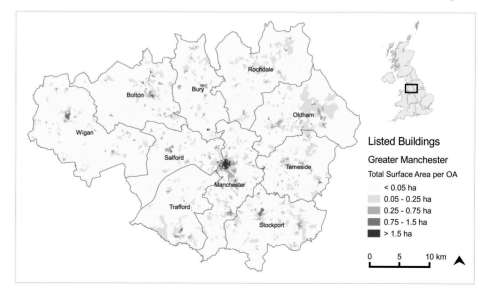

Variables	Variable Description, Aggregated per OA Code
Adjacency effects	
1. Major Roads	Percentage of the area of buildings that the centroid is within 100m of a major road to the total building area. We defined major as those of type 'Motorway', 'A Road' and 'Primary Road'.
2. Arterial Roads	Percentage of the area of buildings that their centroid is within 100m of an arterial road to the total building area. We defined Arterial roads as those with type 'B Road'.
3. Pedestrian Roads	Percentage of the area of buildings that their centroid is within 100m of a pedestrian road or footway to the total building area.
4. Railway Tracks	Percentage of the area of building units that their centroid is within 100m of railway tracks, excluding tunnels to the total building area.
5. Woodland Areas	Percentage of the area of building units that their centroid is within 100m of woodland features to the total building area.
6. Surface Water	Percentage of the area of building units that their centroid is within 100m of surface water (inland) and seafront (calculated by the distance from the coastal line), but excluding small rivers and streams, to the total building area.
Intermediate effects	
7. Railway Stations	Percentage of the area of building units that their centroid is within 600m from the centroid of a railway station to the total building area.
8. Parks and Gardens	Percentage of the area of building units that their centroid is within 600m from the registered site extents to the total building area.
9. Retail Centres	Percentage of the area of building units that their centroid is within 600m from the retail centre centroid plus 200m to the total building area.
10. Schools	Percentage of the area of building units that their centroid is within 600m from the sites that are identified as primary through secondary education to the total building area.
11. Higher Education	Percentage of the area of building units that their centroid is within 600m from the sites that are identified as further and higher education to the total building area.
Direct measures	
12. Detached Ratio	Percentage of unshared households that are classified by the 2011 Census as detached housing to the total building area.
13. Semi-Detached Ratio	Percentage of unshared households that are classified by the 2011 Census as semi-detached housing to the total building area.
14. Terraced Ratio	Percentage of unshared households that are classified by the 2011 Census as terraced housing to the total building area.
15. Flat Ratio	Percentage of unshared households that are classified by the 2011 Census as Flats to the total building area.
16. Density	Ratio of persons to total building area (people/ha).
17. Cul-de-sac	Ratio of cul-de-sacs (dead-end street points) to the total OA area (points/ha).
18. Registered Buildings	Ratio of listed buildings to the total OA area (points/ha).

Table 13.2
Built and physical
environment
attributes used
in the classification.

type. Population density was calculated using a ratio of persons per total building area, which potentially would give more accurate results regarding housing dynamics. The final OA attributes along with their descriptions are provided in Table 13.2.

13.3
A small-area classification of urban morphology features

Methodologically, the cluster analysis follows the conventional geodemographic approach, as detailed in Harris et al (2005); however, only the physical and built environment data, detailed above, are used to create the typology. A common clustering technique used in geodemographic analyses is the iterative allocation–reallocation algorithm, known as K-means. Although this algorithm has been used in a variety of geodemographic applications, this dataset is characterised by very sparsely populated attribute values, which is not fit for K-means applications. Essentially, the majority of values are zero, indicating the absence of the particular built environment or physical characteristic from that area.

Due to these shortcomings, an alternative technique was used: a Self-Organizing Map (SOM). A SOM is an unsupervised classifier that uses artificial neural networks to classify multidimensional observations in two-dimensional space based on their similarities (Kohonen, 2001). A SOM typically organises observations by projecting them as grid units onto a plane, and through consecutive iterations finds the best configuration of observations so that every observation is most similar to the others closest to them. Typically, the SOM mapping process employs a lattice of squares or hexagons as the output layer, and the results are therefore easily mapped as they retain their topology. SOMs have many applications in a broad range of fields, from medicine and biology to image analysis and computer science. SOMs have also been tested as an alternative classifier

of Census data where they seem to perform well for socio-economic data at the US Census tract scale (Spielman and Thill, 2008).

Prior to clustering, the input data, consisting of 18 variables and summarised in Table 13.2, were transformed into z-scores in order to standardise their measurement scales.

This SOM implements a hexagonal grid within which OAs are projected and thus create the classification based on the resulting topology. A relatively unexplored built environment classification with too many clusters would be difficult to interpret, so a selection of a 4-by-2 hexagonal grid was made, which produced eight distinct clusters. Once areas were assigned to clusters, mean attribute values were assigned to radar plots in order to map cluster characteristics and label them accordingly, as seen in Figure 13.4.

Radial plots are used extensively in geodemographics as they are very intuitive in identifying the nature of formed clusters. A radial plot essentially depicts the cluster centre; it is a vector representing each attribute mean (in this case for 18 variables) within the cluster. Each attribute mean can be traced along every radial axis at their intersection, forming a unique pattern for every cluster. Since values were standardised to z-scores, values of zero suggest that the cluster attribute mean is equal to the national mean, while values above or below zero suggest that cluster attribute means are above or below the national average respectively. It also suggests that the values shown are measured in standard deviations.

To illustrate, assume that Cluster C is under consideration. The radial plot shows that Cluster C has an above average prevalence of major roads (1.0), pedestrian streets (0.4), parks and gardens (1.4) and retail sites (1.5). It has below average values of detached and semi-detached housing ratios (-1.6 and -1.7), but a high concentration of flats and

High Streets and Promenades

Central Business District

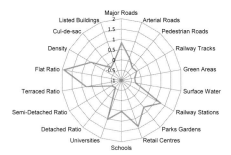

The Old Town

Railway Buzz

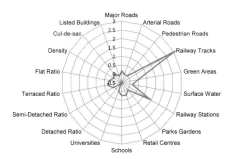

Victorian Terraces

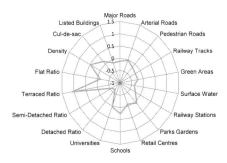

Suburban Landscapes

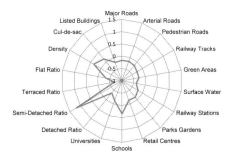

Countryside Sceneries

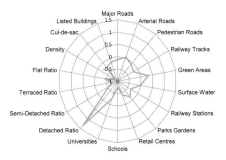

Waterside Settings

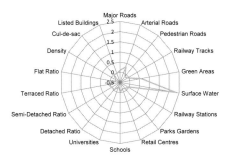

Figure 13.4
Radial plots of cluster
attribute centres, as
produced by the SOM.

terraced housing (1.4 and 1). The defining aspect of this cluster, however, is the listed buildings attribute, which has an average value of 5.1 within the cluster. From the mean values of attributes of Cluster C, it is suggested that these neighbourhoods are in the periphery of the city centre, proximal to some major roads and retail activities. The number of historical buildings and the presence of flats and semi-detached housing suggest neighbourhoods that have been historically affluent, potentially with a strong presence of churches or administrative buildings that have been repurposed to housing (e.g. flats) or recreational facilities (e.g. pubs and restaurants).

Mapping the classification can also provide further insights in cluster labelling. For instance, looking at the Liverpool city centre, some of the OAs of Cluster C are located within the Georgian Quarter, a historic affluent housing neighbourhood built in the 1800s. Cluster C appears to be dominating the geographical extents of the City of London as well, possibly due to the high number of historical sites in the area. In a similar manner, the rest of the clusters were examined in order to identify defining characteristics. This enabled cluster types to be labelled and the following short descriptions to be created:

1. High Streets and Promenades
These clearly depicted areas represent the main retail centres of urban regions located along the main commercial streets. The main characteristic of this cluster is the very high ratio of pedestrianised street networks, not only around retail clusters but also along seafronts, where traditionally a lot of recreational and leisure venues can be found.

2. Central Business District
The area often called city centre. Typically, high-rise buildings with a lot of commercial and office spaces, hence the relatively low net population density. These areas have proximity to the majority of public amenities, and have plenty of access via major roads and railways. For moderate-size cities the title holds true, but in areas such as London they tend to be too expansive to be labelled as central.

3. The Old Town
The traditional town centre or historically affluent residential developments, usually in the periphery of the main high street. The cluster is strongly defined by the number of registered buildings. Typically, a lot of recreational facilities can be found here, like pubs and restaurants, along with many administrative buildings and some historical major roads. Although the cluster does have a considerable number of flats, densities remain low, potentially due to refurbishments and change of usage.

4. Railway Buzz
The areas that are dominated by railway tracks and railway stations. They have no other major distinguishing attributes, which may suggest that they are actually rather heterogeneous in physical and socio-economic structure.

5. Victorian Terraces
These are typical neighbourhoods with terraced housing, average densities and moderate access to public and private services. In general, this is one of the most central clusters in the classification; excluding housing types, all attributes are very close to average. It is also one of the few typologies that can be found anywhere.

6. Suburban Landscapes
These areas are typically of semi-detached houses, with good access to parks. They tend to be quite distant from retail centres. Densities are higher than average as a result of the few non-domestic properties found within (since population density is calculated per building surface). They are primarily residential areas, and tend to be close to schools. Cul-de-sacs are relatively common, possibly because of organised developments and gated communities.

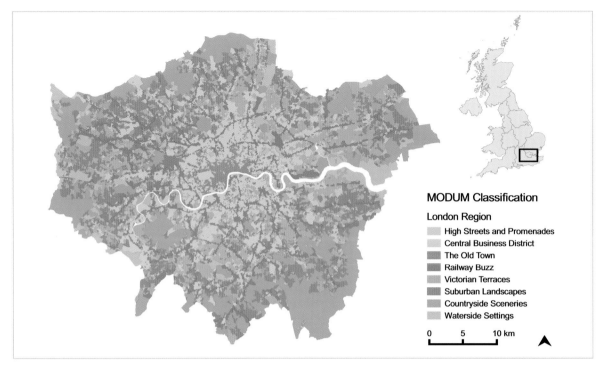

MODUM Classification

London Region
- High Streets and Promenades
- Central Business District
- The Old Town
- Railway Buzz
- Victorian Terraces
- Suburban Landscapes
- Countryside Sceneries
- Waterside Settings

0   5   10 km

7. Countryside Sceneries

These areas are dotted with detached houses, and are located either near or within open countryside. This typology is also defined by the higher than average access to green spaces. Most rural villages fall into this category, along with some city fringe developments that lie beyond the classic suburbs.

8. Waterside Settings

The principal defining attribute of these neighbourhoods is their proximity to surface water such as rivers, canals or sea (these are very distinctive in the East of England). Some of these neighbourhoods, however, can also be found within close proximity of ports, industrial or post-industrial sites (hence the low densities). Among the distinctive infrastructure are arterial roads, i.e. secondary roads wide enough to be used by lorries for the distribution of goods.

A visual interpretation of the classification is always meaningful in evaluating emergent clusters, as illustrated by the map of the Greater London Region (Figure 13.5), as identified by the MODUM classification. As discussed previously, the core of the metropolitan region is identified as Cluster C: The Old Town, expanding outwards along major transport corridors as Cluster B: Central Business District (although in the case of London, this cluster may be too expansive to provide any useful differentiation). In general, axial zones exhibit much more strongly in an urban morphology classification derived from built environment and physical features which are linear in nature, such as roads, railways and rivers.

13.4
Conclusion

The development of the MODUM classification illustrates that the production and analysis of a classification of the built environment using Big and Open Data can offer unique insights into some aspects of geodemographic structure of urban areas. The results capture, through the multidimensionality of the data, both

Figure 13.5
The Greater London Region as identified by the MODUM Classification.

microscopic and mesoscopic identifiers of urban morphology. Potential applications of the MODUM classification involve not only enhancing current socio-economic classifications by appending it to conventional geodemographic systems, but also it can prove useful in itself; it can provide a simplified structure of the physical properties of geographic space that can be used to explore correlations with other spatial phenomena, potentially in a variety of applications, from real estate and house prices to health and wellbeing. In a dynamic sense, it can be used by urban planners and investors in the built environment to identify the areas in which the physical preconditions exist for neighbourhood renewal or upscaling.

On the other hand, the classification process described here is very specific to the underlying data and methodology. An inherent disadvantage of all geodemographic classifications is that lack of a single global optimisation function, making them highly susceptible to the operational decisions during the classification procedure (Openshaw and Gillard, 1978). Nevertheless, this type of classification can be valuable in many circumstances. The classification is easy to use, and offers the ability to append and update data as they become available, while keeping the same model infrastructure intact. In general, it meets the growing need for geodemographic systems that are open and versatile enough to handle the abundance of big data that are currently available.

Further Reading

Barbosa, O., Tratalosa, J. A., Armsworth, P. R., Davies, R. G, Fuller, R. A., Johnson, P. and Gaston, K. J. (2007). Who benefits from access to green space? A case study from Sheffield, UK. *Landscape and Urban Planning, 83*, 187–195.

Graham, S. D. N. (2005). Software-sorted geographies. *Progress in Human Geography, 29*(5), 562–580.

Green, P. E., Frank, R. E. and Robinson, P. J. (1967). Cluster analysis in test market selection. *Management Science*, 13, 387–400.

Harris, R., Sleight, P. and Webber, R. (2005). *Geodemographics, GIS, and Neighbourhood Targeting.* Chichester, UK: John Wiley & Sons.

Hui, E., Chau, C., Pun, L. and Law, M. (2007). Measuring the neighboring and environmental effects on residential property value: Using spatial weighting matrix. *Building and Environment, 42*(6), 2333–2343.

Kohonen, T. (2001). *Self-organizing Maps.* Berlin: Springer.

Martin, D., Nolan, A. and Tranmer, M. (2001). The application of zone-design methodology in the 2001 UK Census. *Environment and Planning A, 33*, pp. 1949-1962.

Openshaw, S. and Gillard, A. A. (1978). On the stability of a spatial classification of census enumeration district data. In P. W. S. Batey (Ed.) *Theory and Methods in Urban and Regional Analysis*, London: Pion, 101-119.

Ordnance Survey (2015). *Open Map – User guide and technical specification* v1.4. Crown Copyright, London: HMSO.

Rijnders, E., Janssen, N. A., van Vliet, P. H. and Brunekreef, B. (2001). Personal and outdoor nitrogen dioxide concentrations in relation to degree of urbanization and traffic density. *Environmental Health Perspectives, 109*(3), 411–41.

Spielman, S. E. and Folch, D. C. (2015). Social area analysis with self-organizing maps. In A. Singleton and C. Brundson (Eds.) *Geocomputation*, London: SAGE Press, pp. 152–169.

Spielman, S. E. and Singleton, A. D. (2015). Studying neighborhoods using uncertain data from the American community survey: A contextual approach. *Annals of the Association of American Geographers, 105*(5), 1003-1025.

Spielman, S. E. and Thill, J. C. (2008). Social area analysis, data mining, and GIS. *Computers, Environment and Urban Systems, 32*(2), 110-122.

Acknowledgements

The authors would like to thank Local Data Company Ltd for providing retail unit data for this research. This research was also funded by the Economic and Social Research Council awards 1390251.

Epilogue:
Researching Consumer Data

Paul Longley, James Cheshire and Alex Singleton

The contributions to this book provide wide-ranging evidence that consumer data are both pervasive and have the potential to generate a deeper understanding about our society. This extends their importance far beyond the realm of identifying customer tastes and preferences into substantive contributions to the social sciences in particular. For example, the chapters in this volume demonstrate that consumer data can help to provide insight to issues as diverse as urban vitality, community carbon footprints, or the collective consumption of public transport services. However, for their potential to be fully realised in tackling issues of broader societal concern, the quality and provenance of consumer datasets need to be fully understood. Developing this understanding is part of the process of assimilation and documentation of diverse sources and forms of consumer 'Big Data' into appropriate digital data infrastructure; a core mission of the Consumer Data Research Centre (CDRC). For example, the desire to generalise patterns – as recorded within consumer data – to the population at large necessitates triangulation and validation with more conventional sources of data, such as the Census of Population and Mid Year Population Estimates. Whilst this work integrates consumer data into the national data infrastructure routinely utilised by the academic community, it also offers insights relevant to data providers, many of whom may not be fully aware of the precise sectors of society that they serve. It is also of relevance to government in its efforts to integrate consumer data sources into official statistics. From this perspective, consumer data are in a significant part a public, rather than a private good. They are also non-rival – that is, the use does not undermine the **competition** concerns of individual business organisations, but they contribute to the overall **competitiveness** of the economy.

For this to be operationalised in the best interests of data providers as well as society as a whole, the CDRC is finding it helpful to subsume particular consumer data sources into composite indicators, similar to existing widely used indices of multiple deprivation and geo-demographic classifications. The CDRC research agenda thus includes the creation and maintenance of indicators relating to retail dynamics, use of digital channels and media, demographic structure, mobility characteristics, local health and carbon footprints.

In these respects, it is important to be aware of an important deviation of CDRC interests from those of commercial data providers and those of government. Academic research has concern not only with the short-term gyrations of consumer-led markets but also with their long-term evolution and potential socio-economic implications. In consolidating large assemblages of data into summary indicators, the CDRC is aware that it is important to have well-founded data infrastructure that is also enduring and facilitates comparisons across time and space. As such, the diverse data sources and case studies reported in this volume coalesce into a long-term vision that reshapes the way in which we think of digital data infrastructure in the social sciences.

Index

First published in 2018 by
UCL Press
University College London
Gower Street
London WC1E 6BT

Available to download free: www.ucl.ac.uk/ucl-press

A CIP catalogue record for this book is available from
The British Library.

ISBN: 978-1-78735-389-3 (Pbk.)
ISBN: 978-1-78735-388-6 (PDF)
DOI: https://doi.org/10.14324/111.9781787353886

Printed by Albe de Coker, Antwerp, Belgium